Sergio Scataglini's passion is for the  *e Twelve Transgressions* cuts to the hear decisions and our behavior can truly p radical holiness, an urgent and timely b

—... WAGNER, CHANCELLOR
WAGNER LEADERSHIP INSTITUTE

Many today blame the lack of revival in the United States on sin in the streets. Sergio Scataglini, a man acquainted with revival, has clarified the issue in this new book. We, God's church, are the greatest hindrance to revival. We need not wrestle revival from the hands of a reluctant God. Revival is a gift, not a goal. God is simply looking for a decent place to put one. As we become that holy place, we will see the knowledge of His glory cover our nation as the waters cover the sea! Thank you, Sergio!

—EDDIE SMITH
U.S. PRAYER CENTER

I know that God loves America because He sent us Sergio Scataglini. Sergio's love for holiness and his passion for Christlikeness do more than teach; he inspires. It is one thing to provide Christians with religious information; Sergio brings transformation. I can say with confidence that those who apply themselves to the truths in his book will become more Christlike as a result.

—FRANCIS FRANGIPANE
AUTHOR AND SENIOR PASTOR, RIVER OF LIFE MINISTRIES

Pastor Sergio Scataglini is a dear friend of mine and a great man of God. He truly burns with the fire of holiness, and his ministry is a blessing to the body of Christ.

This book will move you internally to make decisions that will change your destiny. His message, which is deep, biblical and rich in illustrations, will cause you to run to a new altar of consecration and brokenness. It will help you overcome all of the obstacles to living in holiness.

Yes! Holiness is possible. Prepare yourself to live a new time with God!

—REV. CLAUDIO FREIDZON, SENIOR PASTOR
KING OF KINGS CHURCH
BUENOS AIRES, ARGENTINA

Sergio has written a prophetic book that will motivate us by the grace of God and the power of the Holy Spirit to live holy lives for His glory. May this book be a catalyst for another Jesus movement!

—CHE AHN, SENIOR PASTOR
HARVEST ROCK CHURCH
PASADENA, CALIFORNIA

Sergio Scataglini's new book *The Twelve Transgressions* is confrontational yet so refreshing. This is not a book for junk food lovers. It is getting back to the meat and potatoes of an evangelistic message from the heart of an evangelist that God is using in a powerful way in the closing hours of the church age.

—JOHN A. KILPATRICK, SENIOR PASTOR
BROWNSVILLE ASSEMBLY OF GOD
PENSACOLA, FLORIDA

Throughout our spiritual lives God places people and products in our path to help keep us in His perfect will. Sergio Scataglini is one of those people. This book is one of those products. *The Twelve Transgressions* speaks clearly about sin and radiates hope to everyone who desires to live a holy life.

—STEPHEN HILL
EVANGELIST

This is a book that will be a blessing to every Christian leader who sincerely desires to grow to become more and more like Jesus Christ our Lord. Sergio is that kind of Christian leader. He has a deep passion to become Christlike—and he invites us to learn and benefit from what our Lord has been teaching him in his adventure of following Jesus.

—DR. PAUL CEDAR, CHAIRMAN
MISSION AMERICA COALITION

The Twelve Transgressions is an excellent reminder of some of the spiritual pitfalls great servants of God experienced. The biblical examples used will alert you to these transgressions and help you to avoid them in your own life as you walk with the Lord. The revelation God has given Sergio reveals how revival within the church begins when we are first cleansed of our transgressions as we humbly seek to obey Him.

—ELIZABETH (BETH) ALVES, PRESIDENT
INTERCESSORS INTERNATIONAL
BULVERDE, TEXAS

The Twelve Transgressions

SERGIO SCATAGLINI

Charisma HOUSE

THE TWELVE TRANSGRESSIONS by Sergio Scataglini
Published by Charisma House
A part of Strang Communications Company
600 Rinehart Road
Lake Mary, Florida 32746
www.charismahouse.com

Unless otherwise noted, all Scripture quotations are from the Holy Bible, New International Version. Copyright © 1973, 1978, 1984, International Bible Society. Used by permission.

Scripture quotations marked NAS are from the New American Standard Bible. Copyright © 1960, 1962, 1963, 1968, 1971, 1972, 1973, 1975, 1977 by the Lockman Foundation. Used by permission. (www.Lockman.org)

Scripture quotations marked KJV are from the King James Version of the Bible.

Cover design by Eric Powell
Cover illustration by Eric Joyner

Library of Congress Catalog Card Number: 2002107693
International Standard Book Number: 0-88419-873-1

02 03 04 05 06 — 8 7 6 5 4 3 2 1
Printed in the United States of America

To devoted Christian workers around the world:

*May God use this book to encourage you in the
path of holiness and to dramatically reduce the
number of spiritual casualties in the body of Christ.*

And to my home team:

*Kathy, my beloved wife and helper
Pablo, my son in the Lord
Nathan, Jeremy and Miqueas, my sons and disciples*

Acknowledgments

T*his* book is a team effort. I am grateful for the many hours that Kathy put into gathering, organizing, typing and retyping the original manuscript. Thanks to Jeannie Stutzman who typed for us as well with such a willing heart.

My deep appreciation goes out to my friend Lee Grady for his passion to see this book published and his personal involvement in seeing it through. I also want to thank my friend Steve Swihart for his insightful and precise remarks and all of our intercessors who constantly surround us with prayer.

I want to express my gratitude to leaders around the world who encouraged me and inspired me to publish the message of this book.

I want to acknowledge our great team at Scataglini Ministries. Each one of them is an effective helper in the ministry.

Most of all, I thank God for my family that accompanies me in this exciting lifestyle of traveling, preaching and writing.

Contents

Foreword

T*here* will be people who finish this book and state, "I wish I'd read this a long time ago!" In retrospect they will appreciate the wisdom found in these pages.

This book is like a road advisory telling us where previous travelers crashed—and why! Often after an accident, whether on the roadways or airways, there is always an investigation. Lessons learned can preserve future of future travelers intact.

This book by my friend Sergio Scataglini dissects in detail twelve "crashes" on the course of life. When we do not learn from history, we may repeat history. If you, like myself, are tired of reading the headlines of the most recent Christian catastrophe, then study this book carefully!

Sergio Scataglini's insights will undoubtedly salvage someone. I believe this book also has insight enough that it might just "save" someone from "falling." Sergio joins with Jude in saying that the merciful heavenly Father will "keep you from falling"—*if you will practice "cautious Christianity."* Don't go speeding through where "angels fear to tread!" To be "kept" is better than to be "delivered."

I appreciate the ambulance at the foot of the cliff after an accident, but how much better the barrier at the top of the precipice.

I think all of us would agree it's better to bounce off a barrier with bruises than crash down the cliff and be crushed. This book is better than a bandage at the bottom of the cliff; it's a roadside barrier to catastrophe at the top! Don't let the crisis subject matter intimidate you into not reading this book—you need this information, fellow traveler.

Sometimes a book is made even better by knowing the life of the author. Sergio passionately lives what he has written. It could be said of him as it was another—"an Israelite in whom there is no guile." Sergio has a pure spirit. This word from heaven is uncontaminated. I took what I read to heart, because I know both the Source and the vessel.

—TOMMY TENNEY
GODCHASER

Preface

Apprehended by His Fire

In May 1997, I greeted my congregation in the city of La Plata, Argentina, and said, "I will return to you in a week; I am going to see the revivals in a couple of places in the United States. I will bring reports back to you of what the Lord is doing in the world." Basically, I thought I was doing so well with the Lord that all I needed was another touch from Him at these places of revival. I assumed that these encounters would simply strengthen my ministry. I didn't have any idea that God was about to bring a revolution into my life.

However, there had been a cry, a very strange prayer that I had been praying for the previous months. Several times as I knelt down in prayer, I found myself praying, "Lord, if You are not going to bring another revival, take me home. I do not want to live anymore." Each time I tried to rebuke my soul because I have three children and a wife; the ministry was not doing so badly either. I thought, *I should not pray this way; the Lord might answer my prayer!*

Then I realized that the Holy Spirit was putting a burden in my heart to see revival. There was a holy hunger for more of God. John Knox used to say, "Lord, give me Scotland or I will die." I pray that you will desire revival more than your own life; that you will desire, more than being alive, to see your entire nation shaken under the power of God.

Like many others, I was *praying* for revival, but I was not *preparing* for it. I was going to bring reports of revival back to my congregation. So I went to a place of revival and rejoiced in the Lord with what I saw. I was excited, and then I left the next morning very early for northern Indiana, where my wife's family lives.

Two days later I stood up to greet the people in a church in Indiana. I only had a few moments in the program because they had another guest speaker that Sunday morning. It was not my turn to preach there; as a matter of fact, I was supposed to leave very quickly to go to another church to preach. But the Lord had other plans.

I shared a greeting, and then the pastor said, "I'm going to ask Pastor Sergio to come up front. We are going to pray for him before he goes to the other church so he can carry fire to them."

Some young people began to pray very calmly. Everything was quiet and orderly, and the service was going nicely according to the church bulletin. I closed my eyes, and my mind was not on revival or anything else. I was in a rush to go to the next church to preach. But suddenly my clasped hands began to shake without my permission; I could not control them. In our denomination, and especially in the training my father gave me, we maintain control when we are on the platform. We let the Lord use us, but we don't get out of hand. We were concerned that if we get out of control, the rest of the congregation might lose control as well.

But something was happening to me for the first time that I could not control. I thought, *This is out of place!* I opened my eyes and looked at the congregation before me. No one else was shaking. So I tried to stop the trembling. I gripped my hands more tightly trying to stop the movement, yet my entire body began to shake. I remember locking my knees and making them really stiff, and then I fell on the floor.

Something strange was happening, and I said, "This is not right; I must get up." I was on the floor, shaking completely out of control.

I looked at the people, and they were looking at me. No one was praying any more! The pastor began to lead a few songs. I was weeping and the next moment I was laughing. I felt very, very embarrassed, quite shocked and extremely happy—all at the same time.

I said, "I must get out of here!" Three times I tried to stand up. The third time two ushers helped me to my feet. The associate pastor was next to me. The pastor came down from the platform to where I stood in front of the platform. Crying, I said, "Pastor, do not let me interrupt this meeting; please take me out of here."

This brother put his arm over my shoulder and said, "You are not interrupting, Brother. This is the presence of God." His words were like a healing balm over my soul. I knew how important it was that when the new glory of the Lord came, there be godly people witnessing the experience to understand what is going on.

They finally carried me out. I thought they were carrying me to a separate room because I wanted to be alone with God. But they had the bad idea of seating me on the front row! I continued shaking, and every few minutes I would fall on the floor. Someone would pick me up and put me back in the chair. I tried to control myself as much as I could, but the more I tried, the stronger the waves of the Holy Spirit would come upon me. There were surges of power over my entire body. His glory was there. I did not know what to call this experience.

Someone, without consulting me, went back to the church office and called the pastor of the other church that was expecting me to preach. The pastor was told, "It does not look like Sergio is going to make it today." It took me two weeks to get to that church to preach!

At that point of my experience, though, my mind was not changed; my thoughts had not yet been renewed. My body was shaking, and I could feel the waves of the glory of the Lord. But I did not know yet what this meant. The Bible speaks to us about miracles, signs and wonders. I believe that my experience was a sign from the Lord to get my attention. And He certainly did! I was available twenty-four hours a day to Him for the next six days.

Then a brother came and asked me a question that was a little humiliating. "Brother, do you need a ride home?"

"Yes," I said, "I think I do." I only had one prayer as we were driving to my in-laws' house. As I continued to shake, cry and laugh, I prayed, "Lord, please do not let my in-laws see me like this." I was praying that they would not be there when I arrived. There had been some theological tension with my in-laws, and I did not think they would agree with my unusual encounter with the Holy Spirit. I also prayed, "Lord, do not let this cause any division." But the Lord did not answer my prayer not to be seen.

When we opened the door to my in-laws' house, standing right there before me were my mother-in-law and my father-in-law. I could not walk very well, so the brother who had driven me home was sort of carrying me, almost as if I were intoxicated. I was perspiring, and I could not speak clearly, but I remember saying to my mother-in-law, "Mom, I am OK; don't worry, but please do not look at me."

Immediately my mother-in-law raised her hands to heaven and began to praise and glorify God. She entered into a three-day fast because she knew God was touching me. As I made my way to my room, I heard her say, to my great surprise, "This is what we need in our churches!"

The man who had driven me home began explaining to them what had happened at the church. That gave me an opportunity to go upstairs to my room. I closed the door and was so happy to be alone. I continued to shake and weep, and I did not know what was happening.

Two hours later, the physical manifestations ceased completely; there was no more shaking, and everything was fine. I said to myself, *Boy, do I have things to tell my church in La Plata.* I thought that was the end of the experience.

Since I was "normal" again, I went downstairs to explain to my in-laws what had happened. Before I could explain, my mother-in-law set a plate of food before me and said, "Isn't the Lord wonderful?" When she said that, I could feel the glory of the Lord coming upon me again. I fell backward to the floor and began shaking. Once again I crawled up the stairs to my bedroom!

I was supposed to confirm with another pastor in the area that I would preach in his church, but I could not even make a phone call. I prayed, "Lord, if this experience is from You, why am I not doing Your work? I should be more busy than ever before." Sitting on top of my desk was a list of things to do. The airplane ticket I had purchased to get to that next church was expensive, so I felt I had to get back to work. I was looking at that list, and that list was looking at me. I wanted to get busy for the Lord, but I did not understand that the Lord had a different plan for me. He did not regard my agenda; He ripped it to pieces!

For six days I was in the presence of almighty God, weeping and crying in the bedroom at my in-laws' house. When I thought I was normal, I would put on my tie and jacket and get ready. Before I would touch the doorknob, the power of God would come upon me and throw me on the floor so I could not get up. At times I would be there for hours before I could get up.

The next day after my experience at the church, the presence of the Lord was even more powerful. About 7:00 A.M. I began to iron my shirt, because I wanted to do things for God. I did not finish ironing my shirt until about 3:00 P.M. In between my attempts to iron the shirt, the glory of the Lord would fill the room, and I would fall on the floor and worship Him. I didn't realize it at the time, but I would later understand that I was having an encounter with the fire of His holiness.

John the Baptist explained this phenomenon clearly in Matthew 3:11:

> I baptize you in water for repentance. But after me will come
> one who is more powerful than I... He will baptize you with
> the Holy Spirit and with fire.

God is not equal to us—He is more powerful. That is why He cannot fit in our old religious patterns. That is why we cannot have a fresh outpouring of His Spirit on our lives and keep the same old wineskins. We have to have a change of wineskins before the Spirit can descend. If you are so bound to your ways and your patterns, and the Holy Spirit comes, this will break the old wineskins. But new wineskins are different because they stretch.

So many people say, "Oh, I received the Holy Spirit fifteen years ago." I believe that the Holy Spirit comes to our hearts when we receive Jesus. That is the beginning. His presence is with us. We could not be Christians without the Holy Spirit. But somehow we have managed to separate the baptism of the Holy Spirit from the fire of the Holy Spirit.

I sensed waves of the Holy Spirit over my life those first few days, but my mind was not changed until the third day that I was under this fire of the Lord. That day, everything changed. I woke up, and there was a sadness in my room. The same beautiful presence of God that was loving me and hugging me the day before now was rejecting me and coming so strongly, so dangerously close to me.

That morning, the holiness of God was so close and so strong in my room that I became frightened. I began to retreat. I backed up until my back touched the wall; then I thought, *What am I doing? This is the presence of the Lord; I cannot hide from it.* I prayed, "Lord, please, no more." That was the first time I had ever prayed that prayer. I was so frightened that I said, "Lord, I don't think I can take any more. You are too holy."

I continued, "Lord, what is it? I know there is something wrong. Please have mercy on me; don't kill me here." That afternoon I went for a walk outside of the house. The power of God very suddenly came over me, and I sank to my knees on the ground. It was so sudden and so unpredictable that I broke down into tears immediately. Then the Holy Spirit began to show me pictures of sin in my life—issues that had been unresolved.

I was born and raised in a Christian home. My parents used to read the Bible to me even when I was still an infant. They taught me the ways of the Lord. But now God was dealing with what I had thought were "evangelical sins"—things I had thought He would not mind. I had accepted a lie of the devil, one that said that we will always have a percentage of willful sin in us. Now the Holy Spirit was resisting me. He was not hugging me.

While I was there on the ground, the Lord pointed out many specific things in my life that were not right. I thought time would erase them because they were so minor. But I was reminded that *little sins* are still sin. All sin is sinful and destructive. Memories of times I had hardened my heart against a brother flashed through my mind. I could see the very place that it had happened. I had never mistreated him, but I had made a silent pledge never to get close to him again. I was also reminded of times when my eyes had lingered too long on images of things that were not pleasing to the Lord.

As I lay there I began to weep for my sin. I felt such remorse that I felt sick, as if a fever were coming over my body. The Holy Spirit began to speak to me, and now my mind was beginning to catch up with what the Lord was trying to do. I recalled the verse that says, "Because you are lukewarm—neither cold nor hot—I am about to spit you out of my mouth" (Rev. 3:16).

I was shocked. "Lord, I have been in the ministry for years. I am a preacher of Your Word. I fasted last week, and I pray every day. How have I been so deceived? Why have I never seen this before?"

The Lord said to me, "I wish you would be cold as a pagan, so I could save you again, or hot as a believer who has given 100 percent to me. Then I could use you in My own way." Then the Lord answered my question about why I had not seen this before: "Deceitful is the heart of man, and desperately wicked." I was terrified; I could not believe that moment. Then the Lord spoke again to me and said clearly, *"Ninety-eight percent holiness is not enough."*

In a sense I was a Pharisee of Pharisees. I grew up in a Christian church. My goal was to be fairly holy, to do pretty well, to pass the examination with an 80 percent, or a B average. But the Lord had different demands.

He rebuked me for my self-righteousness and exposed the lie of my heart. I then realized my greatest error: I was not trying to be like Jesus; I was just trying to be fairly good. At that moment I felt that all of my religiosity, all of my discipline was like filthy rags in

His presence. Before this, I had not believed the Lord called me to be a fairly good person—I knew that He had called me to be like Jesus. The week before my trip to the States, I had fasted and prayed a lot, and I felt so good about myself. I felt I must have been 90 percent holy or more. Now I realized that was not enough.

Sometimes we let seemingly insignificant sins get into our hearts. But we have to ask ourselves, "With how many sins do you think the Lord will allow us to get into heaven? What percentage of evil do you think He will allow us to take with us when the day of the Lord comes? How many idols will we carry to heaven with us?" If we are going to be like Jesus, every compromising attitude toward sin must be confronted and defeated.

As I was in His presence, God spoke to me in terms that even a child could understand. At that moment, I could not understand anything more complex. He told me, "Nobody gets up in the morning and prepares a cup of coffee or tea with just one drop of poison in it, and then stirs and drinks it." Then He began to speak to me about the church. "There are people in the church who allow poison in their hearts and in their minds, and it is destroying them. No one would consider buying a bottle of mineral water whose label read, '98 percent pure mineral water; 2 percent sewage water.' Yet that is just what many Christians have allowed in their lives."

So many people wonder, *Why do I lose the power of God or the strength of the Lord so quickly? Maybe it is because I am a failure, or maybe it is because I am not trained.* I will tell you that even if there is only 1 percent of willful sin in our lives, that small amount can eventually destroy the whole devotion in our lives.

I wept, I confessed and I repented. The Lord pointed out to me specific sins in my life. He did not point out generalities; He was painfully specific.

Satan has a false ministry that he uses especially in the church. His ministry is a ministry of bringing guilt and condemnation. The Bible tells us that Satan is the accuser of the brethren. He comes to give us a general sense of guilt. He never helps us to resolve it. Then all we do is feel bad. There are some leaders, some workers, some servants of the Lord in the ministry whose hearts are trying their best, but they are tortured by guilt. Before they preach they have to get rid of that guilt for one hour, and then it comes back on them. That is not the ministry of the Holy Spirit.

The ministry of the Holy Spirit is to bring conviction of sin (John 16:8). He speaks very directly and specifically, and His word is so clear to us. He will tell us what is wrong with our hearts, our thoughts and our affections, and He will demand repentance from us. He will change us. That is the work of the Holy Spirit. It is very different from the work of Satan.

Satan comes to destroy lives, to pull entire ministries into depression and loneliness. There are people who say, "I hope that nobody will ever know me the way that I am personally." But I will tell you this, when the fire of the Holy Spirit comes upon you, you will say with the apostle Paul, "My conscience is clean." Your life will be purified because of Jesus. How desperately we need this fire!

That day I went back to my room and gradually began to recapture the joy of the Lord. Now instead of landing in the same place as before, I had changed to a new address. The joy of the Lord was in that room.

I am sharing my testimony with you not only to tell you about something that is happening on the other side of the world. I am sharing it because I know the Lord wants to impart to you what He has given to me—the fire of holiness. It is something He longs to pour out upon His church in this crucial hour.

WHAT I HAVE LEARNED ABOUT HOLINESS

Moses, Joshua, Elijah, David and Peter—what similarity can we find in the lives of each of these biblical leaders? Perhaps it was the great faith each of them—and other great biblical leaders—exhibited as they lived their lives in commitment to God. Maybe you would say it is the great impact each man had on his nation—and on Christians today.

But there's another thread that ties these men together, a thread shared by others like Eli, Jacob, Samson, Saul, Solomon, Jonah and the rich young ruler whom Jesus told to sell all his possessions. It is the thread of transgression! Each of these leaders felt the pain of failing God because of a sin they committed in a moment of disobedience to the God they loved and served.

These men were not evil people. Each had been called by God to lead His people into righteousness. Still, some of these leaders were destroyed by their sin; others repented just in time. Each paid a high price for his transgression. And their failures provide vital warnings to us today.

As God drew my attention to the biblical accounts of these servants of God, I began to think about why these transgressions were included in the record of what these men did for God while they lived on earth. None of their sins are in the Bible just to entertain us. Rather the Bible says that these things have been kept in His Word to encourage us and to admonish us. God included their stories not to discourage us, but to protect His people from falling into the same traps. (See 1 Corinthians 10:11.)

So many dedicated believers struggle with trying to live lives of obedience to God. As I have thought about our struggle with obedience, I have realized that it is not our inability to keep the Ten Commandments that is our biggest problem. Our biggest problem, as I will outline in this book, is avoiding what I have come to describe as "the Twelve Transgressions."

I believe a tremendous spiritual revival is coming. In some parts of the world this has already begun. It may be the greatest revival the history of the world has ever seen. It is a revival of holiness combined with the anointing and the gifts of the Holy Spirit. God is doing something that is new and unprecedented on the earth.

Often when I tell people that God is sending a revival of His holiness, they associate this with something harsh and negative. When I speak of holiness, they imagine that I am talking about living according to a legalistic set of man-made rules about clothing and hairstyles. They think this because, sadly, the church in times past has defined holiness simply by whether a person refrained from smoking cigarettes or watching worldly entertainment.

This is not true holiness! The Bible does not define holiness as a man's attempt to live according to certain man-made rules or regulations. True holiness, in fact, is an inward work of the Holy Spirit in the heart of a believer. Only God can make us holy, and He is more interested in shaping our heart attitudes and delivering us from wrong desires than He is about conforming us to some man-made code of behavior. He wants to form Christ in us! And this work of refining can only be done by His Spirit.

God, in His mercy, puts His arms around His church and says to her, "I want to protect you. I don't want you to keep falling. I don't want any more wounded casualties—casualties of spiritual war. I don't want My servants to be wounded. I love them, and I grieve when they are defiled by sin."

I pray that this book will encourage and challenge you to rise to a new place in God. I have not written this book with the attitude that I have "arrived," or that I am not susceptible to falling into these twelve transgressions. I am one of you. I weep when you weep, and I rejoice when you rejoice. I do not claim to have obtained perfection, but the Lord has been teaching me to walk on the "highway of holiness" as He enables me. I wish for you, my fellow servants in the kingdom of God, to be able to look into Jesus' eyes with no guilt or hidden sin and to hear Him say, "Well done, good and faithful servant."

I hope you will allow this book to help you avoid several spiritual pitfalls in your life and to open the door to an exciting, fruitful life of holiness. I pray that the Sanctifier, the Spirit of God who is described in Hebrews 12:29 as a "consuming fire," will visit you—and transform you into His image.

Introduction

The Twelve Transgressions: An Overview

In 2000 I moved my family to the United States from Argentina and purchased a house. The house was not new, so we decided to take advantage of the home inspections they were offering us to see if the house was in good condition.

The realtors mentioned the possibility of doing an inspection for radon gas. "Yes, I want an inspection done for that," I told the real estate agent.

"Do you know what that is?" my wife, Kathy, asked, looking at me in surprise.

"I just heard the real estate agent say that it is a form of dangerous gas that sometimes is present in homes," I responded. "He said it's not good for people, so we need the inspection." Radon gas is invisible and has no smell, but it can cause lung problems and cancer.

"But this inspection is going to cost us," Kathy cautioned me.

I decided to do it anyway, just in case. After several days of testing, we discovered that the level of radon gas in the basement was very high, especially under certain weather conditions. I was sad to hear that radon gas was present in the house, but I was happy that we had gone ahead with the test. We were able to discover and fix that invisible problem. The problem was solved with the addition of a permanent meter that controls the level of radon as well as a pipe venting it to the outdoors.

Sometimes the Bible works like that radon test. It checks hidden areas of our lives that we don't see. We may be totally unaware of the presence of a potentially destructive attitude, sinful habit or unbiblical desire. Then suddenly God tells us, "Test this. Check this out. Be sure about this. Give careful attention to your steps. I will guide you, but you must pay attention."

In this book I outline twelve invisible transgressions that have been serious obstacles for God's people since sin came into the world. We do not want any of these unnoticed errors or invisible sins to poison our marriages, our lives or our homes. The Bible tells us:

> Like a muddied spring or a polluted well is a righteous man
> who gives way to the wicked.
>
> —PROVERBS 25:26

We want to have the purity of heaven in our minds and in our hearts. Even though we are still on earth, our passport is stamped: "Heavenly." We are citizens of heaven (Phil. 3:20). We are called to operate under a different set of rules.

I have a double citizenship. I am an Argentine by birth and an American by choice. In my country you do not lose your citizenship when you become a citizen of another country. I travel with a passport from both countries, and I use either of these two passports when I pass through customs in different countries. However, I know that there are different laws and rules in both nations.

In the same way, if you have been born again, you are bicultural. You have a passport of your nation, but you also have a passport from the kingdom of heaven. Daily we are learning more about the rules, commands and regulations of the kingdom of heaven.

I do not want to delay God's revival move in the world, and I'm sure you do not want to delay it either, simply because our obedience is delayed. This is why it is so important for us to expose and root out these twelve transgressions from our lives.

Why Revival Doesn't Come

Many times we consider our world, our neighborhoods and our own lives and ask ourselves, *How can there be revival? My city isn't being transformed for Christ. Lives are not being transformed or touched. What is hindering a mighty move from God?* Many of us are waiting for a revival that will touch every part of society. Yet it seems to elude us. Why?

Revival is the renewal of the church. It's also the awakening of unbelievers and the reforming of society. When God moves in awesome power, the light of His Word will prevail against darkness. Whenever there is genuine revival in a nation, sooner or later the history of that nation will be changed. Not only will the church be renewed—entire cities and nations will be wrapped in the arms of the Holy Spirit.

Some of you may have trouble believing that this is possible. Let me encourage you with an example in the Bible. Look at the city of Nineveh (Jon. 1-4). When Jonah took the word of the Lord to that city, the whole city was impacted. The Ninevites declared a fast, and everybody fasted—including men and beasts alike. As a result, God relented from judgment, and His mercy prevailed.

The first revival described in the Book of Acts changed the history of this planet. The revival that promises to shake our generation will also transform the whole world. But the bottom line is this: *For this revival to begin within the church, we must first be cleansed of our transgressions.*

What are the twelve transgressions? The Lord birthed these principles in my spirit so that I may encourage the church to overcome sin totally and live "from glory to glory" (2 Cor. 3:18, KJV). In each chapter I will present the trauma of missing His will and how well-known Bible characters allowed these sins to trap them. I will also show how God can help you to turn your own failures into a testimony of God's amazing grace.

Let's look closer at these twelve transgressions.

1. When weakness becomes sin

We get a firsthand look at the tragedy of this transgression in the life of Eli, the priest whose own sons strayed far from the Lord. Eli knew his sons were in sin, yet he was too weak to do anything about it. Eli ended up dying a tragic death, as did his sons, even though he had been serving Israel in the priesthood for forty years.

2. Using carnal means to obtain divine blessing

Although Jacob had been promised a blessing from the moment of birth, he used his own scheming plan to get the blessing from his brother. How tragic it is today that so many of God's people believe they can manipulate or trick God and friends into granting them their unsanctified desires.

3. Charisma without character

Samson is an example of a man who had an obvious call of God upon his life, along with unusual spiritual power. Yet, because he lacked godly character, his transgressions cost him the sight of his eyes and, eventually, his life. We learn from his sad story that impressive physical and spiritual abilities do not replace the need for inward integrity.

4. Using godly anger in an ungodly way

Moses gave us an example of this transgression. The first time the children of Israel needed water, Moses was told to *strike* the rock. So he struck the rock and water came. The second time they needed water, he was told to *speak* to the rock, but he struck it in anger. Amazingly, water still gushed forth, but because of his anger and partial obedience, he lost the privilege of going into the Promised Land. How many leaders today have frustrated the grace of God by misusing their authority in this way!

5. Embracing disillusionment

Elijah defeated the four hundred fifty prophets of Baal on Mount Carmel and saw the revival fire of God descend in front of an entire nation. Yet afterward he sank into a deep depression. He succumbed to a stubborn spirit of discouragement, and although God renewed his spirit, Elijah was instructed to anoint his own replacement. So often we are tempted to entertain thoughts of discouragement and even suicide. But if we are walking in true holiness we will not allow this negativity to rule our hearts or steal our joy in Christ.

6. The sin of presumption

Shortly after a great victory at Jericho, Joshua, under God's commission to conquer the land, took his army to battle against Ai—where the Israelites were soundly defeated. Unaware of the sin that was hidden in the camp, Joshua presumed that God would grant them victory. Many people struggle with anger over an Ai experience. They don't understand why God allowed them to fail. Perhaps it was because sin was hiding in the camp, and they did not think to check their motives and desires. It does not matter how many victories you have experienced in your past. An unexplained defeat will always come back to haunt you.

7. Allowing foolishness to become sin

King Saul became a victim of his own calling because he rushed things. Unable to wait patiently for the prophet Samuel to offer the sacrifice to the Lord, King Saul took matters into his own hands and offered the sacrifice himself. That foolish, carnal rush triggered the rejection of his kingship and the destruction of his kingdom.

8. Failing to set boundaries

David harbored secret sin in his life. After a time, it became hidden even to himself. It took someone else, the prophet Nathan, to awaken him to the reality of his sin. Even though his sin was hidden, he still paid the consequences of that sin. During that process, he moved from unnoticed sin to conviction of sin and, finally, to genuine repentance.

9. Fatal distractions

The primary sin that destroyed Solomon's relationship with God was not sexual immorality. The main sin was this: Solomon ignored God's warning that marrying foreign women would bend his heart toward their pagan idols. As with Solomon, there are distractions in our lives that, in time, will bend our hearts toward evil. If we are not vigilant, these distractions will destroy us.

10. Serving God with reluctance

Jonah was called to preach to the city of Nineveh, but he did not want to go. Through the supernatural intervention of God, Jonah was finally convinced he should go. He went from disobedience to being a reluctant servant. He went to Nineveh unwillingly. His feet were there, but his heart was not. When our hearts do not accompany our obedience, frustration will surely follow. Often we feel we are "doing God a favor" by obeying Him, but the truth is that we are dragging our feet all the way—and hindering His purpose as we complain!

11. Fearing man more than God

Peter was a man-pleaser, and his actions revealed his error. When he was with the Gentiles, he showed them acceptance. Yet when backed into a corner by religious legalists, he refused to get together with the Gentiles. He had double standards based on fear. It was hard for him to portray truth. His hypocrisy influenced others and compromised his integrity. Man-fearers become man-pleasers. If man-pleasing is allowed a place in our hearts, we will eventually stumble.

12. Refusing to give up the last idol

The last transgression always comes in the form of an idol. In the New Testament, a wealthy and successful young leader came to Jesus to inquire about eternal life. He had an impeccable religious background, yet the Lord went past his religious status and found an idol in his heart. External obedience alone will not do. We always must identify and eradicate the one area in which we refuse to follow Christ.

Each of these biblical leaders failed God in an area of obedience—just as we all have done. But as we begin to look closely at each of these transgressions, I want you to discover the keys to overcoming these transgressions so that you can experience the grace of God enabling you to live a life of holiness. By the indwelling power of the Holy Spirit, you can overcome the failure of transgression and become a forerunner of revival in your community.

Chapter 1

The Transgression of Eli: When Weakness Becomes Sin

In 1999, presidential elections were held in my home country of Argentina. After being under the rule of the Peronist party for ten years, the people threw their support behind the other political party—the Radical party. Fernando de la Rua, the candidate for the Radical party, was voted in as president. He, of course, inherited the country in the situation in which the Peronists had left it. That was a difficult situation. Argentina had accumulated more than $100 billion of foreign debt during a period when the peso was artificially determined to have the same value as the dollar. Many of the government-run services, such as telephone companies, airlines, railroads and petroleum companies, were sold to private investors.

De la Rua could have succeeded. He was not known to be a corrupt man, and he had very good intentions for the country. But his lack of decisiveness, timely action and sound strategies caused him to lose the trust of the Argentines. When the people realized that he was not providing strong leadership for the country and that the economy was beginning to deteriorate and unemployment was rising, their disappointment turned into desperation. Soon the frustrated people took to the streets in protest, which resulted in twenty-seven deaths. The government froze personal bank accounts. Mobs stood outside banks to demand that the government reverse its policies. De la Rua had to resign after serving only two years of his four-year term. He fled the presidential palace by helicopter. His political weakness cost him his presidency.

In this chapter we are going to take a look at a biblical leader who faced a similar dilemma. And we will learn that good intentions alone will not excuse us when we have been irresponsible.

ELI'S PROBLEM: COMPROMISING WITH THE SINS OF OTHERS

In 1 Samuel 2, we find the story of Eli, a leader who guided Israel for forty years. He basically was a good person. He wasn't committing adultery or stealing from the offering plate. We know from the Scriptures that he was a peaceful man. However, he ended his days in tragedy.

Eli was a good man who failed. Why did this happen? In 1 Samuel 2 we also read the record of Eli's wicked sons, who had no regard for the Lord:

> Now Eli, who was very old, heard about everything his sons were doing to all Israel and how they slept with the women who served at the entrance to the Tent of Meeting. So he said to them, "Why do you do such things? I hear from all the people about these wicked deeds of yours."
>
> —1 SAMUEL 2:22–23

It appears that when Eli became aware of his sons' wicked deeds, he simply gave his sons a proverbial "slap on the wrist":

> No, my sons; it is not a good report that I hear spreading among the LORD's people. If a man sins against another man, God may mediate for him; but if a man sins against the Lord, who will intercede for him?
>
> —1 SAMUEL 2:24–25

But even though Eli gave his sons a mild rebuke, they did not listen to their father's correction. Their hearts were already hardened.

Although Eli had good intentions, he was weak in his dealings with sin in others. He had the mantle and the calling to guide Israel. It appeared that he was in the right place. However, Eli's toleration of sin became his downfall.

THREE ERRORS OF ELI

Eli did not have the moral strength to deal strongly with his sons' wickedness. Because of his own weakness, he fell into three errors. These three errors greatly impacted his effective leadership not only of his own sons, but also of the nation of Israel. These errors will impact the leadership of any person who does not deal strongly with wickedness when it surfaces within the lives of people for whom that person is providing leadership. We must avoid these errors at all cost.

1. He was too tolerant.

Eli allowed immoral men in the ministry. Hophni and Phinehas were serving in the temple, yet they were having sex in the doorway of the tent of meeting! Their consciences were so seared that they were committing fornication in the sight of God and His people! Eli's error was that he tolerated this. There comes a time when the servant of the Lord must bring correction.

2. He was too timid.

Scripture tells us that Eli "was very old" (1 Sam. 2:22). We must beware of the sins of old age. Perhaps Eli felt that he was just too old and too tired to take a strong hand with his wicked, independent sons. Perhaps they acted belligerently toward their old, weakened father.

Age does bring physical weakness, but it does not have to bring spiritual weakness. It should be a time of great spiritual maturity. By responding timidly to the situation, Eli was revealing his own lack of spiritual maturity. How tragic that a man of God could fail so miserably at the end of his life simply because he allowed his physical weariness to disqualify him.

3. He was too late.

By the time Eli even bothered to rebuke his children, they did not listen to him. It was already much too late for Eli to try to deal with the wickedness of his sons. Perhaps Eli assumed that his sons would serve the Lord faithfully simply because he was a priest or because they grew up near the temple. No doubt he had failed to call his sons to obedience from the time they were small boys—long before they entered the priesthood and began impacting the nation with their wickedness. Their wickedness was so great that Scripture says it was the Lord's will to put them to death (v. 25).

VITAL LESSONS ON SPIRITUAL AUTHORITY

Responsibility and authority are so important that God will hold the irresponsible accountable. Here are eight lessons from which we all can benefit:

1. God holds leaders accountable.

There is no doubt that Eli's sons were wicked men. Scripture says, "They had no regard for the Lord" (1 Sam. 2:12). They were immoral. They were involved in scandalous sin. Yet God speaks to *Eli:* "Why do *you* scorn my sacrifice and offering that I prescribed for my dwelling?" (v. 29, emphasis added).

The sins Eli permitted had become his sins! Avoiding this transgression is not about forcing our Christianity on our children, but it will require our taking wicked men out of the ministry when it is our authority to do so—even if they are our children. In other words, to avoid this transgression we must make things right before God when there are things that are not right within our area of responsibility.

I know of pastors who employ their adult children on the staff of their churches. This can be a wonderful experience, of course. But there are cases where a pastor will tend to overlook his own son's sins simply because he wants to protect him or to protect his family's reputation. This is tragic, because the lack of biblical discipline will allow sin to grow like a cancer in that church.

A senior pastor cannot avoid having an immoral son, but he can avoid having his son in a place of ministry. The same rule would apply even if the person was not his son. A spiritual leader should not tolerate immoral people in places of ministry—even if they give large tithes, are influential in the congregation, have seniority or are relatives.

2. God will not accept second place.

God asked Eli, "Why do you honor your sons more than me?" (v. 29). God will not play second fiddle. He demands to be first. He tells us that clearly: "For the LORD your God is a consuming fire, a jealous God" (Deut. 4:24).

By not dealing with the wickedness in his sons, Eli was placing their desires and wishes—and sin—above the desires and commandments of God. We can never allow what is precious to us—even our children—to take precedence over God's will. This is idolatry.

3. God has a right to break promises.

Many of God's promises always come with a price tag—our obedience. Even though the Lord had promised Eli that his family would minister forever, because of Eli's disobedience God changed His mind and canceled the promise. God's promise was replaced with a curse:

> Therefore the LORD, the God of Israel, declares: "I promised that your house and your father's house would minister before me forever." But now the LORD declares: "Far be it from me! Those who honor me I will honor, but those who despise me will be disdained. The time is coming when I will cut short your strength and the strength of your father's house, so that there will not be an old man in your family line and you will see distress in my dwelling. Although good will be done to Israel, in your family line there will never be an old man. Every one of you that I do not cut off from my altar will be spared only to blind your eyes with tears and to grieve your heart, and all your descendants will die in the prime of life."
>
> —1 SAMUEL 2:30–33

4. God can find a substitute.

God's callings and gifts are irreversible. His destiny for us is meant to be permanent, but our disobedience can override His best plans. After cursing Eli and his family's ministry, God said:

> I will raise up for myself a faithful priest, who will do according to what is in my heart and mind. I will firmly establish his house, and he will minister before my anointed one always.
>
> —1 SAMUEL 2:35

Then God raised up Samuel as a faithful "priest" unto the Lord. How different was Hannah's determination to raise her son to wholeheartedly serve God from the attitude of Eli, who timidly slapped his sons on the wrist for their flagrant sinning before God. Hannah had vowed that her son would serve God, and Him alone: "O LORD Almighty, if you will only look upon your servant's misery and remember me, and not forget your servant but give her a son, then *I will give him to the LORD for all the days of his life,* and no razor will ever be used on his head" (1 Sam. 1:11, emphasis added). We should remember that Eli actually made fun of Hannah's prayers for a child. He did not understand her travail, nor did he respect her desire to raise up a deliverer for Israel. He demonstrated this same attitude by raising sons who mocked God.

May we learn to carry a "Hannah attitude" so we can avoid transgressing as Eli did.

5. God may seem unduly severe.

Why did God levy so much punishment upon Eli? Because God had placed so much trust and authority upon him. We read in James 3:1:

> Not many of you should presume to be teachers, my brothers, because you know that we who teach will be judged more strictly.

God's Word is clear: "From everyone who has been given much, much will be demanded; and from the one who has been entrusted with much, much more will be asked" (Luke 12:48). Eli had been entrusted with the nurture and care of God's beloved people. He could not carelessly abdicate his responsibility by looking the other way while his sons committed acts of wickedness against those people. He broke God's trust, and he felt the sting of God's severe response. Of course we know that God is merciful and will forgive our sins when we humble ourselves in repentance. But God's mercy does not always restore to us His special promises. Leaders who walk in disobedience can be disqualified.

6. The lack of moral energy is dangerous.

Eli's compromising with sin was the cause of his demise. God will not turn His eyes away from the presence of wickedness in His church. He will not deal lightly with those who will not deal strongly to rid His church of sin. Hophni and Phinehas both died for their disobedience. Eli's family line was cursed—and Eli himself would be filled with grief as he saw his family reap the rewards of his sons' wickedness:

> The time is coming when I will cut short your strength and the strength of your father's house, so that there will not be an old man in your family line and you will see distress in my dwelling. Although good will be done to Israel, in your family line there will never be an old man. Every one of you that I do not cut off from my altar will be spared only to blind your eyes with tears and to grieve your heart, and all your descendants will die in the prime of life.
>
> —1 SAMUEL 2:31–33

7. Irresponsibility in leadership brings Ichabod in the land.

Ichabod means, "the glory has departed." Many times God's glory departs because a leader has allowed corruption to enter when it was in his power to change it. In many examples in the Bible, not even the ark of the presence of God could save God's people from the consequences of corrupt leadership.

After the Israelites lost four thousand men in a battle against the Philistines, they decided to bring the ark of the covenant back from Shiloh to keep them safe from their enemies. (See 1 Samuel 4:1–10.) They sent for the ark. Eli's two wicked sons were present with them in the camp with the ark. The Philistines came against them again, and this time thirty thousand foot soldiers were killed, the ark was captured and Eli's two sons died. The presence of the ark did not protect the Israelites from God's judgment upon them at the hands of the Philistines.

The presence of God in your church will not cover sin. Increased worship will not overturn the judgment of God when corruption is present. We can turn up the volume of our music, preach louder and shout longer. But if we are hiding sin, the glory of God will not rest in that place.

8. The one who has the gift of leadership needs to lead with diligence.

Even though our bodies are getting old, we must remain strong in the spirit. The apostle Paul said:

> Though outwardly we are wasting away, yet inwardly we are being renewed day by day.
>
> —2 CORINTHIANS 4:16

We need to say *no* to getting old spiritually. We are being renewed, and every day we resemble Jesus more and more—until the very last day of our lives. God never gives us permission to "retire" spiritually.

By the time Polycarp, the bishop of Smyrna, was in his eighties, he had developed bone spurs in his knees from being in prayer so much. But he didn't lose his spiritual authority or get old morally. The principles he had followed during his entire life were maintained diligently until the very end.

One night this bishop of Smyrna dreamed that his pillow caught on fire. The next morning he told his companions, "I must be burnt alive." The dream did not shake him. He had the power of God upon him. Even at the age of eighty, his frail body had a powerful spirit within it, and he was eagerly waiting for the resurrection of his body in Jesus.

Three days after Polycarp's dream, soldiers came to arrest him. They took him away, tied him to a stake and prepared to burn him.[1] They lit the fire under him, and while it burned, Polycarp worshiped the Lord with such intensity that he forgot he was standing in the flames. The old saint discovered that the flames of the fire of God in his heart were stronger than the fires of persecution.

Polycarp was being executed in a stadium filled with blood-thirsty spectators. They were there to watch another "martyr for the cause" die at the stake. *But he wouldn't die.* The military leaders were amazed that Polycarp was not being consumed by the flames. Finally they ordered the soldiers to pierce his body with a spear. History records that Polycarp was killed by the spear—not by the fire![2]

Before his death, the authorities of the city had admonished Polycarp: "Listen, you can save yourself from the bonfire. All you have to do is to deny Jesus."

Polycarp's words echo down through the annals of history: "Eighty and six years have I served him, and he never once wronged me; how then shall I blaspheme my King, Who hath saved me?"[3]

Each believer today must make a decision to stand firm for Christ. We must determine not to be weak morally. We need a rock-solid commitment to live—and die, if necessary—for Jesus.

MIXED RESULTS

It is confusing for believers to see servants of the Lord who appear to be doing great things for the Lord suddenly betray their spiritual commitment in an act of devastating sin. Such scandalous behavior seems inexplicable. How can godly people do ungodly things?

We've all heard stories of Christian leaders who have been caught in immorality, cheating the government, extorting church funds and the like. In recent days, the American church has been plagued with scandal. Ministers in so-called Spirit-filled churches have fallen into adultery, homosexuality and child molestation. And in some cases, these fallen ministers were quickly "restored" to their positions in the church.

Our actions can even become violent if we harbor hidden weakness. Over the years I have counseled some servants of the Lord who say to me, "Pastor, I don't know what happened, but I was just about ready to hit somebody. The violence within me surprised me." It is shocking to discover that domestic violence is a serious problem in the church today—even in some ministers' homes. Spiritual weakness can cause dangerous reactions in our lives, and we need to strive continually to walk in the strength and power of God's Spirit. How do we avoid these devastating failures? Why is there such a moral crisis in the church today? I believe it is because of the sin of spiritual neglect.

Day after day, year after year, we neglect our bodies, our families and our churches; then, in a panic, we ask God why we are failing. I learned years ago that spiritual strength is a decision and a choice each person must make. Strength is not a gift. Strength is not a special talent. It is a choice of our faith. The Lord spoke these words to Joshua:

> Be strong and courageous. Do not be terrified; do not be discouraged, for the LORD your God will be with you wherever you go.
>
> —JOSHUA 1:9

Not only will God give you strength, but He will also motivate you to be courageous.

The Book of Proverbs compares the righteous man who gives way to wickedness to a "polluted well" (Prov. 25:26). This pollution comes when we do not draw our spiritual strength from God, but instead neglect time in His Word, prayer and developing an intimate relationship with Him. Because of this neglect we begin to give place to the wicked. Although Eli was a righteous man, a priest in God's temple, he neglected his relationship with God, fell into spiritual lethargy and gave place to the wicked—his own children. As a result he destroyed his life and the lives of his children, and he brought spiritual ruin to a nation.

In the year 2002, a horrible scandal was uncovered in the Roman Catholic Church. It became obvious, as reports surfaced, that Catholic bishops who were aware of clergy sexual abuse were excusing these immoral priests and even sending them to other parishes in order to hide the sin. Priests who were preying sexually on innocent boys were allowed to continue ministry in the church.

Similar spiritual compromise goes on in many churches today. There are pastors who have committed terrible injustices through spiritual neglect. They have negotiated and compromised with people—sometimes members in their own churches. Some pastors have failed to remove ungodly people from ministry positions because they feared that person's removal would bring financial ruin to the church. At times a pastor may fail to deal with error in the church or staff because it seems that even in the midst of known sin the church is still growing and flourishing.

I believe the devil desires to make a pact with us. He bargains with us by saying, "You take care of the growth in your church. Don't worry so much about immorality; don't get fanatical about holiness. Don't go to those extremes. You take care of your congregation, and I'll take care of your city."

The devil is not afraid of church growth. He doesn't care how big our churches become—just as long as we don't enter into revival and holiness. Some Christian leaders have held revival at arm's length while they paid taxes to the devil. Before long, these pastors begin to wonder where the anointing has gone. They don't even realize that God has written "Ichabod" on their door!

Eli desired to maintain peace in the family. How could he denounce his own children and publicly scold them and send them out? After all, that might destroy his reputation! He had the authority of God to take care of the temple, but he didn't make timely decisions. Perhaps he was thinking, *Someday I'm going to have to do something about those boys of mine!* But he never dared to do so. "Someday" never came. Maybe he thought it was going to cost too much. Whatever his reason, Eli knowingly allowed sin to continue under his mantle of leadership.

If you have allowed the wicked to stand next to you in leadership, even if your ministry is flourishing now, sooner or later destruction will come upon your life and upon your ministry. If you allow the children of iniquity in your midst, then you are cursing your church and your ministry. May God give us the strength and wisdom to be leaders who can model integrity and character.

Even if it costs you your salary—or even your ministry—determine to live in the holiness of God. Don't sell yourself out for anything. Don't make transactions with the devil.

When you unleash your life and your ministry to live in holiness and purity, it's not just church growth that you will experience. The glory of God will descend upon your church. And not just upon your church, but upon your whole city also. God is looking for people who will stand in the gap—in the gap of holiness—so that He does not have to send judgment to your city.

A Special Word to Those in Authority

If God has placed you in a position of spiritual authority in His body, like Eli, it is vital for you to examine your life for any areas of moral or spiritual weakness. In the body of Christ we must work in partnership with other believers. If you recognize an area of weakness in your own life, determine to work diligently to strengthen yourself in the Lord. The following recommendations will help you to remain strong and pure during the season of transition into deeper holiness:

Seek the counsel and mentorship of someone in authority.

When you lack spiritual authority, seek out someone who does have that authority and place yourself next to that person. When I was at Bible school in Argentina, I decided that I would not go to chapel meetings. They were compulsory, but I thought I could better use my time by being alone. I wrote Christian songs, I prayed, and I read the Word.

One day the president of the school, who was also my friend and mentor, asked me about my absences from chapel. I answered with great self-confidence (and youthful arrogance), "All I need is God, the Bible and myself," implying that I did not need to fellowship with others at the chapel services.

The president looked firmly at me and said, "Sergio, the spirit of independence is not the spirit of Christ." That rebuke from a man

I respected as a teacher and mentor instantly settled the issue in my life. From that day on, I identified selfish independence and isolation as a sin. My heart began to work toward unity, respect and cooperation more than ever before in my life.

If you are leading a ministry but do not have the confirmation or the strength of the Lord, you need a servant to stand with you. Run to that person and say, "I've lost my moral strength. I've lost the authority to exert discipline in the church. I'm confused. Help me."

This willingness to be vulnerable and submissive will heal the church. It is the way Christ's body is designed to function best. Paul described this attitude in his first letter to the Corinthian church:

> God has combined the members of the body and has given greater honor to the parts that lacked it, so that there should be no division in the body, but that its parts should have equal concern for each other. If one part suffers, every part suffers with it; if one part is honored, every part rejoices with it.
>
> —1 Corinthians 12:24–26

Imitate Christ, who did not show moral weakness.

The Bible says that there was no defect in the Lamb of God (1 John 1:5). He walked in perfect holiness, not just so we can admire Him, but rather that we might imitate Him (Eph. 5:1). If we believe that Jesus walked in purity, and if we are His followers, then we will walk in purity also.

If you give one minute to the devil he will destroy your life. To watch over my own moral integrity, I have made a covenant with my eyes. I travel throughout the world, passing through airports continually and having many sights pass before my eyes, often in a moment when I least expect it. But I have made a covenant with my eyes that I will never look at a woman and covet after her. If at any moment my eyes rest on something that is wicked for more than a second, I kneel right where I am and ask for forgiveness. I want to enjoy the same standard of holiness that Jesus enjoyed.

I travel often, and I must spend many evenings in hotel rooms. This can be a great temptation for traveling ministers because so many hotels offer pornographic movies on the television. So when I check into my room, I typically drape a towel over the television and make it into an "altar" by placing my Bible on the top of it. This is my way of consecrating the room—and my life—to God in a fresh way so that I will not give in to any temptation.

I have learned that we must get radical about holiness! So I say, "Lord, even if I have to kneel every five minutes, even if my pants wear out, even if they're all wrinkled when I'm preaching, I prefer to wear wrinkled pants and ensure that there is not one wrinkle on my soul."

Many precious servants of God today are being lured to look at pornography on the Internet because it is so easily available. I tell these men to get ruthless with sin. If you must, unplug your computer and get rid of it! It would be better to do without the Internet if you are close to losing your ministry because of spiritual compromise. If you will make the same commitment and practice it day by day, moment by moment, greater power and authority will come upon your life. The Lord will cause a holy indignation to rise up within you against sin. He will give you an intolerance against sin, but a great love toward sinners.

Be quick to react against sin.

A pastor or leader who recognizes that there is sin in his congregation—or a believer who recognizes sin in his or her own life—but does not feel strong enough morally to deal with it should make plans right away. That person can begin to fast, pray and seek counsel. He or she may go to another pastor and say, "There's sin in my church (or in my life). If I discipline the person with sin in his or her life, half of my church is going to leave. (Or, I do not have the strength to discipline myself.) Help me, Pastor. Give me strength, because I desire to live in holiness."

Many leaders practice personal holiness, but fail to practice *ministerial holiness.* Eli had great intentions. He led the people of Israel for forty years, but the final results of his ministry were devastating—his family was judged forever. God not only judges us because of our personal wickedness; He also judges the wickedness under our authority that we have refused to cleanse.

Make this day a day for purification. Bathe your finances in holiness. If there are fraudulent transactions in the economy of your church, or if you have told the treasurer to lie a little to conceal the details, then make a decision to change today.

If you do not deal with sin in your midst, you will walk in the way of Eli. Sin always brings death!

Receive the fire of God to restore moral authority.

Some people have the Holy Spirit, *but they don't have His fire.* They feel the presence of God, and it gives them goose bumps and charismatic manifestations, but they don't have the moral authority to correct sin in their own lives or churches.

God is calling each of us to a life of total integrity—no matter what the cost. Everyone who wants to live in righteousness will suffer tribulation. Peter tells us clearly:

> Therefore, since Christ suffered in his body, arm yourselves also with the same attitude, because he who has suffered in his body is done with sin.
>
> —1 PETER 4:1

What does this mean? Perhaps the words of Christ are easier to understand: "In this world you will have trouble" (John 16:33). Don't refuse tribulation and persecution.

Holiness often begins with suffering and persecution. But an indescribable glory falls upon those who endure suffering and persecution and maintain holiness. So don't be afraid of being persecuted. Even if they send you to jail, like Paul and Silas, begin singing worship to the Lord. Holiness is on the way! A deliverance earthquake will come upon your household, your jailer will be converted, and your city, like the city of Philippi, will be revived with the fire of God.

A PRAYER OF REPENTANCE

Father, forgive me for the times when I have become spiritually weak and lethargic. I don't want to fail You because of the transgression of Eli. Grant me grace to avoid the pitfalls of sin. When I am tempted to ignore sin or to tolerate it, help me to confront it lovingly. Give me boldness to speak out when I know that someone is spreading sin like a cancer in your church. And help me to speak the truth in love when my friends or family members need godly correction. In Jesus' name, amen.

Chapter 2

The Transgression of Jacob: Using Carnal Means to Obtain Divine Blessing

A pastor in a large city planted more than fifteen daughter churches. Although they all started out as mission churches, eventually each was given independence and established its own autonomous congregation. One leader who was in charge of one of the daughter churches decided he was not comfortable with being in an associate position. Instead he wanted to be a senior pastor.

So one day he resigned, taking with him all the furniture the pastor had placed in his church. He backed his truck up to the building where the church services were held and then loaded all the chairs, the pulpit and the sound system in the truck. He even took the plants and the decorations that were around the front of the platform!

In actuality, eventually this man would have become a senior pastor when his church was given its independence. But he was too impatient to wait—so he named himself *pastor.*

When I first heard this story, I was still young and had not learned what I now understand about the twelve transgressions. I was sure this guy would last only a few months as self-appointed pastor of a congregation. I was waiting to hear that he had failed miserably. However, he didn't. He began his own congregation with the few members he stole and continued to have moderate growth.

However, there is an addendum to the story. About fifteen years later, when the wounds were healed or forgotten, he faced a time of treasonous actions from his own board members. Some of his young leaders treated him in a worse manner than he had treated the senior pastor under whom he was serving while associate pastor of the daughter church. His previous sins came back to haunt him. He eventually reaped what he had sown.

There is a spiritual law that cannot be broken—even if we carry the anointing of God. We may heal the sick and perform miracles, but the Bible says:

> Do not be deceived: God cannot be mocked. A man reaps what he sows.
>
> —GALATIANS 6:7

It may take fifteen years, or it may not happen until the time of Christ's return, but someday we will give an account for everything we do. That is why it is so important that we never fall into the transgression of Jacob.

SUCCESSFUL YET UNETHICAL?

Have you ever wondered why some people succeed in the church even though they have an apparent lack of ethics? I have seen disloyal people with a fair amount of success. I have even known of men who enjoyed a level of "success" while they were living in adultery.

In the Scriptures, Jacob is an example of someone who broke the rules of ethics and yet experienced an amount of success because of the calling upon his life. In Genesis 25 and 27 we see how Jacob went from being a manipulator to being a usurper. He actually stole someone else's position. He was also a negotiator—he negotiated at Bethel (Gen. 28). *Bethel* means "house of God." A lot of people are stuck at Bethel. They are stuck in religion, in the house of God, which is good, but they never go beyond that point.

Years later Jacob camped at Peniel where he wrestled with the angel of God and became a broken man. Until we get to that part of our life, to our spiritual Peniel, any success we have will be relatively untranscendental in the kingdom of God.

We all have an appointment for a wrestling match with the angel of God! It's a match we will lose, and he will hurt us in our flesh. That is when the actual purposes of God begin to be fulfilled in our lives. All of us need God to wrestle us to the ground so that He can fatally wound our pride.

In the last few years, God has brought a new level of brokenness into my life. Just when we think we have graduated out of brokenness, He comes to break us again. Living our Christian lives in a state of brokenness is the best way to walk with God. It is not damaging, nor is it destructive. The state of brokenness is good, because in brokenness our flesh is wounded, *but our spirits are healed.*

After Jacob's encounter with God, he walked with a limp. He did not walk with a cocky attitude. God had broken his pride. How desperately the church today needs a Peniel encounter!

GOD'S WILL AT THE WRONG TIME

The Bible tells us that Jacob's brother, Esau, actually forfeited his call and destiny because of impatience. In Genesis 25:29–34 we read:

> Once when Jacob was cooking some stew, Esau came in from the open country, famished. He said to Jacob, "Quick, let me have some of that red stew! I'm famished!" (That is why he was also called Edom.)
>
> Jacob replied, "First sell me your birthright."
>
> "Look, I am about to die," Esau said. "What good is the birthright to me?"
>
> But Jacob said, "Swear to me first." So he swore an oath to him, selling his birthright to Jacob. Then Jacob gave Esau some bread and some lentil stew. He ate and drank, and then got up and left. So Esau despised his birthright.

Both the Old and New Testaments tell us that Esau cried bitterly over this impulsive act. (See Genesis 27:34; Hebrews 12:16–17.) He tried to get the birthright and blessing back, but it was too late. He negotiated and exchanged it for instant gratification.

Esau was also looking for instant success. He became an *apostate,* someone who denies the faith.

Here is a word of caution for us who have promises, prophecies and the call of God on our lives. If we become impatient, if our appetites for recognition, position and success get the best of us, chances are we are going to do something desperate just as Esau did. He sold his blessing for a bowl of lentil soup.

Jacob was called by God to inherit the blessing that Esau forsook. God was going to give it to him anyway. Yet it is interesting that in the kingdom of God the end does not justify the means. We might think that if God promises something to us, we should go ahead and get it. But He wants us to wait until it is His perfect time.

Some church splits originate with the attitude of Jacob. Someone who is serving in minor leadership in the church may announce that God has called him or her to preach. The senior pastor might suggest to that person that he or she should go to Bible school to prepare for the ministry and wait for two years to enter the ministry. Rather than take the longer road of preparation, that person leaves in a huff and splits the church. Some members follow, and the person begins preaching on the next Sunday, expecting the Lord to anoint the ministry. He cannot wait for His blessing.

The perplexing thing is that sometimes the Lord does anoint that new work. We begin to feel like asking the Lord to change His way of doing things. Maybe we pray, "Make him fail, Lord. Make his life miserable so people will see Your justice." Well-meaning Christians sometimes get discouraged in situations like this. They expect the justice of God to kick in right away. They want to see the justified failure of that traitor within a matter of a few weeks. But God doesn't work that way—at least not all the time.

Jacob chose to "help" God with a plan—he used carnal means to obtain divine ends. The promises were for him. When he was born, the Lord had told his mother, Rebekah, "The older will serve the younger" (Gen. 25:23). In other words, Esau was going to be a servant of Jacob someday. In essence, God said, "Jacob is My man. I have predetermined that." Jacob knew of God's prophecy to his mother. His mother knew. His father knew. Yet Rebekah and Jacob tried to "help" God—to hurry up His plan—and they ran into trouble as a result. We must come to the realization that we cannot "help" God with our carnal, fleshly manipulation!

LAWFUL BUT NOT RIGHT

Actually, Jacob took two dishonest shortcuts. One of them was the manner in which he manipulated his brother, who was starving. He took advantage of his extreme hunger, figuring his plan was lawful. Although many things may be lawful, not all of them are right. In modern society, we can use lawsuits or legal threats to bring damage to people and to gain more money than we should. This may be legal, but it's not righteous. It is a temptation we need to avoid. It can become a carnal means to obtain financial blessings.

I have heard angry Christians talking about filing a lawsuit so they could make a lot of money. If they had lost a thousand dollars, they were ready to make twenty thousand dollars. That kind of legal battle can be very unfair. As Christians, we need to put a fair limit on our demands. We need to seek justice—but not act out of greed.

The sense of integrity, equity and fairness is lost for so many Christians. The problem is that many times they can succeed in the work of the Lord or in their business without practicing righteousness. They compare themselves to humble people who are always repenting and trying to do things right before God, and when compared to their own successes, numbers and money, they assume their own measurable blessings are a sign of God's approval.

When a nation is called by God to revival, an obvious denunciation of sin can be seen in that nation. The church, due to its own lack of spiritual discernment, may be unaware of the kind of inner sin that can destroy relationships and break trust. Jacob was able to win the birthright from Esau, but he lost trust. His relationship with his brother was lost—nearly for the rest of his life. Because he used carnal means to obtain the will of God in his life, his actions split the family.

WHEN AMBITION REPLACES VISION

Impatience is the fruit of carnality. At times we become very irritated by delays—not knowing that some delays are actually engineered by God. We live in an age of instant gratification. We search for instant solutions at any price, and when we do that, we can be sure carnality is present. Carnality causes our vision to be replaced by selfish ambition. It will lead us to sell what is best to get what is only good.

There is a better way to walk in the ways of the Lord; that is, on the highways of holiness and righteousness and in His timing. It is the path of godly patience and total surrender.

Jacob not only won the birthright, but he also received the blessing from his father. In order to trick his father to bless him, he devised a plan with his mother:

> Jacob said to Rebekah his mother, "But my brother Esau is a hairy man, and I'm a man with smooth skin. What if my father touches me? I would appear to be tricking him and would bring down a curse on myself rather than a blessing."
>
> His mother said to him, "My son, let the curse fall on me. Just do what I say; go and get them for me."
>
> So he went and got them and brought them to his mother, and she prepared some tasty food, just the way his father liked it. Then Rebekah took the best clothes of Esau her older son, which she had in the house, and put them on her younger son Jacob. She also covered his hands and the smooth part of his neck with the goatskins. Then she handed to her son Jacob the tasty food and the bread she had made.

He went to his father and said, "My father."

"Yes, my son," he answered. "Who is it?"

Jacob said to his father, "I am Esau your firstborn. I have done as you told me. Please sit up and eat some of my game so that you may give me your blessing."

Isaac asked his son, "How did you find it so quickly, my son?"

"The LORD your God gave me success," he replied.

—Genesis 27:11–20

Jacob sounded like such a religious man, but he was lying to his father's face. Isaac was old and not able to see his son clearly, so he said to Jacob, "Come near so I can touch you, my son, to know whether you really are my son Esau or not" (v. 21).

My own three sons have discovered a way to trick me. When I call home while I'm traveling, one of my children is able to imitate the voice of the other two. When I ask, "Who is this?", with a little voice he says the name of his younger brother. One or two times I really thought I was talking to my youngest son. Their playful deception has given me a better understanding of how easy it was for Jacob to imitate Esau's voice and appearance, especially since Isaac had grown so old and, no doubt, no longer had good eyesight and hearing.

Jacob went close to his father, Isaac, who touched him and said, "The voice is the voice of Jacob, but the hands are the hands of Esau" (v. 22). Isaac did not recognize Jacob, for his hands were hairy like those of his brother, Esau, so he blessed him. "Are you really my son Esau?" he asked.

"I am," he replied. The result of his lie? He got blessed.

That's hard to assimilate. The man was lying and deceitful, yet he got the blessing. He got the blessing because he was going to get it anyway. It was destined for him. He used carnal means to try to accomplish God's ends. A precious blessing descended upon him, but this does not mean that God ignored Jacob's craftiness.

When Esau realized that he had been cheated, "Esau said to his father, 'Do you have only one blessing, my father? Bless me too, my father!' Then Esau wept aloud" (v. 38). Isaac his father answered him and gave him a difficult word. (See Genesis 27:39–40.)

In verse 41 we see the result of Jacob's carnal manipulation:

> Esau held a grudge against Jacob because of the blessing his father had given him. He said to himself, "The days of mourning for my father are near; then I will kill my brother Jacob."

Jacob's trickery actually put him in serious danger. If our past is not immersed in the blood of Jesus, it can bring future persecution. We need to confess any deceitful dealings we have had with people. May the Holy Spirit bring revelation into our hearts if we have stolen something, lied or manipulated people to obtain personal gain. If we have said something that is not true, God will give us the grace to bring it under the blood of Jesus.

PAY ATTENTION TO THE WARNING SIGNS!

One day I left my office in La Plata, Argentina, to begin a short drive to my house. Argentine traffic is a bit different than it is in some other nations—if you don't go, they push you! I was trying to avoid an accident, but I did not see a red light, not even the traffic lights at all, and went right through it. Another fifty cars went through that red light with me. But soon I saw a different kind of light behind me, one that flashes! It was a policeman!

If you are a pastor or minister, you will be able to sympathize with the silent prayer that I uttered: "Lord, please don't let him ask me about my occupation." I stopped the car, the officer came, and I explained my innocence to him. Hoping to touch a compassionate spot in his heart, I said, "Officer, to be honest with you, I didn't see the red light. I did not even see that there was a traffic light there." He wasn't impressed with my answer, because the consequences of running a red light—whether I saw it or not—could have been devastating.

God has some spiritual red lights that we must heed. He wants us to be attentive, to be alert, to be watching. We need to ask ourselves, "Am I an honest person, or am I a tricky, manipulative person like Jacob? Are my dealings with people honest, or am I constantly telling little white lies and half truths?"

Half truths are the same as lies. Ignorance will not save us. We can't try to plead ignorance when we arrive at heaven's gates by saying, "Lord, I am sorry; I didn't read the story of the life of Jacob."

The Lord might reply to you, "But you have Bibles in ten versions."

Some people have given their lives in order to be able to hold the Bible in their hands. Church history records the examples of people who died to preserve the manuscripts of God's Word. Because of that, we now have the Word of the Lord available to us. God is calling us to be instructed in righteousness, to be wise and knowledgeable in His Word. We may use ignorance as an excuse, but it will not get us off the hook. We cannot ignore the warning signs when they are right in front of us.

Bethel: Negotiating With God

The same person who manipulated his brother, Esau, then tried to manipulate God. He tried to make a deal with God. He probably thought that since he had been able to manipulate so many circumstances in his life, he could now trick God.

Jacob had a dream at Bethel of the presence of the Lord.

> When Jacob awoke from his sleep, he thought, "Surely the LORD is in this place, and I was not aware of it." He was afraid and said, "How awesome is this place! This is none other than the house of God; this is the gate of heaven." Early the next morning Jacob took the stone he had placed under his head and set it up as a pillar and poured oil on top of it. He called that place Bethel, though the city used to be called Luz. Then Jacob made a vow, saying, "If God will be with me and will watch over me on this journey I am taking and will give me food to eat and clothes to wear so that I return safely to my father's house, then the LORD will be my God."
>
> —Genesis 28:16–21

Upon awakening, Jacob made what I call a "conditional vow." When revival comes, these things come to light very quickly. When the move of God begins to flourish in our midst, suddenly people like Jacob will say, "If I get this, I will serve God." People we thought were totally committed to God turn out to be conditional Christians. They make covenants with God at their own dictates. "If the Lord does this for me, I will follow Him, and if not, I'm out."

I remember one Christian lady who brought her mother, who was sick, to church with her. But when her mother did not get healed, the lady quit the church. Because of what happened—or didn't happen—she turned away from the gospel. She thought she could bargain with God and convince Him to condescend to her terms!

People like this woman are the Jacobs of today. They negotiate with God and are conditional in their commitment. They do not say that the Lord will be their God even if they die in the process. Rather, they try to be God themselves. This is the essence of pride.

Jacob could have said, "You will be my God even if I never make it to my father's house. I just want to know that I am pleasing You." But he went from dishonest dealings with his brother to being conditional in the presence of the Lord. We may make progress even with dishonest shortcuts, but eventually we will reap a bitter harvest.

WRESTLING YOUR WAY TO STRENGTH

Jacob, who had acted so deceitfully against his father and brother, reaped a harvest of deceit and betrayal against him from others. When he got older, his father-in-law, Laban, deceived him. His wedding week was a crisis for him. After his wedding night, he realized Laban had given him the wrong lady! He had to work another seven years to pay the bridal price for Rachel, the woman he loved.

Jacob, the deceiver, was now being deceived. He was reaping what he had sown. And it was a bitter harvest. Even with the blessing of the Lord…even with the awesome calling from God to be the father of nations…the deceiver was being deceived.

Jacob became so discouraged that he left his father-in-law's home. No longer welcome at Laban's house—or his father's house—he was in no man's land. The deceiver had become isolated. He had no ministry and no apparent future. He was just trying to survive and not get killed by his brother. The man who always had a trick up his sleeve had now run out of ideas. He was desperate.

I believe that God in His mercy allows such desperation and crisis because He wants to take us up a level—out of conditional Christianity. Jacob was about to have an encounter with God that would end forever his conditional surrender to the will of God. We read of this special moment in Genesis 32:

> That night Jacob got up and took his two wives, his two maidservants and his eleven sons and crossed the ford of the Jabbok. After he had sent them across the stream, he sent over all his possessions. So Jacob was left alone, and a man wrestled with him till daybreak. When the man saw that he could not overpower him, he touched the socket of Jacob's hip so that his hip was wrenched as he wrestled with the man. Then the man said, "Let me go, for it is daybreak."
>
> But Jacob replied, "I will not let you go unless you bless me."
>
> The man asked him, "What is your name?"
>
> "Jacob," he answered.
>
> Then the man said, "Your name will no longer be Jacob, but Israel, because you have struggled with God and with men and have overcome."
>
> Jacob said, "Please tell me your name."
>
> But he replied, "Why do you ask my name?" Then he blessed him there.
>
> So Jacob called the place Peniel, saying, "It is because I saw God face to face, and yet my life was spared."
>
> —Genesis 32:22–30

Notice that Jacob, who earlier had stolen the blessing from his brother, was still seeking the blessing. This time he obtained it— but on God's terms, not his own. Many Christians have used all kinds of tricks, but are still void of the blessing. In an article in *Leadership,* Allan Redpath gave some interesting observations about this moment of struggle that Jacob had with God, which came twenty years after he fled to Aram:

> An angel wrestled with him—encountered him in the very point in which he was strong. He had been a taker by the heel from his very birth, and his subsequent life had been a constant and successful struggle with adversaries. And when he, the stranger, saw that he prevailed not over him, Jacob, true to his character, struggles while this new combatant touched the socket of his thigh so that it was wrenched out of joint. The thigh is the pillar of a man's strength and its joint with the hip and the seat of physical force for the wrestler. Let the thigh bone be thrown out of joint, and the man is utterly disabled. Jacob now finds that this mysterious wrestler has wrestled from him, by one touch, all his might, and he can no longer stand alone. Without any support whatever from himself, he hangs upon the conqueror, and in that condition learns by experience the practice of sole reliance on one mightier than himself. This is the turning point in this strange drama.[1]

Until we have a defining encounter with God, it is as though nothing has meaning in our lives. The encounter with God is for everyone. Every Christian should have a life-changing encounter with God, a moment in which we are "marked" by Him. After his desperate struggle, Jacob was no longer Jacob. His name, *Jacob,* which means "deceiver," was changed to *Israel,* meaning "prince."

The will of the Lord for our lives, our ministries and our characters is to be changed from Jacob to Israel. This was not the first time Jacob had rested for the night from his travels and subsequently encountered the Lord. Twenty years earlier, after fleeing from his angry brother he stopped for the night to rest. That night he encountered the Lord in a dream, standing at the top of a ladder. It was then the Lord promised Jacob: "I am with you and will watch over you wherever you go, and I will bring you back to this land" (Gen. 28:15). When he left that place, he called it *Bethel,* which means "house of God."

The problem with many Christians is that we have become so close to Bethel that we don't want to move anymore. Like Jacob, some people arrive at Bethel and say, "This is the house of God. I have good dreams here. I can see the angels going up and down from the presence of the Lord. This is beautiful, I have what it takes, so why bother with another step?"

Unless we take the next step, our land will not be healed. We must all move from Bethel to Peniel. After Jacob's encounter with God at Peniel, he traveled on to meet his brother, Esau. This time there was no war, no killings and no disaster. He didn't have to fight with Esau—he had wrestled with God.

It is so important for us to learn that there are many battles in the flesh we need to avoid. There is only one struggle that counts—the struggle with God. With the tenacity of Jacob, we need to wrestle with God in a holy way, in a fearful way, and say, "Lord, I will not leave You until You bless me." We need to allow God to crush our self-will and our manipulative nature.

Several years ago, my church in Argentina faced a year of very serious conflict. Until that time we had operated in unity, but due to some internal conflict, suddenly the staff was divided. Some staff members took one side of the issue, and others lined up with the opposition. It became so divisive that a few people began to talk about splitting the church.

As the senior pastor, I did my best to resolve the issue. But the more I tried, the worse the problem became. I set up meeting after meeting to negotiate a resolution, but all to no avail. Although we did a lot of praying, we also called a lot of meetings, trying to get the two primary parties in the conflict to talk out a solution. Some of those meetings became very intense.

One night I was tired and weary of the whole thing. Here I was, traveling to the nations of the world to take the message of holiness, righteousness and the fire of God, and my own church was divided in opinions. "Lord, this is not good!" I cried out. I felt that I had run out of any ideas that could help. Some of our ideas for resolution had been really creative. We tried hard to end the conflict. But no matter what we tried, nothing worked. Everything we touched just turned worse.

That night I fell on my face and said, "Lord, I will not go to sleep until You answer." I had entered my wrestling match with the angel of the Lord. "You must bless me and my church," I prayed. Hour after hour I continued in prayer. I was determined to hear from God. I would rather faint than fall asleep.

Finally I sank down on the sofa with my Bible in my hands and fell asleep exhausted. Less than two hours later it was morning. The Lord, in His mercy, was about to bless me. He led me to one particular scripture. As I read the verse, I knew I had received my answer.

Immediately I got on the phone and called one of the offended parties to meet me as soon as possible. "We have a solution to the problem," I told him when I saw him. From that moment on, although it took a carefully thought-out process, we walked out of that conflict—without losing one member over that issue or experiencing a painful division. The two ministries led by the parties involved in the conflict are still together today, and they don't want to separate. Because of God's pure grace the mercy of the Lord descended on us.

How like God it was to bring me to the point of desperation. He showed up when I had not one more idea to try. Not even the fourteen-page agreement we had drafted could solve the discussion because nobody wanted to sign it. But when I finally decided to struggle with the angel of the Lord, the answer came.

Brokenness Attracts God

God is looking for Christians with wounded flesh. The Word tells us, "God opposes the proud but gives grace to the humble" (James 4:6). God is looking for a people whose name is no longer *Jacob*— no longer seen as the smart one, the fast one, the one who takes the advantage right away. God's people must be broken before God. He is looking for people who say, "Lord, I am hurting, but I am so desperate for You that I am going to keep struggling until I get my answer."

Your answer will come! Don't be afraid of your wrestling match with God. It doesn't matter if you walk out of that confrontation limping in your flesh. I hope you will! The tricky ways of the flesh need to collapse. In the account of Jacob's wrestling, we are told that the angel of the Lord touched Jacob's *thigh*. The thigh contains the largest bone and muscle in the body. It represents human strength. But in order for Jacob to be truly strong in God, God had to break his human strength.

We need our pride to be shattered. We need to say, "Lord, use us as a generation of people who are pure not only in our objectives, but also in the way we pursue those objectives. Make us people who keep our word."

Jesus warned us, "Let your 'Yes' be 'Yes,' and your 'No,' 'No'" (Matt. 5:37). In our litigation-conscious world today, with its required signatures and safeguards of every kind in place, people still don't keep their word. The covenants made at weddings with vows, rings and pictures are broken all the time. People walk away from business deals, break their word in relationships and deceive to get what they want all the time.

Become a man and woman of your word. Say, "From this day on, God Almighty, I will be a man or a woman of honor; I will be a man of honesty, a man of my word. When I say yes, people will know I mean it."

Don't Get Ahead of God's Will

Jacob waited more than twenty years for God's will to unfold in his life. It may not always take twenty years, but we often experience a dry period, a season of desert waiting, for God's will to unfold in our lives. Don't get ahead of God's will for you.

Many Christians do run ahead. Don't be the young man or woman who can't wait for marriage to become physically intimate. Don't think, I *can't wait until my marriage; I am so tempted. I love my fiancé(e) anyway, I know that (s)he is the one that God promised to give me.* Thinking like that will lead you into fornication.

And don't be impatient for God to place you into the ministry to which you have been called. Don't try to rush Him by getting started "on your own." The one who cannot wait for ministry doors to open will not be respectful of authority. We can call it the Frank Sinatra syndrome—because he sang, "I did it my way." We have enough self-will in the church!

When the fire of the Lord came in my life in 1997, one thing was sure—it wasn't my way. It was His way. I was perplexed, embarrassed and scared, but it also brought a period of great rejoicing as I saw God unfold His plan to me. Give God time to work in your life. Come to the place of Peniel, then prayerfully and carefully wait for your destiny to be unveiled. God will lead you into your blessing!

I dream of a nation of righteousness, yet many times the ways of the church are not righteous. Before I received the fire of God in my life, I felt good. I felt confident that I didn't have any spectacular sin in my life. But then God showed me my corrupt heart, and things began to change. We need to rid ourselves of any pretending, falsehood, lying and cheating. We need to confess any specific sins in any area God brings to mind. Surrender it all to the Lord. Make a decision that from this day on, you will be a person of integrity—no longer Jacob, but Israel.

As you empty yourself of these ways, the Lord will show you His ways. Every lie and every pretense in the body of Christ should be changed into total honesty. My prayer is that God would put a mark on us, a wound in our flesh, so that we will not dare to do ministry again in carnality. May we do ministry in the power of the Holy Spirit. May we limp as a reminder that we are totally dependent on His power alone.

I see an army being trained that will be so well equipped that no casualties will be necessary. This is the only army in which our Commander-in-Chief, God, assures us we will not become casualties. We need only to obey His instructions. God is preparing His army.

More than two hundred years ago, revivalist John Wesley enrolled more than two hundred thousand people in small groups. He referred to these groups of people as "holy clubs." He gave them twenty-two questions to use during their daily devotions. Two of these questions were: "Are you consciously or unconsciously pretending to be something or someone you are not?" and "Have you made yourself out to others as being better than you actually are?"

We need to return to honesty in the body of Christ. We must return to sincerity and truthfulness. Some of you may need to take steps of restitution. Ask the Lord for wisdom. Sometimes the prayer of repentance is not the final step, but rather the first. You may have to take several steps toward God.

If you are not sure how to do this, consult your pastor and your leaders for help. As you are trained in a new dimension of righteousness, you may find you need to make restitution. If the Holy Spirit prompts you to do so, make a list of the specific steps you plan to take. Doing this will produce fruit in keeping with repentance. (See Luke 3:8.)

A Prayer of Repentance

Father, find in me any dishonest ways. Search me in my deepest parts, O God. You are preparing me for something that is so great, so beyond my own carnal strength. I want to give up my carnal weaponry. I put it at the altar of the Lord, and I pray for Your mercy now.

I am about to wrestle with You. Change me from Jacob to Israel. Move me from Bethel to Peniel. Change me completely. I renounce selfish ambition, fear of man and the desire to please everyone all the time. I take a stand against falsehood, against lying spirits, deceitfulness, the lack of transparency and the lack of sincerity in Jesus' name. I pray that You will purify my mind, my way and my eyes, Lord. Wound my flesh.

Cause me to walk with a limp. I would rather have my flesh wounded by You, Lord, than destroyed by Satan.

Come, O God, in Your mercy. I want to move from negotiation to surrender, from conditional commitment to unconditional consecration to You. Receive me; accept me; I give You 100 percent of my life! In Jesus' name, amen.

Chapter 3

The Transgression of Samson: Charisma Without Character

A few years ago, we heard about a pastor who was experiencing some tremendous supernatural manifestations of God in his congregation. The power of God often manifested while he was on Christian radio. People began calling the station to tell him that as he prayed and talked about the things of God, golden dust fell in their homes. As he heard these tremendous reports, he looked around the studio to tell the soundmen and other employees, but they were all on the floor under the power of God.

He told about other unusual signs and wonders in his congregation. As people worshiped, precious stones would fall into the choir loft. The choir members were picking them out of their hair! Other members of the church discovered their teeth had been filled with gold fillings. We knew of some people who had seen the gold fillings, as well as the precious stones.

After these things began occurring, this pastor was invited to travel to other nations to share his story. The reports were sent back to us of golden dust falling within an area of one hundred feet around the buildings where he was preaching.

It was obvious that God was manifesting Himself in the ministry of this pastor. His church was experiencing supernatural signs and wonders, and many people were being added to his congregation. It was growing by leaps and bounds.

A few years after these signs began, we heard other very different news about this man: He had left his wife, had run off with another woman and was no longer pastoring the church! No doubt you would want to ask the question, "Did this scandalous behavior begin suddenly?"

I would have to answer, "No, it takes more than one swing of the ax to fell a large tree." Apparently there had been some unfaithfulness for a long time, but finally the tree could no longer stand. Sadly, this is an example of a man who had charisma and supernatural gifts, but no solid Christian character to back it up.

FLIRTING WITH DISASTER

Unfortunately, this transgression is very common with people in our churches. We could also call it "the transgression of flirting with the world." It happens when we become too friendly with the things of which God does not approve or when we establish ongoing relationships that do not please Him. In the life of Samson we see a man who destroyed his own life because he flirted with the world. He was dancing with the enemy, just playing around with the godly anointing the Lord had given him.

There is no doubt that Samson had charisma. He received the gifts of the Spirit with signs and wonders. He was a leader, called from birth for God's service. God entrusted him as a judge to lead his nation.

This man was graced with a good background. His parents feared God. They had received an angelic visitation to announce his birth. Signs and wonders accompanied his birth. The angel of the Lord, the presence of God manifested as an angel, said to the parents of Samson: "The boy is to be a Nazirite, set apart to God from birth" (Judg. 13:5). Samson was dedicated to the will of God before his birth. He was special.

Samson had the right prophecies, the right training and the

godly background. Many things were right with Samson, but he lacked a foundation of godly character. It is a dangerous thing to have charisma without good moral character.

It often seems that the body of Christ is divided between those who embrace the gifts of the Holy Spirit and those who don't. I have friends on both sides. I respect both evangelicals and Pentecostals, and I learn from both. But it is sad to see that some people exhibit gifts with no godly character. As a result, they become stumbling stones for those who are trying to walk in the Spirit.

As you read this book, may God grant you special grace to be embraced by His complete holiness. I invite you to embrace radical holiness. Do not wait for a later date; it may never come. If you sense the Holy Spirit speaking to your heart about embracing total holiness in your life, no matter what your age, start today.

IT TAKES TWO WINGS TO FLY

When my youngest son was about six years old, we lived in Argentina. One day we had a competition flying paper airplanes in our living room. My son decided to build a very original plane— one with only one wing. "It's not going to fly," I predicted to him.

"Daddy, you don't know; let me do it," he responded.

"OK," I said, and let him try it. In great anticipation he threw that paper plane with all his might. It gave only one disappointing half loop in flight, then fell with a flop on the floor. As I predicted, it did not fly.

Unfortunately, some people follow that same pattern. They think they can "fly" in the ministry, but they insist on doing it with only one wing. They have a lot of anticipation, but become bitterly disappointed. That's because it takes two wings to fly in the will of God—*charisma* and *character.*

It's impossible to fly with only one wing. Yet some Christians decide to be people of upright moral character, dedicating themselves solely to teaching the Bible. They forget the anointing, miracles, signs and wonders. Some have even been taught that miracles only happened in New Testament times. Others decide that because they feel the presence of God and are used in supernatural signs and wonders, they are completely right before God. They forget character.

Neither extreme is biblical. God is calling the body of Christ to dare to believe we can have both things. We can be filled with the Spirit and have His gifts in our lives—and also have a character of integrity.

SEVEN SPIRITUAL ADVANTAGES

Each of the following spiritual advantages was a part of Samson's life. They may also be a part of the experience of a man or woman of God. But without character, none of these advantages will assure success in your spiritual life.

1. The calling of God

Samson was called from birth to be a Nazirite and leader:

> The angel of the LORD appeared to her and said, "You are sterile and childless, but you are going to conceive and have a son. Now see to it that you drink no wine or other fermented drink and that you do not eat anything unclean, because you will conceive and give birth to a son. No razor may be used on his head, because the boy is to be a Nazirite, set apart to God from birth, and he will begin the deliverance of Israel from the hands of the Philistines."
>
> —JUDGES 13:3–5

It is wonderful to have a call from God. But do you know that many who have been called have disqualified themselves? Some did not answer the call. Others sought to fulfill the call in their own carnal way or according to their own timetable.

2. Being well prepared

Samson's parents equipped and trained him just as they were instructed to do by the angel of the Lord. They obviously took their parenting responsibility seriously:

> Then Manoah prayed to the LORD: "O LORD, I beg you, let the man of God you sent to us come again to teach us how to

bring up the boy who is to be born." God heard Manoah, and the angel of God came again to the woman while she was out in the field; but her husband Manoah was not with her. The woman hurried to tell her husband, "He's here! The man who appeared to me the other day!"

—Judges 13:8–10

Having a godly heritage is a wonderful advantage. But it does not assure success. Just because our parents taught us the Word of God does not automatically mean that we will choose the path of holiness.

3. Signs and wonders

An angel appeared to announce Samson's birth, and then ascended in the flames on the altar where Manoah had place a sacrifice to God.

As the flame blazed up from the altar toward heaven, the angel of the LORD ascended in the flame. Seeing this, Manoah and his wife fell with their faces to the ground. When the angel of the LORD did not show himself again to Manoah and his wife, Manoah realized that it was the angel of the LORD.

—Judges 13:20–21

God may go to great lengths to get your attention and to affirm your calling. But even great miracles do not guarantee success.

4. The blessing of God on your life

Samson had the initial blessing of God upon his life.

The woman gave birth to a boy and named him Samson. He grew and the LORD blessed him.

—Judges 13:24

The fact remains that we must choose to walk in God's blessing. If we flirt continually with the world or choose to walk in flagrant disobedience, we can forfeit all that He has planned for us.

5. The tangible presence of the Spirit

Samson felt the Spirit stir within him to do mighty deeds, and people were obviously impressed with his unusual victories.

> And the Spirit of the LORD began to stir him while he was in
> Mahaneh Dan, between Zorah and Eshtaol.
>
> —JUDGES 13:25

Just because we can "feel the Holy Spirit" in a meeting does not
automatically mean that the preacher leading the service is walking in holiness. We cannot allow feelings to determine how we
evaluate a ministry.

6. Awesome supernatural miracles

The Lord allowed Samson to tear a lion apart.

> The Spirit of the LORD came upon him in power so that he
> tore the lion apart with his bare hands as he might have torn
> a young goat.
>
> —JUDGES 14:6

So many ministers have fallen because they assumed that miracles
were a sign that they were right with God. After a few healings, they
became impressed with their own ministries—as if they caused the
healings—and then pride eventually became their downfall.

7. Longevity in the work

Samson led Israel as a judge for twenty years. But we cannot
assume just because someone has been preaching for many years
that the Holy Spirit still backs up everything they say or do.

GO BEYOND THE INITIAL BLESSING

To succeed in the ministry that God gives us, we need to go
beyond the initial blessing. All the apparent advantages that
Samson had in his life were not enough to keep him from spiritual
disaster. Pastor Pedro Ibarra, a pastor who counsels many people
in ministry, once said to me, "It is a law of life: The character carries the anointing, and not vice versa."

A few years ago we began hearing news stories on television
and in the newspapers about many traffic accidents that were
occurring, especially in SUVs using a defective tire. If that flaw had
gone undetected, it could have caused the lives of many to be lost.

We can observe several character flaws in Samson that eventually became part of his downfall. We would do well to learn from this story in Scripture and avoid the same traps.

Impulsiveness

One of Samson's moral flaws was his impulsiveness. Judges 14:19 says that Samson was "burning with anger." Samson had been called to set Israel free from Philistine oppression. It was God who had called him, but he was not operating in the calling of God when he struck down the men of Ashkelon. He may have felt the strong presence of the Lord—but that was not his driving force. His motivation was an anger that was not tempered by the Holy Spirit.

There are people who operate in the strength of their anger. There are Christians who have not forgiven the people who wronged them, and there are so-called believers who still hate someone else. They have not learned the lesson of Jesus, who, even while being crucified, prayed that God would forgive His tormentors. Anger can be a destructive driving force.

Samson also became reactionary and vengeful.

> Samson said to them, "This time I have a right to get even with the Philistines; I will really harm them."
>
> —JUDGES 15:3

> Samson said to them, "Since you've acted like this, I won't stop until I get my revenge on you."
>
> —JUDGES 15:7

He was a leader, but because of his impulsiveness, instead of being proactive in his behavior, he became reactive. He began to react to whatever offense came against him.

Personalizing the ministry

Another moral flaw that Samson had was the problem of personalizing ministry. He began making up his own plan of attack without the Lord's direction. We read in Judges 15:11, "I merely did to them what they did to me."

There are people in the church who cannot find their place in the church. They serve for a while in one ministry, then they get upset and angry and move into some other church. They switch churches as we switch channels. If we are the people of God, equipped to be solid and strong in ministry, why is there such a lack of fidelity in ministry? Why do so many Christians wait year after year and never find their place?

One of the problems is personalizing ministry. Self-absorbed Christians think the work of the church revolves around them. "If they offer me this much..." "If my responsibilities have to include that..." "When I get this or that accomplished first..." We think that God gives us a blank page and we fill it in. We forget that it is the other way around—we hand God the blank page of our lives, and He fills in the details. We think ministry is something we own. We forget that God owns us.

Disloyalty

When things went wrong or got too tough, Samson was uncommitted and disloyal. In Judges 14:19-20 we read, "He went up to his father's house. And Samson's wife was given to the friend who had attended him at his wedding." Earlier, Samson had married a Philistine girl. During the wedding feast, in a burst of boastfulness and pride, he gave his new Philistine friends a riddle to solve. He was sure they would never be able to solve it. But because his wife and new Philistine friends ganged up on him to get the answer deceitfully, he became very angry and walked away from his marriage, leaving his wife behind. He just simply packed up his bags and left, showing absolutely no loyalty toward his new wife.

During a conference in Argentina, one young pastor came to me to make a confession. The message of holiness had pierced his heart. He said, "My wife and I had separated, but when I heard the message of total holiness, I went to my apartment, packed my belongings and went back to my wife." Unlike Samson, this young pastor had learned that God requires loyalty.

In Luke 3:8, John the Baptist said, "Produce fruit in keeping with repentance." The fruit of our repentance should be evident and obvious for others to see. We cannot walk in disloyalty, ignoring commitments and promises we have made. We cannot walk away from responsibilities and people in an outburst of anger. I know of an evangelist who was traveling all over the United States conducting revivals. People were impressed with his messages and miracles. But later it became known that this man had divorced two women and was actually wanted by police in another state because he had not been paying child support. If men are not taking care of their own families, they have no business representing God from the pulpit.

Sensual gazing

Samson had a flaw in the way he dealt with women and relationships. Judges 16:1 tells us, "One day Samson went to Gaza where he saw a prostitute. He went in to spend the night with her." As a Nazirite, Samson knew that he had been called to moral and sexual purity. But he was unable to avoid the temptation that Satan brought to him through the lusts of his flesh.

In Judges 16:4 we read, "Some time later, he fell in love with a woman...whose name was Delilah." No doubt you already know the story of Samson and Delilah. Sensual gazing and immature romance were sure steps to his destruction. Be aware of the power of the lust of the eyes and the lust of the flesh to destroy you. Sometimes it is only one gaze that can lead a man into adultery.

Losing common sense

Samson became so callused to God's leading that he got to the point of playing around with his anointing. When Delilah asked him the source of his strength, he playfully lied to her about the source, and then used that strength of the Lord to get out of the situation. This is dangerous!

Samson told her, "If anyone ties me with seven fresh thongs that have not been dried, I'll become as weak as any other man" (Judg. 16:7). Of course he "snapped the thongs as easily as a piece of string snaps when it comes close to a flame" (v. 9). God had instructed Samson not to give away the secret of his strength, which was his long hair.

But his enemies would not give up. Delilah continued to ask Samson what the source of his strength was. Finally he told her the truth; he shared the secret given to him by the Lord. He threw his precious pearls before swine.

He still thought that just like before, when the enemies came, he would be able to overpower them with his great strength, break free and destroy them. But things were different this time—his strength was gone. As an old-time pastor in Argentina once said, "The essence of sin is stupidity." Samson heard Delilah ask him, "Tell me...how you can be tied up and subdued" (v. 6), and in a most irrational decision he began to tell her. He lost common sense.

A false sense of security

Samson was morally unstable. He could not take constant pressure. But Delilah nagged and prodded him day after day until he was exhausted (Judg. 16:16). When people flirt with the world, there will come a time when their soul gets tired to death. When they reach that point, they will say, "I cannot resist this temptation anymore. It is just too strong."

Many believers play with their godly anointing in much the same way Samson played with his. They fool around with relationships that are out of the will of God. They watch their own kind of entertainment—even when it is displeasing to God. They do the wrong things, speak wrong words, go to wrong places. Yet they think they are not such bad sinners. But, like Samson, their strength is limited. There comes a time when they cannot fight anymore.

Becoming spiritually numb

Samson became numb to the things of God. He thought his life would never change. He had mastered the art of balancing the anointing of God with the sin in his own life. He had become a man of many passions. We can read the sad evidence of just how numb Samson had become to the things of God in Judges 16:20:

> Then she called, "Samson, the Philistines are upon you!" He awoke from his sleep and thought, "I'll go out as before and shake myself free." But he did not know that the LORD had left him.

He did not know that he had played with the anointing and the things of the world for so long that, without any more warnings, the Holy Spirit withdrew from his life.

We need to remember that Jesus promised He would never leave us. He may actually withdraw His blessing from our ministries, but He will not take His grace and forgiveness away if we repent. A man once came to my parents' home weeping and in utter desperation. "I think I have committed the unpardonable sin," he cried out to them. He was filled with terror that the Spirit had left him forever and that there was no more forgiveness.

I have good news for people who may feel that way. If you are concerned about committing the unpardonable sin...if you are crying out to God about it...that is a sign that the Holy Spirit has not left you. Spiritual concern for your soul can only come from the Holy Spirit.

WALKING THE HIGHWAY OF HOLINESS

You may ask, "Are you telling me that God expects me to walk in total, absolute holiness?" Yes, I am! We must be totally holy or totally repentant. Is that even possible? Not in ourselves. You and I cannot produce that kind of holiness. That's why I preach holiness as a miracle from heaven. The same One who saved you miraculously will sanctify you miraculously. The same Jesus who died for your salvation also died for your justification, righteousness, wisdom and sanctification. Salvation is by faith, and holiness is also by faith.

I am not writing this book to tell you how holy I am. Believe me, I could tell you how wretched my soul can be. My flesh is as corrupted as anybody else's flesh. If not for the mercy of God, even though I am a fourth-generation Christian, I would still be on my way to hell. But it was God Almighty who purified my soul, my eyes, my mind and my body. Even though I was never an official backslider and was raised in the Christian church, there were times I was a backslider at heart.

What is a *backslider?* Here is a new definition: It's a person who has his or her feet in the church and his or her eyes on the world. You can be in every ministry in the church and still be a backslider— if your heart is longing for something else.

Before he went to be with the Lord, singer Keith Green wrote a popular song titled "You Love the World (and You Are Avoiding Me)." When we love the world we avoid God. Samson loved the world, and he was avoiding the will of God. He never declared himself a backslider. He never officially said, " I quit…" He never said, "I don't want to have anything to do with the God of Israel." As a matter of fact, he thought he was doing fine. He did not even notice when the Spirit of God left him. He thought everything was normal.

As I said before, the stories in the Bible are not recorded for our entertainment. We need to learn from the mistakes of those who have gone on before us. These resolutions will point you in the right direction:

- *Resolve not to use the anointing at the expense of character.* Do not cover sin with signs and wonders. Don't allow miracles to overimpress you. Even if God is using you powerfully, if there is sin in your life, you need to repent.

- *Resolve at once to stop flirting with the world.* We have read about young people in America who say they have not committed sexual immorality or actual acts of fornication, but who flirt with each other in an indecent way. We need to reexamine our habits of dating and physical involvement. In his book *I Kissed Dating Good-Bye,* Joshua Harris makes this point:

  > What is really the point of most dating relationships? Often dating encourages intimacy for the sake of intimacy—two people getting close to each other without any real intention of making a long-term commitment …Intimacy without commitment awakens desires— emotional and physical—that neither person can justly meet.[1]

- *Resolve to reduce all passions to only one—God and His kingdom.* Samson was a man of many impulses and many passions: the passion of anger, the passion of revenge and many romantic relationships. But God calls His people to have only one main passion, God Himself.

- *Resolve to move from occasional victories to permanent victory in Christ.*

- *Resolve to move away from your weakness to be strong and solid in your character.*

- *Resolve to become a complete person.* To your anointing, add holiness; to the gifts of the Spirit, add the fruit of the Spirit. To the baptism of the Holy Spirit, add the fire of holiness. To charisma, add character.

- *Resolve to take advantage of the opportunity for restoration.* Judges 16:22 says, "But the hair on his head began to grow again after it had been shaved."

Jesus paid the sacrifice for our restoration on the cross. He died for us so that we don't have to die for our sins. At the end of Samson's life, he asked a servant to lead him to the main columns of the pagan temple, where the Spirit of the Lord once again came upon Samson. With his restored supernatural strength he destroyed the entire building. It collapsed upon him and more than three thousand Philistines. The Bible tells us that with his death Samson accomplished even more than with his life (Judg. 16:30).

How wonderful it is when we can honor God with our obedience rather than out of our disobedience. Yes, there is repentance and forgiveness. Yes, there will be grace. But how much better it is when we invest our lives in godliness now—while there is time to serve God. How much better it is when we are used as vessels of honor and not vessels of dishonor.

If you know that you have an ongoing friendship with the world, which is not God's will, I ask that you take a moment right now to repent. There is nothing wrong with being a friend to sinners—Jesus was. But the purpose for our friendship must be to bring them closer to God, not for them to take us further away from God. Relationships out of God's will put your soul at risk.

Whatever there is in your life that you are trying to balance along with the blessing and anointing of God, deal with it right now. Get it out of your life before it causes God's Spirit to leave you as He left Samson. It may be unholy entertainment that is polluting your eyes. It may be sensual gazing or disloyalty. Get rid of it now.

In many of the conferences where I preach, we actually set up a "spiritual trash can" and invite people to purify their homes and lives by bringing the things that are offensive to God to throw in the trash can. We have filled several barrels of spiritual trash in these conferences. People bring ungodly videos, demonic CDs, drugs, condoms, pornography, jewelry kept from an illicit affair and many other things. The list is endless.

We need to cleanse our souls. It doesn't matter if you consider yourself "sort of holy," "kind of holy" or "fairly good, but without the holiness of Christ." You need Jesus to touch your soul and purge you from every trace of sin in your life. Take a moment, and ask Him to do that right now.

If your eyes are not pure...if you dwell on evil and do not possess the purity Jesus possessed...Jesus can impart His holiness to you. Jesus said, "Whoever comes to me I will never drive away" (John 6:37). If you come to the Lord with a broken heart, it doesn't matter how dark your sin has been—Jesus will meet your need and restore your soul.

I will never forget what happened at one conference where I ministered on holiness. In the midst of the glory of the Lord descending in that place, one man pushed close to the edge of the platform. As I moved close to him to pray with him, he said, "Pastor Sergio, I have molested a child. I don't know that there will be forgiveness for me."

The amazing truth about the work of Christ on Calvary is this—Jesus' sacrifice included every sin. I said to that man, "If you repent, our God will forgive you."

Whatever you may have done that is still torturing you, whatever it is that has you bound, if you repent, God Almighty will forgive you. He will embrace you and give you the strength to renounce your sin forever.

In the hours just before His crucifixion, Jesus asked the Father,

"Lord, if it is possible, let this cup pass from Me." Jesus knew that cup from which He must drink held all the bitterness of the world. It contained homosexuality, hatred, wrath, vengeance, pornography, envy, jealousy and fits of rage—they were all there. Every sin of mankind—past, present and future—had been placed in the cup of Christ's sacrificial death.

For you and me, Jesus became the flesh of sin. He became a trophy of sin. He never sinned in His own life, but He drank the sin of humanity. He became the final offering for our sins. After that happened, the veil in the temple was torn. There was no more division between the holy place and the holy of holies.

Sin's hold had been broken. A direct entrance to the throne of God had been established—one that could be used by any person anywhere who came to Christ in repentance. Jesus opened the way for sinners to come directly into the presence of God where they could be forgiven and could receive the gift of eternal life.

There is no reason for us to end up as Samson did.

A PRAYER OF REPENTANCE

Lord, thank You for the warnings in Your Word about the dangers of sin. Thank You for giving me an opportunity to make things right with You. Father God, forgive me for the times I might have played with Your calling in my life and with Your anointing upon my life. Forgive me for my unholy alliance with the world.

Lord, have mercy on me. I need Your purification. I need to be transformed into Your image. Save me before it is too late. Have compassion on my soul. In Jesus' name, amen.

Chapter 4

The Transgression of Moses: Using Godly Anger in an Ungodly Way

Beware of anger in the pulpit! Several years ago, we knew of a Christian who played an instrument with the worship team of his local church. He was probably not a very mature Christian, and there were some areas in which he needed to grow.

One day during a church service, the pastor, in a moment of anger—perhaps even righteous anger—stopped the service and told this person that because of his sin and rebellion, he needed to put down his instrument and leave the platform right then and there. Of course, the man did leave—he practically crawled off of the platform. He was so devastated by that display of public humiliation that he left that church, never to return. He went straight into the world—he could not handle that display of "godly" anger.

This man wasted several years in the world, doing things he would live to regret. Thankfully, this story has a good ending. Eventually he returned to the Lord and began attending a different church. However, there are thousands more stories about men and women just like this young man that do not end as well. So many people have actually suffered spiritual abuse in the house of God.

So many well-meaning Christians are irritable, angry and danger-ously frustrated in their personal lives. In time, this frustration can bring terrible consequences. Moses provides an example of this. He was a man with a temper. When his temper flared, in a burst of anger he killed an Egyptian and then had to flee the land of his birth for many years. He paid a heavy price for his temper, yet he became a meek man of God.

His life is an example of what a not-so-godly man can eventually become. He gives us hope. God can deal with our hostile nature so that we can become more self-controlled and useful if we have this kind of transgression in our life.

There are some people who have a great measure of God's anointing upon their lives, but they lack self-control. Their anger has not been bridled. The ministries of these people will go well for a season, but often their homes—and ministries—end in disas-ter. Unless we have character in *both* the ministry and the home, it is going to be very difficult for us to succeed.

THE WRATH OF MOSES

Moses was set apart for God's purposes at birth. He was ordained to become a mighty leader for the people of Israel—and he did lead them out of the land of bondage. However, even the meekest of men can sometimes slip into an unjustified anger that produces serious consequences. Moses was a great deliverer, but he was not able to lead his people into the Promised Land because of his anger problem. The Scriptures tell us:

> Now there was no water for the community, and the people gathered in opposition to Moses and Aaron. They quarreled with Moses and said, "If only we had died when our brothers fell dead before the LORD! Why did you bring the LORD's com-munity into this desert, that we and our livestock should die here? Why did you bring us up out of Egypt to this terrible place? It has no grain or figs, grapevines or pomegranates. And there is no water to drink!"
>
> Moses and Aaron went from the assembly to the entrance

to the Tent of Meeting and fell facedown, and the glory of the
LORD appeared to them.

—NUMBERS 20:2–6

Recently I read in a newspaper the story of a father who beat
his son's hockey coach to death at a hockey game over a disagreement on game calls.[1] This story refocused our attention on
violence in sports. This dramatic situation highlights the amount of
damage that lack of self-control can cause.

The good news is that several organizations are addressing this
need. On May 25, 1999, at a summit sponsored by the Josephson
Institute of Ethics, the Character Counts! Coalition and the United
States Committee, Coaching Division, nearly fifty influential sports
leaders issued the Arizona Sports Summit Accord. Some principles
of the Accord are:

- To promote sportsmanship and foster the development of good
  character, sports programs must be conducted in a manner that
  enhances the mental, social and moral development of athletes
  and teaches them positive life skills that will help them become
  personally successful and socially responsible.

- Sports programs should establish standards for participation by
  adopting codes of conduct for coaches, athletes, parents, spectators and other groups that impact the quality of athletic programs.

- All sports participants must consistently demonstrate and
  demand scrupulous integrity and observe and enforce the spirit
  as well as the letter of the rules.

- The importance of character, ethics and sportsmanship should
  be emphasized in all communications relating to the recruit-
  ment of athletes, including promotion and descriptive materials.

- In recruiting, education institutions must specifically determine
  that the athlete is seriously committed to getting an education and
  has or will develop the academic skills and character to succeed.

- Everyone involved in athletic competition has a duty to treat the
  traditions of the sport and other participants with respect.

Coaches have a special responsibility to model respectful behavior and the duty to demand that their athletes refrain from disrespectful conduct, including verbal abuse of opponents and officials, profane or belligerent trash-talking, taunting and unseemly celebrations.

- The profession of coaching is a profession of teaching. In addition to teaching the mental and physical dimensions of their sport, coaches, through words and examples, must also strive to build the character of their athletes by teaching them to be trustworthy, respectful, responsible, fair, caring and good citizens.[2]

The National Alliance for Youth Sports advocates that "parents complete an orientation to understand the important impact sports have on their child's development." They also recommend that parents sign and abide by a Parents' Code of Ethics, which states in part, "I will practice good sportsmanship by demonstrating positive support for all players, coaches and officials at every game, practice or other youth sports event."[3]

Many people move very quickly from excitement to anger. Latin America has seen much violence—and, unfortunately, a number of deaths—as a result of raging emotions during soccer games.

Bitter anger and extreme frustration can have terrible consequences. Controlling our emotions and character is very important for everyone—especially for Christians who are trying to develop a Christlike spirit. Explosive anger often takes us by surprise. I remember that I thought I was a very good Christian as a young man in high school in Argentina. But I also remember the times when we were required to line up to file into school in the morning, a custom for schools in Argentina. Often the students in line behind me would provoke me by pushing and shoving as we waited in line. Time after time I would stand there and say to myself, "I will not get angry; I will not get angry; I will not get..." But before I could finish saying the phrase the third or fourth time, I was fighting with the guy behind me! He had bothered me a little, and I exploded!

VIOLENCE VS. MANHOOD

When I was younger, I accepted anger as part of my manhood. In Latin America there is a lot of talk about being *macho,* and sometimes we mix up the concept of violence with manhood. Some Latin American men actually think that violence is a virtue! They assume that the more you lose your control, the "mightier" you are—stronger and more valiant. This is why wife beating is a common problem in some Latin American countries.

But as the years went by, I realized that I had an anger problem. Even when I did my best to control my temper, sometimes I could not. Knowing that you are not fully in control of your own emotions makes a man insecure. You can't be certain how you will react the next time.

During one little argument I punched a door to vent my anger. Every once in a while when I lived in Argentina I would do that, just bang the door with my fist, but not all of the time. Nothing happened as a result. But when I punched the door this time, I was in the United States—where some inexpensive doors are a lot thinner! They looked like solid wood, but they were paper-thin. Although the door looked very strong, as I punched it, I made a hole in the door.

I stepped back and looked at that door and simply could not believe my punch had been the cause of so much damage. That's when I realized something must be wrong. Maybe this "macho anger" was not such a virtue after all. This flaring of my anger was something that I could no longer control.

By that time I had already prayed many times to overcome my anger. I had to struggle very hard to overcome the tendency to lose my temper. Maybe many of you consider yourself easily frustrated or prone to anger. It is a problem with a high price, unless we bring it to the Lord and allow God to perform a miracle in our lives.

FROM ANGER TO DISOBEDIENCE

As a young child, I read the story of Moses striking the rock for water and then being told by God that he could not enter the

Promised Land because of his disobedience. I could not digest that
story. I thought it would forever remain a mystery to me. How
could God be so strict with a man as pious and honorable as
Moses? Moses followed God faithfully for so many years. Why
would God give Moses such strong discipline if all that Moses did
wrong was get a little angry? After all, all he did was hit a rock—in
much the same way that I had punched a hole in that door!

Read this account where Moses responds to the complaints of
the people:

> The LORD said to Moses, "Take the staff, and you and your
> brother Aaron gather the assembly together. *Speak to that
> rock* before their eyes and it will pour out its water. You will
> bring water out of the rock for the community so they and
> their livestock can drink."
>
> So Moses took the staff from the LORD's presence, just as he
> commanded him. He and Aaron gathered the assembly
> together in front of the rock and Moses said to them, "Listen,
> you rebels, must we bring you water out of this rock?" *Then
> Moses raised his arm and struck the rock twice with his
> staff.* Water gushed out, and the community and their live-
> stock drank.
>
> But the LORD said to Moses and Aaron, "Because you did not
> trust in me enough to honor me as holy in the sight of the
> Israelites, you will not bring this community into the land I
> give them."
>
> —NUMBERS 20:7–12, EMPHASIS ADDED

Today I understand the implications of God's response to
Moses' act of disobedience. Now I know that uncontrolled anger
dishonors God. Anger is a sign of distrust. Uncontrolled bursts of
anger are the impulses of disobedience. When we move in fleshly
anger, we reveal that we are trusting in ourselves rather than God.

In the verses above, we see Moses move from frustration and
anger to disobedience. Because of his disobedience he was told he
would not enter the Promised Land. Notice that the miracle of
water gushing out of that rock happened anyway. Miracles are not

necessarily a sign of holiness. Our character can be out of the will of God, but because we have faith to do what God told us to do, we see a miracle.

No punishment could have been more hurtful to Moses than being denied entry into the land he had longed to enter for forty long years of wilderness wandering. In His mercy, God did not bring Moses to eternal destruction, but Moses ruined the last stage of his career. A great part of his life—almost forty years—had been spent dreaming of the day he would cross the river and go into the Promised Land. He had lived the latter years of his life with the promise from God of reaching that land.

As a result of his disobedience, Moses was only allowed to view the Promised Land from a distance, from the top of a mountain. He never entered it. And all because of anger!

The encouraging news is that Moses became a man of meekness and an example for all of us. But we can never forget this crucial error he made. His anger was justifiable, but his lack of control in his reaction was not. He used a God-given anger in an ungodly way.

Ungodly reactions are a temptation for many servants of God. People who have a good standing before the Lord in all other ways can be betrayed by a lack of control over their character or temper. In fact, sometimes people think they are entitled to react in anger because they hold positions of authority. Yet God requires leaders to walk in humility.

RESIDUAL FRUSTRATION

Moses had residual frustration. This was not the first time the people of Israel had complained against Moses. There had been similar situations before. Apparently when it happened earlier, their complaining did not affect Moses greatly. However, when it became a recurring complaint from the people, it got on his nerves. Are you in a situation where you do not know how long you will be able to take it? Are the pressures from other people, the nagging, the complaints, the criticism or the disapproval building up in your heart so dangerously that you are about to explode in anger? Beware of handling your anger in an ungodly way that dishonors God.

Losing control in your reactions to the situations you face is like saying, "Lord, this far I have trusted You, but this is too much. From now on, I will have to handle this my own way. It seems as though You have no answer to this problem."

We are dealing with the issue of anger in my family. I have three boys who are nine, eleven and thirteen years old. I have seen the dynamics of anger at work in them. I have prayed, "Lord, do not let any of my anger in previous years be inherited by them." But that bent toward unholy anger can be seen.

There can be a tendency to a quick temper in any of us—young children, adults or leaders in ministry positions. But that does not make it right. Extreme angry outbursts are often the result of inner pain. Before a person will act out of control there has to have been an ongoing source of irritability. Something has been disturbing and bothering that person, and he or she has taken that irritability personally to heart. The person has finally reached a point whereby he or she can no longer give a measured, controlled response to the situation—so there is an outburst as the person "loses his cool." Not only is this a problem for unbelievers; it's also a problem with believers.

I often hear of ministers who have explosive tempers. Sometimes these men of God preach on Sunday and then treat their wives and church employees abusively all week. I have even heard of ministers who were charged with assault for striking someone during an argument. This should not be! Perhaps we forget that the apostle Paul said that a man who is "given to anger" is not qualified to serve the church (1 Tim. 3:3).

I take anger very seriously. Recently, I persuaded one of my boys to get help. I was kind and firm until my reluctant son agreed to visit a Christian counselor. I went there not only to help my son, but also to learn more. Yes, the fire of holiness has descended on my life and remains with me, but holiness is never isolationist. I depend upon my brothers and sisters like never before. The counselor gave us some practical clues for my son to handle his angry reactions. We have seen a change ever since then. The problem is under control. We prayed about the problem, then we acted and got help. There are times when God may not give you a "revelation" about how to solve a situation, but He will give you insights regarding people to whom you can go for help. Be open to both. God knows how to help us.

If you are carrying a sense of chronic frustration or if you become angry every time you remember a specific situation or person, then you need healing. That chronic frustration could hinder your ministry and short-circuit the purpose of your life.

Maybe you are frustrated with your church or church leaders. Perhaps you are a Christian leader who is frustrated with your followers. Frustration is not unnatural; it will happen in this life. Anger will also happen. The Bible gives us permission to be angry. Anger was not the sin of Moses; his sin was anger rooted in distrust, disobedience and dishonoring of God's name. The Bible tells us that we should not *sin* in our anger (Eph. 4:26). We should not let our anger be manifested in ungodly ways.

One day a believer who called himself a prophet came to my office, soon after I had just been named senior pastor of a congregation. With condemnation he pointed his finger at me and said, "You are not the pastor of this church, and you never will be."

When I first heard his words, a chill went down my spine, and I thought, *Maybe we made a mistake.* But then I realized that this man did not love my ministry very much. The way he talked against me, it seemed he would rather see me dead than pastoring a church. By the time he left I had frustration in my heart, and I knew it was the beginning of bitterness. But then I knelt down and said, "Lord, I will not get up from my knees until You break my heart."

I knew very well that if I let that resentment continue, it would turn into a root of bitterness. The unholy thought crossed my mind: *I will never let another prophet in my church. I am going to get rid of everything that is prophetic.* I entertained those thoughts because one person had acted aggressively against me.

A few minutes after kneeling down, I began to weep and pray for

God's mercy on that prophet. My heart was changed. But in spite of my prayers, the prophet grew worse spiritually. Weeks later, he began insulting some of my leaders with words of cursing. Things went from bad to worse. So we devised a strategy. We made up our minds that we were not going to give this man to Satan. We decided to surround him with our prayers until he was spiritually safe. Six months later this man was restored through the imparting of spiritual wisdom, the application of some correction and a lot of patience. One day he came to see me again, and this time he said, "I know that you are the servant of the Lord for His church." What a miracle it was to see a spiritual turnaround!

Momentary Anger to Permanent Loss

I believe that the capacity of Moses to get angry was part of his God-given character. He became angry at things that hurt the honor of God. He became angry when people disobeyed the laws of God. But this time, he used his anger in an ungodly way. Because he did, his momentary anger resulted in serious loss. There were four primary reasons why this happened.

1. Moses misused his authority.

The Bible tells us that the Lord told Moses to take the staff from the Lord's presence. This was the rod of Aaron, which had miraculously budded in an earlier encounter with God and which God had directed should be kept in the tabernacle. (See Numbers 17.) This rod signified authority and anointing. God had directed that Moses should carry this rod with him as he stood before the people and when he spoke to the rock, as God had commanded him to do. It was an important time in the life of Moses, and he misused the authority God had given him by using Aaron's rod to strike the rock.

We knew a young woman (whom we will call Nancy) who was very talented and who played the keyboard at her church. She played for the church services, for the choir and for all of the special music. She was almost a celebrity in the church. She was nearing her high school graduation, and many of the other young people her age in the congregation were preparing to leave for college to prepare themselves for their careers.

Nancy talked to her pastor about her desire to attend Bible school in preparation for ministry. The pastor replied to her, "No, you can't go. Who would play the keyboard for us?" Although the pastor had been put in that church to keep a watch out for the spiritual condition of the people in his congregation, he misused his spiritual authority for his own personal comfort—not having to look for a new music person.

Nancy stayed there at the church and continued to play the keyboard. But as she saw others leaving for Bible college and university, she felt her personal plans had been thwarted by her pastor's words to her. Pretty soon, although her hands were at the keyboard, her heart was in the world. She ended up marrying an unsaved man. The last I had heard, she was on her second marriage.

Church leaders need to be careful that the spiritual authority God has given to us is not used in areas that are out of our spiritual jurisdiction, especially when it involves a decision made for our own personal comfort. When we misuse authority, we go from helping people find God's will to dictating to people what His will is for them.

I believe the church is in a season when we do not need to "strike the rock" in ministry—we need to "speak to the rock." We do not need to stand on "Mt. Sinai" with a message of condemnation. We need to position ourselves on "Mt. Calvary," preaching a message of hope and salvation.

Once I went to minister in a nation in Central America. On the way from the airport to the meeting place, my host said to me, "Pastor, we would like to mention to you that the word *holiness* is not a good word to use in the place where you are going to minister." He went on to explain the word was being used in a mean and negative way by many churches. "They are beating young people over the head with this word," he told me.

I went to my room to pray before the meeting, and I asked the Lord if He would still be with me if I did not use the word *holiness*. I needed His permission to preach without using this word.

It was a burning message about holiness that the Lord had placed on my heart. The Lord gave me permission.

Instead of using the word *holiness,* I used the words *consecration, purification, dedication to the Lord* and so forth. But by the third meeting with the people, I felt at liberty to use the word *holiness.* The power of God came in that meeting. More than six thousand teenagers were in attendance at the meeting, and I was still on the second point of the message when hundreds of them began to walk to the front. I was not even sure at first what they were coming to do. They stood in the altar area. Many of them knelt at the front, weeping as I finished the rest of the message. They asked God to baptize them with holiness.

Holiness is not bad, but in that instance I did not need to keep hitting the rock. God had changed His anointing. Just as God said to Moses, "Speak to the rock," He had given me a new way to do ministry in that circumstance.

Although God told Moses to speak to the rock, Moses was so angry at the rebellious Israelites that he struck the rock anyway. I can just hear him saying, "You want water? OK, here's your water," as he struck the rock.

In whatever ministry role God calls you to fulfill, be sure that you listen carefully to His instructions so that you stay within the anointing He has placed upon you. Each of us is called to serve the Lord. But don't misuse the authority God gives you by attempting to fulfill His calling in your own way. Many believers have been hurt by someone who "strikes the rock" instead of "speaking to the rock."

Misusing authority is easy to do. I can remember the first few months after my wife and I were married. It was a season when I was trying to settle the issue of the husband's authority in the home. But I wasn't sure just how to do that. I had asked God for a virtuous wife, one who was intelligent and who would be able to confront me when I needed her wisdom. But now that God had given me someone like that, I wasn't sure what to do with her! I had to learn not to misuse my authority as a husband.

Grandpa Scataglini, who is of Italian descent, used to say his temper had something to do with his Italian background. Many people blame their tempers on their ethnic backgrounds—especially if it is far away from where they live! When my grandpa would get upset, he banged the table with his fist. As a little child, I remember watching the plates and silverware jump as Grandpa banged his heavy fist on the table. It was a scary sight. But that was as far as he ever went with his temper. That was as bad as he got.

I'm not sure if my grandpa ever misused his authority by banging his fist on the table. If God has not told you to bang your fist, but you do it anyway, you could be misusing authority. We must be careful to respond in the ways God tells us to respond in our relationships with others. Authority can be misused.

One area where we can misuse our authority is as parents. When a parent faces an out-of-control teenager who is acting belligerently and rebelliously, it is amazing the threats that a parent can come up with in response. But it is very likely that if we start to use strong words and screaming to make our point, we will abuse our authority as a parent. Raising our voices will do little to raise our level of authority in that situation.

One day I asked one of my associate pastors to call the home of a family that had not been coming to church for a few weeks. When he called, they told him, "No, there is no problem; we are all doing well. Everything is just fine." Then they hung up the phone. However, their small child had pressed the speaker button on the phone, and the phone line did not disconnect.

The associate pastor could not believe what he heard. Coming through the phone lines were insults, screaming and cursing—in a supposedly Christian home. The associate pastor was taken aback by what he heard.

Later he told me, "They talked so nicely to me. I thought everything was truly fine, until the moment they thought they had hung up the phone. Then aggressive words began flying toward each other."

Friend, there is a continuous open line from your house. Heaven is hearing every word. There must be servanthood authority in the home. Screaming, rage and vain threats have no place in God's family. We must speak to the situation and no longer strike it.

When a man is leading but his heart is hurting permanently, there is no peace. It is very hard to lead effectively when we have outbursts of anger. It is such a serious offense that Paul tells us, "The acts of the sinful nature are obvious...fits of rage...and the like. I warn you, as I did before, that those who live like this will not inherit the kingdom of God" (Gal. 5:19–21).

I used to think that although God would get really mad at a person who commits adultery, an occasional outburst of anger here and there was OK in His book. But that is not the case. God wants His people to demonstrate the meekness of Jesus Christ. Moses' anger led him to disobedience, and he was not allowed into his Promised Land. Don't let your outbursts of anger keep you from God's destiny for your life.

Frustration is so common among some Christians. Perhaps it is because people think they can get more done with frustration and anger. Years ago, a young man on a missions trip to Argentina was asked, "Why are you so serious? You look upset all the time."

His answer was, "Because when I am serious and mad, I seem to learn better."

Screaming or threatening may seem to work for a while. When it does work, you may develop the tendency to keep doing it so you continue to get results. However, our anger and God's righteousness do not mix:

> For man's anger does not bring about the righteous life that
> God desires.
>
> —JAMES 1:20

At times we are all tempted to misuse the authority we have been given. The Bible teaches us that the time to strike is never when we are angry. That is the time to speak carefully as God directs us to speak. God instructed Moses to speak to the rock, not to strike it.

We are living in the age of God's grace. We are to speak the word of the Lord—it is the strongest rod of correction.

2. Moses ministered in frustration, not in obedience.

Moses' service could be called "resentful service." It was done in the midst of his cumulative frustration. Instead of seeing the promise of God that said, "I will pour water from the rock," Moses saw only the problem.

It is our decision whether we see the problem or the promise. Either we focus on our problem, or we focus on His promises. We cannot avoid some of our problems. But if we focus on God's promise for our life, He will speak to our hearts and give us a *rhema* word. That word will be a word of hope, one that enables us to embrace God's promise and continue to be faithful to Him. As we focus on God's promise, we will learn to trust Him more and will not have to lose control. If we do lose control, it is because we have lost trust.

3. Moses missed the new opportunity by reverting to the past.

When Jesus visited Jerusalem, He expressed regret that the people of Jerusalem had missed the time of God's visitation to them. In the New Testament there are at least two words to define time. One is *chronos;* the other is *kairos. Chronos* is the time we measure by the calendar or the clock. *Kairos* is a "God moment"—a specific time of God's intervention into our lives.

The opportunity presenting itself to Moses when the people were clamoring for water was a God-given opportunity for Moses to show the character of God to His people. But Moses did not understand the function of that *kairos* moment; he saw only the *chronos* opportunity.

Another opportunity to decide between a *kairos* moment or merely the *chronos* timing of events can be seen in the story of the crippled man at the pool of Bethesda in John 5. The Bible tells us that an angel would come occasionally and stir the waters in the pool. When that happened, the first person to get into the water would be healed. So a paralytic man would sit next to the pool waiting, not for the *chronos* time, but for the *kairos* time— the time when the waters would be stirred—so that he could get in the water and be healed.

Because the paralytic man could not jump into the water on his own, he did not get into the pool first when the angel stirred the water. When Jesus saw him lying there and found out that there was no one to put him into the waters, He asked him this question: "Do you want to get well?" In essence, Jesus was saying, "Are you looking for merely a *chronos* moment, or are you ready for a *kairos* event in your life?" Then Jesus healed him directly.

I believe that many of us have been waiting for a *kairos* moment, for some angelic presence to bring a blessing to our home, to bring the miracle we are expecting, to bring the strength to go on or to bring our backslidden children back home. Even if we have waited for a long time, there is a *kairos* time from God when Jesus comes and visits us. If we do not miss the time of His visitation, He will perform miracles in our midst.

At the *kairos* moment in Moses' life when he was to speak to the rock, he became selective in his obedience and missed the opportunity. He talked to the people and did several things the Lord asked him to do. However, he missed the opportunity to speak to the rock and so honor God with a new kind of miracle (not to mention obedience). He ended up striking it in anger.

Sometimes when we are angry, we tend to revert to the past. You might be walking along in the Christian life, with things going just fine, but discover that because you are accumulating frustration and anger, your tendency is to go back to the old style of things. Some of us grow very slowly in the things of God, but God is still shaping our characters and helping us to control our anger. If we want to be in the fast lane, we need to forsake anger and embrace meekness.

Located in the fast lane is the altar of the Lord, the place where we give 100 percent of ourselves to Him. There at His altar we renew our dedication to God and to the people of God. That is where we say, "I will no longer have fits of anger."

We are not capable of keeping that promise on our own unless the power of God descends upon us. His power descends when He knows we will use His power in the right way. Then He sends upon us His baptism of fire and holiness. He gives us the strength we need for the journey.

Moses did not use the anointing and power of God the right way. He resorted to the old way of solving things—by using anger. Yet this same man became such a man of peace. You may be similar to Moses and still harbor a violent character within. I believe, however, that you will be transformed. The fire of God changes our character. If you have generated division or strife in your experiences in life, I believe God will give you a grace to become an ambassador of peace. You could become a *networker*—a person who unites people instead of separating them.

Jesus said to the Pharisees, "You break the command of God for the sake of your traditions... You hypocrites!" (Matt. 15:3, 7). People tend to revert back to their traditions, doing things the old way. One problem hindering some businesses from developing and growing larger is the mind-set of people who say, "We have always done it this way. We don't want to change." The previous revival can become our present rebellion.

4. Moses misrepresented God in front of the people.

The Lord had shown Himself as holy in front of the people. He has always been faithful. The Lord was committed to Israel. He was proving Himself faithful and righteous. Even though we are unfaithful, He remains faithful.

But Moses did differently. The Bible says that he did not trust God enough. He did not honor Him. His behavior brought discredit to the integrity of God among His people. Do not follow this example from Moses. Are you an extremely frustrated person with an aggressive temper? Are your answers to people so edgy that you cut the souls of those to whom you speak? If so, chances are that you are discrediting God in front of His people. By acting out of anger and frustration, you are misrepresenting Jesus to the pagans.

I know of a man of God who started many churches and preached in many nations. He had a passion to reach souls and an infectious zeal for purity. Yet this man also had a tendency to get very angry with the pastors he was training in ministry. He treated them like wayward children and often scolded them publicly. Ultimately, these pastors decided to turn away from this man's authority, and they sought out a new spiritual covering. This man eventually lost his ministry because of his belligerent attitude. Frustration arises from incomplete trust. We become frustrated when we say, "I don't believe that God can change these pastors I have trained. I don't believe that God is powerful enough to overcome their weaknesses. I do not have any hope for these people." This can happen in business, in a family, in a cell group or even in your marriage. Lack of trust will trigger anger.

If this is your problem, confess your anger and frustration to the Lord and repent. You may have dealt with your anger for a long time. You may even feel like saying, "I have confessed and repented a hundred times. It just doesn't work for me." Then repent for the one hundredth and one time—but this time receive the baptism of holiness.

The Right Way to Respond

There was a time when Moses responded differently when confronted by the bickering and complaining people of Israel. What a contrast we see in Moses' reaction in Numbers 20 and his earlier response in Exodus 17:

> So they quarreled with Moses and said, "Give us water to drink."
>
> Moses replied, "Why do you quarrel with me? Why do you put the LORD to the test?"
>
> But the people were thirsty for water there, and they grumbled against Moses. They said, "Why did you bring us up out of Egypt to make us and our children and livestock die of thirst?"
>
> Then Moses cried out to the LORD, "What am I to do with these people? They are almost ready to stone me."
>
> The LORD answered Moses, "Walk on ahead of the people. Take with you some of the elders of Israel and take in your hand the staff with which you struck the Nile, and go. I will stand there before you by the rock at Horeb. Strike the rock,

and water will come out of it for the people to drink." So
Moses did this in the sight of the elders of Israel. And he called
the place Massah and Meribah because the Israelites quar-
reled and because they tested the LORD saying, "Is the LORD
among us or not?"

—Exodus 17:2–7

In this first incident when the people of Israel needed water
and complained, the people distrusted the Lord—but Moses did
not. It was no problem for Moses. But it would become a problem
for Moses by the time it happened again in Numbers 20. Moses
had begun to harbor the anger and frustration of the ongoing pressure—the relentless nagging and complaining of the people he
was leading. He was on the verge of a character collapse.

Are you on the verge of a similar collapse? Has a recurring situation in your life created anger and frustration for you, so that you do
not know how to handle it? Have you begun to take it personally?

Two of my boys had a fight recently. Even though our home is a
holy Christian home, sometimes there are conflicts to resolve. My
children are very young, and we are in the process of training them
in the ways of the Lord. The two boys were competing angrily over
a minor issue. I began to correct my older son, who is twelve years
old. I noticed that he was so angry he could not control himself. I
was not scared of his flesh, but I was scared of my carnality.

At that moment it was a father/son struggle for power. I felt the
check of the Spirit, as though the Spirit was asking me, "What are
you doing, Daddy? Why are you getting into this in a personal way?"

Immediately I cooled off and said, "Son, I am not going to fight
against you. I am disappointed at the way you are doing things
right now." In effect, I retreated. Soon I saw the good effect my
backing off had on my son. His anger began to subside.

A few minutes later he came to my room and asked forgiveness.
Then he went to his younger brother and asked forgiveness from
him. He even fixed tea for his two brothers and me, and the four
of us had a reconciliation meeting. I wish I could tell you that
every time a tense situation arises, I have handled it the same way.

Unfortunately, that is not true. But I savor the memory of the times when I grasp self-control and am able to turn a potential battle into an opportunity to set an example for my boys.

Moses gave us a good example about how to deal with nagging problems in Exodus 17. He did not take it personally. He said to the people, "Why do you put *the LORD* to the test?" (v. 2, emphasis added). He did not get bitterly angry with the people. And he asked God for specific instructions on how to deal with them, and then he followed every one of the instructions.

As you begin praying about the things that are frustrating you, there will be instructions from the Holy Spirit to your heart. He will speak to you clearly. This is one of the realities of Christianity—God can speak to us, and we can hear His voice. There will be a time of instruction from God. The Holy Spirit speaks to us lovingly and shows us the way to follow. We need to follow the example of Moses in Exodus 17, not his example in Numbers 20. If we respond to the Lord and follow every one of His instructions...if we are careful to follow everything that God has already spoken to our hearts...we will see a tremendous breakthrough in our lives. We will see mighty results.

If you sense in your heart that wonderful sense of conviction that comes from the Holy Spirit, do not avoid it; welcome it. It is part of God's mercy to our lives. God sees the resentment in our hearts. If the mention of a certain person's name or the memory of a hurtful situation brings pain to you, then you need a healing done in your heart.

A PRAYER OF REPENTANCE

Lord, thank You for the warnings in Your Word. For as long as You want me to, as long as You instruct me to, I will put up with the frustrating situation in my life. I will not become a violent person. I want to be Your servant. I want to be a person of meekness. I will change with Your help.

Holy Spirit, I invite You to speak to me and instruct

me on how I should respond to this situation. Lord, remove residual frustration from my heart. Help me not to take this problem personally. I ask You to help me change the pattern of my response to frustration. In Jesus' name, amen.

Chapter 5

The Transgression of Elijah: Embracing Disillusionment

Derek had been invited to speak at a Christian conference. The conference organizer, who had heard Derek speak elsewhere, had declared publicly that he had invited Derek to speak at the conference because the Holy Spirit had told him to invite him. Derek accepted the invitation and happily prepared for the conference with prayer and fasting.

However, before the conference took place, Derek and the organizer had a conversation that put the organizer at odds with him. Because of that tension, the organizer began doing little things to undermine the credibility of Derek as the speaker. The organizer talked to the conference pastor to express his concern about doctrinal differences Derek might have with their church. He also began to gossip to the elders of the congregation, couching his gossip in spiritual tones in order to spread suspicion about the doctrinal differences that might exist.

By the time the conference rolled around, Derek, who had heard what was going on, was not sure he should even show up for the meetings. However, he did go, and the Holy Spirit showed up in a powerful way. Dozens of people were touched and changed by the truth that was taught and by the ministry of the Holy Spirit. After the conference, several attendees spoke with Derek to tell him how right on his message had been. People wrote letters to thank him for his ministry.

In spite of all of that, Derek could not stop wondering what the pastor, elders and other leadership people might be thinking about him as a result of the gossip spread by the conference organizer. He decided never to minister at that place again. His ministry at that conference should have been the start of a huge breakthrough and time of victory for what God had just done through his life and ministry. But his own self-doubt and embarrassment, caused by his problems with the organizer, had overshadowed it.

THE POST-REVIVAL SYNDROME

This transgression could also easily be called "The Favorite Transgression of the Choice Servants of the Lord." It happens to many, and I encourage you to learn carefully the lessons we will see from this example in the life of Elijah.

This transgression took place in Elijah's life immediately after his glorious victory on Mount Carmel when he called down fire on the altar of God, humiliating the prophets of Baal who were unable to get their pagan god to respond. As a result of the supernatural victory, Elijah had ordered the killing of more than four hundred fifty prophets of Baal. (See 1 Kings 18.) Elijah had certainly experienced a high point in his ministry. It was a revival experience.

But revival highs are often followed by serious lows. Immediately after his victory at Mount Carmel, we find Elijah fleeing to Horeb for his life.

> Now Ahab told Jezebel everything Elijah had done and how he had killed all the prophets with the sword. So Jezebel sent a messenger to Elijah to say, "May the gods deal with me, be it ever so severely, if by this time tomorrow I do not make your life like one of them."
>
> —1 KINGS 19:1–2

Jezebel, the wicked wife of King Ahab, had threatened the life of

Elijah for his victory over her idol-worshiping prophets. She swore that by the next day Elijah would be killed. Although the prophet had just come from what we might call a "revival," he entered a post-revival syndrome with the receipt of Queen Jezebel's threat.

This sin can usher defeat into the lives of God's servants, even after being in revival. Elijah had confronted an entire nation of pagans and achieved a great victory. When the occult altar of Baal had been proven to be impotent and unresponsive even after four hundred fifty prophets ranted and raved for half a day, Elijah had called down the fire of God upon His altar to the living God in a matter of minutes. The Bible tells us that the people watching had fallen prostrate before God when they saw what happened. They began to cry out, "The LORD—he is God! The LORD—he is God!" (1 Kings 18:39). The entire nation changed religions in half an hour. The nation of Israel repented of its idol worship of Baal and reverted back to worship of the true God in one afternoon. It was a glorious victory, but a subtle defeat was imminent.

A TRANSGRESSION FOR BOTH STRONG AND WEAK

Elijah was a strong man of God. He solved his religious theological disputes by killing all the prophets of Baal. I do not recommend that method today! In the New Testament era, there are other ways to apply the message, but in Old Testament times that was the command of God. Moving in the power of God Almighty, Elijah got rid of the religious curse in Israel.

Yet after the defeat of paganism, Elijah fell into a deep depression. Disillusionment can affect the strong man and woman of God just as much as the weak individual. Disillusionment has a way of diminishing in your eyes everything else you have done in the past. It does not matter how many spiritual successes you have had; disillusionment causes you to see life through a grim, negative, dark glass. When it creeps in, regardless of what you do or what your church does today, you will feel sad and will perceive yourself as defeated. Disillusionment makes you feel as though you have no reason to move forward.

This is what happened to Elijah. This mighty warrior prophet of God who defeated four hundred fifty wicked prophets of Baal at Mount Carmel now received the threats of one powerful woman—and became afraid enough to run for his life.

"I Just Want to Die"

When Elijah fled from the threat of Queen Jezebel, he ran south, into the desert near Beersheba. When he arrived at Beersheba in Judah, he left his servant there while "he himself went a day's journey into the desert" (1 Kings 19:3). He came to a juniper tree, sat down under it and prayed that he might die. "'I have had enough LORD,' he said" (v. 4). You may have found yourself in that same frame of mind. Perhaps, like Elijah, you are saying, "I have had enough; I cannot take any more. My strength is gone. I am not ready to face the future. In a quiet, humble and very evangelical way, I am going to retreat from this whole thing." Perhaps you are not making a scandal and you are not screaming. Maybe you do not have the strength to scream anymore, but you feel you have come to the end of your enthusiasm, faith and courage.

This man of God had killed the prophets of Baal. When he prayed to his God, the fire came, destroying the altar of Baal. After declaring a drought earlier that had lasted three years, he prayed, and the rain came. Through Elijah's powerful ministry, the blessing of the Lord returned to Israel, but Elijah lost sight of all God had accomplished in his life and through his life, and he wanted to die! He even became suicidal!

In many cities where we go, we find Christians who have thoughts of death. Perhaps even this morning, or last night before you went to bed, you wished you were dead. Maybe you were hoping there would be an honorable way to die quickly and to get out of your life. The Holy Spirit can transform this negative type of thinking. Jesus came so that we may have abundant life. The spirit of death and suicide is not from God.

Someday our life on earth will end—but only God knows the day and the hour. It is not up to us to choose the time. God never gives you the right to take your own life. It belongs to Him.

Jesus did not come into our lives to give us depressing thoughts of ending our lives. He said, "I have come that [you] may have life, *and have it to the full"* (John 10:10, emphasis added). If you presently are entertaining, or ever have entertained, thoughts of despair to the point of suicide, I have good news for you! Jesus Christ will set you free from those thoughts.

A CULTURE OF DEATH

Someone has defined our present culture not as a culture of entertainment or technology, but as a culture of death. Our culture is filled with negative rock music, movies, videos and books glorifying suicide and death. This is not God's plan; it is the nature of hell itself.

Once when we were in Germany a concerned mother brought a CD to me that her son had been listening to. She did not speak or understand English, so she didn't know what the words on the CD were. But she said her son had been having a lot of emotional and behavioral problems. When I read the words to the music, it was no mystery to me that he had problems. One of the songs on that recording actually advocated the listeners "to make up your mind whether you are going to live or commit suicide."

When I read that, the anger of God came on me. What kind of demonic minds would devise a song like that for teenagers? Why should teenagers have to worry about making that kind of a decision? The minds of our teens should be filled with choices about what sports to participate in, what band instrument to play and what fast-food restaurant to drive through on the way to the game—not about whether or not to commit suicide. Their minds should be filled with decisions about what career to follow and how they can help out more at church or lead a friend to Christ. That's the will of God for our kids.

Just as in Elijah's day, today there is a strong satanic, oppressive spirit leading people to desire death. But our desire should be to work hard for the kingdom of God while we are here on this earth.

When Elijah left his servant at Beersheba and traveled alone into the desert without food or provisions, it appears he was not planning on returning.

> He came to a broom tree, sat down under it and prayed that he might die. "I have had enough, LORD," he said. "Take my life; I am no better than my ancestors." Then he lay down under the tree and fell asleep. All at once an angel touched him and said, "Get up and eat." He looked around, and there by his head was a cake of bread baked over hot coals, and a jar of water. He ate and drank and then lay down again.
>
> —1 KINGS 19:4–6

How kind is the mercy of the Lord! He even brings fast food to the prophet! Elijah ate and drank and then lay down again because he was so worn out. Depression and despair can wear you out! Our day-to-day activities and demands place incredible physical stress upon our lives. Many people today are familiar with being worn out. Whether it is for business, for Jesus or for your family, being tired and lethargic is a way of life for many people.

When we moved to the United States, for me it truly became a land of opportunity. During my early days in this country, so many opportunities for ministry were presented to me that I realized I could wear out faster in America than anywhere else in the world.

All over the world, now, with the phenomenon of the Internet and the worldwide web, even after working eleven hours you can still spend another two hours answering your e-mails. In Elijah's day, at least he could fall asleep when the sun went down, but today electricity has extended our days. Our lives continually seem to be getting busier and busier. Like Elijah, we become so worn out we crash. And this kind of burnout is especially common among ministers today.

Elijah had been serving God wholeheartedly, but he was worn out. When the angel brought him refreshing food and water, he ate and drank and then lay down again.

> The angel of the LORD came back a second time and touched him and said, "Get up and eat, for the journey is too much for

> you." So he got up and ate and drank. Strengthened by that food, he traveled forty days and forty nights until he reached Horeb, the mountain of God. There he went into a cave and spent the night. And the word of the LORD came to him: "What are you doing here, Elijah?"
>
> —1 KINGS 19:7–9

Elijah gave a reply to the Lord. In fact he gave the same reply two times at least.

> He replied, "I have been very zealous for the LORD God Almighty. The Israelites have rejected your covenant, broken down your altars, and put your prophets to death with the sword. I am the only one left, and now they are trying to kill me too."
>
> —1 KINGS 19:10 (CF. VERSE 14)

I believe that Elijah must have been listening to news on the wrong channel. Everything he reported back to the Lord both times was negative. He only got the bad news—he didn't mention the good news.

In response to Elijah, the Lord said, "Go out and stand on the mountain in the presence of the LORD, for the LORD is about to pass by." As he stood there, he experienced a strong wind, an earthquake and a fire, but God was not in any of those powerful manifestations. Rather He came like a gentle whisper.

NOT READY FOR THE FIRE

Early in my ministry of taking God's fire to the nations, I was anxious to pray for everyone. I would pray and pray, laying hands literally on thousands of people. In a few instances, however, I would feel my hand being withdrawn from someone for whom I intended to pray. It was as if the Lord would not allow me to pray for certain people. I was so concerned. I would go to my hotel room and say, "Lord, what happened there? Why couldn't I pray for that person now?"

The Lord led me to the understanding that some people are not ready for the fire. If the fire would come, they might lose it quickly or it might destroy them because their hearts were full of disillusionment, bitterness and resentment. These people wanted more power, but they had not changed the basic makeup of their hearts.

With this understanding, when the Lord seems to be placing a check in my spirit about praying for His fire to fall on some individuals, instead I first pray for the balm of Gilead to be applied to their souls. I ask the Lord to descend upon them with the anointing, with His healing oil to heal the hearts and wounds of these people. I know that once the Lord has healed them they will receive the fire of God—and they will keep it.

Remember how God ministered to Elijah in this hour of his great need. Instead of speaking through the wind, the earthquake or the fire, He came as a gentle whisper. If you are struggling with disillusionment and have become locked into a negative, melancholic attitude, let God's gentle whisper envelop your soul. If you suffer from chronic depression, let the gentle whisper of the Word of God come to you and heal you.

When Elijah heard the gentle whisper of God, he pulled his cloak over his face, left the darkness of his cave and moved to stand at the mouth of the cave. Then he heard that gentle whisper once again, this time asking him, "What are you doing here, Elijah?" It was at this time that he gave the exact same answer he had given before:

> He replied, "I have been very zealous for the LORD God Almighty. The Israelites have rejected your covenant, broken down your altars, and put your prophets to death with the sword. I am the only one left, and now they are trying to kill me too."
>
> —1 KINGS 19:14

Even though God had been miraculously ministering to the deep needs of Elijah, the prophet had misunderstood his God. He thought he had to keep on worrying, continuing to be sad because everything was going wrong. He felt he had a right to be depressed and disillusioned. But this time God had further instructions for him:

> The LORD said to him, "Go back the way you came, and go to
> the Desert of Damascus. When you get there, anoint Hazael
> king over Aram. Also, anoint Jehu son of Nimshi king over
> Israel, and anoint Elisha son of Shaphat from Abel Meholah to
> succeed you as prophet."
>
> —1 KINGS 19:15–16

Elijah was about to see that the best was yet to come. In
essence, the Lord was telling Elijah, "You have started a religious
revolution in your nation. Now I am sending you to complete the
job, but with a political change." That is the work of revival. Revival
is not complete until we affect the legislation and the leaders of
government in our nation.

REVIVAL IN THE POLITICAL REALM

John Wesley, the founder of the Methodist revival movement,
began preaching to the miners in eighteenth-century England.
History tells us that the miners came to hear him speak with their
faces still black from the coal dust. But as his preaching began to
convict their hearts, the tears ran down their faces, leaving white
streaks. But Wesley was not content to stop his work there.
Eventually his preaching and teaching gained entrance to the
English parliament. The laws began to change. His influence was a
forerunner for freedom for the slaves. Such is the influence of
revival preaching.

God wants to complete the work that He begins in our lives. His
work in us involves more than a religious change in our hearts—
more than a Sunday blessing. His work will affect every aspect of
our lives. The power of God, the joy of the Lord and the holiness
of the Lord has to affect us Monday through Sunday.

God was about to complete the work He had begun in the life
of Elijah. Elijah may have thought he was done. He may have been
so disillusioned that he wanted to quit. He may even have wanted
to die. But the Lord was saying, "I have more work for you to do. It
will not depend merely on your strength. I have already calculated
all that you need. Now it is time for you to anoint your successor;

it's time to train someone to stand next to you."

It's important for us to remember that God's work will be accomplished—with or without us. If we enter the cave of disillusionment and despair and refuse to exit when God intervenes in our lives, He might replace us sooner than expected because of our stubborn disillusionment. I remember hearing my father preach this message when I was just a child. Since that time I keep my mind focused on the fact that I cannot get too disappointed or too disillusioned. I do not want God to remove me from the ministry and put someone else in my place. I want to continue what the Lord called me to do until He is done with me.

Elijah could have been removed from his anointing if he had resisted stepping out of the cave to listen to the voice of God. But because he responded when God whispered gently to him, God allowed him to anoint an assistant to help him with his work. This assistant would eventually inherit Elijah's ministry and receive a double portion of his anointing.

THE CHARACTERISTICS OF DISILLUSIONMENT

Can you recognize the onset of disillusionment and despair? Can you separate the daily frustrations and challenges of your life from the more devastating paralysis of disillusionment? There are seven characteristics that can be found in people who are crossing the threshold into disillusionment. These points will help you to identify whether you are one of them.

1. A disillusioned person is afraid.

Elijah had no reason even to think about death. After all, he was a man who would never even have a funeral—he would be taken up into heaven in chariots of fire! Yet because of disillusionment he was running for his life.

A few years ago, because of sheer exhaustion I experienced a severe physical problem. A doctor from my congregation prescribed for me just the therapy I was afraid he'd prescribe—a seven-day hiatus from my ministry, along with total rest! My wife, children and I went to a farm to rest. During those days a dear pastor friend of mine called me on the phone and asked me, "Are you scared?"

Although he could not have known it, by that time I was besieged with many fears, so I answered him affirmatively.

"I want you to know that Satan is attacking you in the very area where God destined for you to be the strongest," he responded. In other words, he was telling me that I would have tremendous strength and stamina in the future, and that Satan had come to intimidate me in that area. That phrase ushered in healing to me as no other remedy could have done.

Elijah was attacked in the area where God would bring the gift of His special anointing. One of the gifts God destined for Elijah was the fact that he would not die. He would have no funeral—he was going to be taken up into heaven. So Satan intimidated Elijah with the threat to have him killed.

Many of the fears we have are totally unfounded. They have no base. Satan is an abortionist—he tries to avert the gifts of God in us.

The Environmental Protection Agency, which acts to limit the amount of toxins released into the air outdoors, recently released an article saying that some people have more pollution inside their home or office building than what is outdoors. Some of the pollutants commonly found in homes and offices are carcinogenic (which means they can produce cancer). Others can aggravate preexisting medical problems like asthma and heart disease.[1]

The problem of indoor pollution has actually become worse in recent years because of efforts to make homes and offices more energy efficient. This is partly because we have now learned to insulate buildings so thoroughly that they receive no fresh air from outside. That would be good if the air captured inside was mountaintop pure—but it usually isn't. It's usually stale and increasingly toxic. I am one of those people who like to sleep with the windows open. I'd rather take my chances with the air outside. My wife likes the windows closed. We just refine each other!

There are studies that indicate that the general population is exposed to exceptionally high levels of carcinogenic substances in their homes. There are agencies that teach you about the substances and what to do about them. I am not an authority on air pollution, but as I read the article from the Environmental Protection Agency, I thought, *This is just like the church. Some of the pollutants that we have in our hearts, our thinking, our imaginations—all found inside the four walls of our churches—seem to be causing more problems than all the wickedness of the world outside.*

When Jezebel informed Elijah, "I'm going to kill you," Elijah didn't experience the symptoms of "outside pollution"—he experienced the symptoms of "interior pollution." The problem was his own *inner disillusionment,* which was his wrong thinking. Although God had already ordained that he would not die, this interior pollution threatened to destroy his soul and take his life. He needed to be delivered and set free of the fear-producing pollution. He needed a breath of fresh air—the air of God's Spirit and anointing.

Just as He did with Elijah, the Lord is calling us to purify our hearts and minds so that we can be set free from fear.

2. A disillusioned person decides when he has had enough.

It wasn't God who said to Elijah, "You have had enough. I am going to give you rest. I am going to take you to heaven now." Elijah himself made that decision and told God he had reached his limit! That is how disillusionment operates; it sets false limitations. Disillusionment will cause us to tell God when we are going to stop our ministry and service to Him. It will keep us from asking God if we should go on and from seeking Him for His power to continue.

While traveling in Asia, I read an article about people from Hong Kong that said clenching and grinding of teeth is on the rise in that territory. The stressful lifestyle that is common among people in Hong Kong has taken a high toll on their dental health. Those who grind their teeth do not even know they do it; often they do it when they are asleep.

Some people experiencing stress are so tense and filled with anxiety that they cannot rest, even at night. Even if they *sleep* for eight hours at night, their sleep is so restless that they get up as tired in the morning as when they went to bed. Stress is a factor affecting nearly everyone in America—and throughout the world.

Sometimes we become so tired of our stress-filled lives that we tell the Lord, "I have had enough."

Consider this: Perhaps you have had enough stress—but not enough service to God. God has an agenda for each one of us. God has a plan for me, and He has a plan for you. God has a glorious schedule for us to follow. But we create a problem when we decide we are going to quit following God's schedule. That is never the will of God. You are not the owner of your life; therefore, you cannot tell God when you are finished!

I pray that the fire of God will descend on your life and that you will say, "Lord, I will never quit. I know I may cry, and I may be weak, but with the strength of Jesus in my life, I will never quit."

3. A disillusioned person will declare that there has been no progress.

Those who live with disillusionment in their lives are quick to say there is no revival in their church and that there is no presence of the Lord in such and such a meeting. They seem eager to shut things down when God is not through with them.

I remember a pastor who came to my church in La Plata when we were pastoring there. He had heard that we had a visitation from the Lord and of the signs and wonders and convicting power of the Holy Spirit that came over the congregation. We prayed for him while he was there. But as he was going out the door of our church, an usher overheard him saying to one of his associates, "Nothing is going on here. Why did we come here anyway?"

A few weeks later, I heard the rest of the story. When this pastor returned to his own congregation he did not know that he had received the fire of God when we prayed for him. He thought that the fire of God would be displayed through some big emotional outburst, and he had not felt anything. Yet when he opened his Bible to preach, the presence of God invaded the meeting, and a new move of God began. This man learned that the fire of holiness is not an emotion; it's not a feeling—it is a sovereign work of the Holy Spirit in our lives.

I think about my own nation, Argentina, which has experienced several waves of the power of God. God's power was so strong in some of our revival meetings in the past that you would think you had gone to heaven and then come back. However, there are people—even church leaders—in my nation who have been wasting ink by writing articles saying that no revival ever took place in Argentina.

Perhaps there was no revival in their towns. Like Elijah, they are saying, "I have been so zealous for the mighty power of the Lord. I am the only one left. No one else is righteous." People like this make other people depressed. They speak negatively; they actually like to proclaim the death of revival. Rather than exalting what the Holy Spirit *has done,* they point out what the Holy Spirit *has not yet done.* People like this will always find fault and say that no progress has been made.

Perhaps you have had a quiet disagreement with the Lord. You are not openly rebellious about it; you are not screaming at God or your leaders, but in your heart, you are suffering from disillusionment. Perhaps you have withdrawn. Like Elijah you have taken your gifts, time, resources, stamina—everything you have—and retreated to a cave, only to feel sorry for yourself.

You may have reasons. Your reason may not be because a Jezebel is telling you she is going to kill you tomorrow—but it could be a church leader who offended you. Perhaps your spouse left you for someone else. Maybe you have gotten over the pain and sadness, but you cannot escape the disillusionment that invaded your soul. You may be crying out to God, "If You really had been there, things would have been different. What I have learned is that I cannot fully trust You."

Are you trusting in God for your salvation—but for nothing else? Is your disillusionment keeping you from getting emotionally involved in your church because the last time you got involved, things did not go well? People get reluctant to go into their next ministry assignment when they do not understand what happened to their last one. We must resist the pull of disillusionment that causes us to be a part of the "passive audience" found in many churches.

The transgression of disillusionment can attack a Christian who has been serving God for thirty, forty or even fifty years in the church. It can masquerade as a pious complaint and look like a godly thing—but it boils down to being disappointed in God.

4. A disillusioned person will become exhausted by sadness.

There is an emotional sadness that can be so intense and problematic that it makes your physical body wear out. Elijah was so physically tired that he lay down twice. The angel had to come to him twice, waking him up and giving him food each time. Depression is a major sickness in many nations. Did you know that depression can actually weaken your immune system and make you more susceptible to disease? It also leads people to rely on unhealthy medications.

5. A disillusioned person withdraws and hides.

Some depressed people hide in their addictions; others either overeat or do not eat enough. Some bury themselves in entertainment and television, needing to fill up their twenty-four hours of the day—but with things out of the will of God. Disillusionment causes them to do something—anything—to keep their minds distracted in order to dodge reality day after day. How tragic it is that many pastors—who are called to heal the downtrodden—are also plagued by this syndrome!

6. A disillusioned person confuses disillusionment with religious zeal.

Some people are so deceived and confused that they think they are doing God a favor with their negativity. They believe they are hurt, bitter, resentful and ostracized because everyone else is wrong. They believe themselves to be the only right ones. They develop a martyr complex. Whenever I am tempted to think that I am so spiritual and everyone else is not, I know I am in a trap. It is a dangerous road to be on, and trouble will soon come. God is calling us to get off that road; it is a dead-end.

Most people who watch TV surf every channel—myself included. If I'm watching TV, I want to see everything there is at once. We live in the age of alternatives, but it is also the age of restlessness. Some people "surf" churches in the same way they surf their television channels. With just the "press of a button" (or the turn of a key in their car's ignition) they switch churches. Maybe they say, "I did not like the program this month," so they switch. They keep switching, but never plug in. They are not interested in anything.

People who are under disillusionment are often a part of the group known as "church surfers." They tend to be restless, yet think they are protecting their religious zeal. Sometimes they even think that God sent them to a particular church to correct the pastor. But they fail to take root in any church because no church is spiritual enough for them.

7. A disillusioned person doesn't envision the completion of God's plan, ignoring the fact that the best is yet to come.

Elijah did not know that God was about to use him to complete the work the Lord had for him to do. He was about to anoint Hazael and Jehu as kings over nations. He was also to anoint Elisha as his successor. This would probably be the greatest and most lasting work he would do for God and His kingdom. Satan loves to get Christians out of the race, especially if it is during the last lap before the biggest victory. We need to be alert to the schemes of the enemy and pray that God will protect us and keep us until His complete plan for us has been fulfilled.

If you have believed that you had a right to isolate yourself or to distrust God (or your pastors or spiritual leaders), you may have suffered what I call a *religious trauma*. I pray that you will come before the Lord and surrender your trauma at the cross of Jesus. Be willing to trade your disillusionment for hope, faith and power.

BREAKING THE OLD PATTERN

If you have lived a long time with disillusionment, you will need time to change the way you see and respond to the reality around you. Luke 22 reveals some principles that show us how to proceed:

> Jesus went out as usual to the Mount of Olives, and his disciples followed him. On reaching the place, he said to them,

"Pray that you will not fall into temptation." He withdrew about a stone's throw beyond them, knelt down and prayed, "Father, if you are willing, take this cup from me; yet not my will, but yours be done." An angel from heaven appeared to him and strengthened him. And being in anguish, he prayed more earnestly, and his sweat was like drops of blood falling to the ground. When he rose from prayer and went back to the disciples, he found them asleep, exhausted from sorrow.

—LUKE 22:39–45

Let's take a closer look at the principles revealed in these verses.

We must surrender completely to God's will (v. 42).

We must learn to trust God even if we don't understand the whole process. Are you willing to give up your anger and bitterness toward God about issues that caused you hurt or frustration because you couldn't see the total picture as God sees? We cannot see as God sees. Solomon, the wisest man who ever lived, made this statement in Ecclesiastes 3:11: "He has made everything beautiful in its time. He has also set eternity in the hearts of men; yet they cannot fathom what God has done from beginning to end."

The Bible teaches us that God's ways are perfect. Yet how easily we blame God when things go wrong! If anyone made a mistake, it was not God—but man. As Romans 3:4 teaches, "Let God be true, and every man be a liar." In other words, God is right; we are wrong.

As He prayed on the night before He was to be crucified, Jesus expressed a desire different from the desire of His Father when He said, "Father, if you are willing, take this cup from me; yet not my will, but yours be done" (Luke 22:42). Take a moment to give God everything you have. Give it all to the Lord, and He will give you something new.

Do not surrender to sorrow (v. 44).

Luke 22:44 says, "And being in anguish, he [Jesus] prayed more earnestly." Jesus was sad, but He was not bitter. He was not disillusioned. He did not hide in a cave. He was willing to march through the streets with His cross and then be crucified on a hill. We should follow Jesus' example. Do not surrender to sorrow.

Notice that the disciples fell asleep, exhausted from sorrow. Some people in the church are asleep, at least spiritually, because they are exhausted from their sadness. There are some things that we cannot resolve ourselves, but we can come to Jesus with our sadness. He is our great burden-bearer. As His Word teaches us:

> Come to me, all you who are weary and burdened, and I will give you rest. Take my yoke upon you and learn from me, for I am gentle and humble in heart, and you will find rest for your souls. For my yoke is easy and my burden is light.
>
> —MATTHEW 11:28–30

Jesus will embrace you and give you a brand-new heart and a new way of thinking. God's Word also teaches us that we are "transformed by the renewing of your mind" (Rom. 12:2). Jesus will help us to think differently and act differently.

Pray so you will not fall into temptation.

If you are disillusioned, chances are you will fall into other kinds of sin. Pray that you will not fall into temptation. This is an urgent call for people who have taken the road of disillusionment. You need to come back. One of the Bible's strongest warnings is, "See to it that no one misses the grace of God and that no bitter root grows up to cause trouble and defile many" (Heb. 12:15). Bitterness left unchecked can ruin your Christian life.

Tell your soul what to do.

Don't let your soul tell you what to do. The psalmist knew that we can exercise authority over our wayward emotions:

> Why are you downcast, O my soul?
>   Why so disturbed within me?
> Put your hope in God,
>   for I will yet praise him,
>   my Savior and my God.
>
> —PSALM 43:5

The psalmist was talking to his own soul. He was not crazy. He just knew that he had authority to command his own soul.

If we continue to embrace our disillusionment we will continually feel like a victim. We may even feel that we need God to pay more attention to us. Some people want to buy pity from God by feeling sorry for themselves. Some may even expect God to get emotional and come to help them.

From experience, I can tell you that God does not work like that. Whenever I throw a spiritual tantrum or feel like a victim, I do not get results. I now know better—I don't even try that tactic anymore. He has never once accepted my invitation to attend my pity parties! I no longer try to impress the heart of God with my victim mentality. Instead, I try to reach God with my faith.

How about you? Do you want to reach God?

A PRAYER OF REPENTANCE

Father, thank You for untangling our thoughts and taking away confusion through Your Word. Thank You, Father, that You are pointing out the road ahead and removing inferiority complexes and fear from our lives.

Lord God Almighty, in Jesus' name we ask You to come and set us free from disillusionment. For You, nothing is impossible. We pray for a mighty visitation of Your Spirit to transform us. Replace the disillusionment with hope.

Send angels to help us. Thank You for protection against the enemy. Give us discernment of our own thoughts. Set us free from thoughts that do not come from You, and purify us. In Jesus' name, amen.

Chapter 6

The Transgression of Joshua: The Sin of Presumption

One particular church I know of spent a lot of time praying and seeking God as a congregation. Several times they had received a word from the Lord indicating that revival was coming to their region. They fully expected to be a part of that great harvest when it came. The worship times in that church were wonderful and the prayer times powerful, yet the church never seemed to progress. The front door of the church was like a revolving door; when a new family came in, it seemed that one or two families would leave.

After several years of this cycle, it was discovered that the pastor had been involved in illicit sexual activities over the years. It was a devastating shock to the whole congregation. At first, they could not believe it. This servant of the Lord had stood in the pulpit and preached for thirty years! When he was confronted and asked, "How could you continue preaching each week when you knew you were living a lifestyle of sin?", his reply was unforgettable. He said, "I would repent each week and ask God to forgive me before getting back up to preach."

His transgression was hurtful to the congregation. Many members just quit and left for another church—even though the pastor himself had already left. The congregation could not believe that God would leave a person in the pulpit for so many years without exposing his sin. Some people stopped going to church altogether.

Transgressions are sins or weaknesses that sooner or later will pull us out of the Christian way, bringing defeat and disaster to our lives. The transgression of presumption occurs when we believe we have heard from God, yet we have not searched our hearts and followed His commands. Spiritual presumption is acting on the *rhema* word of God while forgetting the *logos* word of God. A *rhema* word imparts specific guidance from God. It may involve a prophecy or a word of knowledge. Many people spend their lives searching for this kind of spiritual knowledge, and yet they fail in life anyway. They develop sensitivity to guiding words, but they do so at the expense of learning and applying the Word of God, the *logos* word.

Joshua had a *rhema* word that told him, "Go and take the land." But he neglected the *logos* word, the law of holiness established by God many years earlier.

When we operate on presumption, our lives and ministries do not go the way we imagined. Some Christians are deeply wounded by having presumed they heard and understood God. Then, when things turn out differently than they anticipated, they feel they can never recover.

SIGNS OF PRESUMPTION

It is possible to recognize when you are stepping into presumption. By looking at an example from the life of Joshua, we can learn important principles that reveal the symptoms of presumption. Learn to identify these symptoms in your own life.

Becoming devastated when things do not go as expected

Immediately after their glorious victory over the city of Jericho, Joshua led the Israelites into another battle with their enemies—this time with devastating results.

> So the LORD was with Joshua, and his fame spread throughout the land. But the Israelites acted unfaithfully in regard to the devoted things; Achan son of Carmi, the son of Zimri, the son

of Zerah, of the tribe of Judah, took some of them. So the LORD's anger burned against Israel. Now Joshua sent men from Jericho to Ai, which is near Beth Aven to the east of Bethel, and told them, "Go up and spy out the region." So the men went up and spied out Ai.

When they returned to Joshua, they said, "Not all the people will have to go up against Ai. Send two or three thousand men to take it and do not weary all the people, for only a few men are there." So about three thousand men went up; but they were routed by the men of Ai, who killed about thirty-six of them. They chased the Israelites from the city gate as far as the stone quarries and struck them down on the slopes. At this *the hearts of the people melted and became like water.*

—JOSHUA 6:27–7:6, EMPHASIS ADDED

When the Israelites were defeated by their enemies, they not only regarded it as a temporal loss—they lost confidence in the future. Their sense of trust and hope was broken.

In my high school years in Argentina I had trouble with one particular subject—English. I had to take an additional test. It was hard. I thought I did not have the "gift" to speak it, and I was discouraged. But in the process of struggling with that subject, I became determined to master both the course and the language. A few years later I could read, speak and think English. At first my experience was traumatic. Then it caused growth in my life.

Christians have experienced a defeat and do not know how to overcome it, so they have hearts that have melted and grown cold for God. But God uses defeats to teach new lessons, not to devastate us. Let's overcome the initial shock of defeat, capitalize on the hard experience and move on in the plan of God.

Experiencing perplexity instead of purpose

It's possible that you are moving toward presumption if you find you are perplexed by the situations that face you. You may try to understand God and what He is doing in your life, but you cannot understand His purpose in your situation. Therefore you have no purpose of your own—only perplexity.

> Then Joshua tore his clothes and fell facedown to the ground
> before the ark of the LORD, remaining there till evening. The
> elders of Israel did the same, and sprinkled dust on their
> heads.
>
> —JOSHUA 7:6

Today we find many members of the body of Christ in a stage of
perplexity. There are churches and families who are grieving over
situations they do not understand. They are stuck in the "Why?"
stage of regret. If you are in that stage, you may be asking questions
like these:

- "Why did I trust that pastor for so long?"

- "Why was I so naive?"

- "Why did I believe God so much? Just look at the results!"

- "Why did I put so much effort into our church?"

- "Why did I really believe the gifts of the Spirit would operate in
  my life?"

- "Why did I have this crazy dream that God was going to use me?"

- "Why did I waste so much time praying for that person to be
  healed?"

- "Why didn't I just mind my own business and take up secular
  things?"

It's very likely that Joshua had some of these questions running
through his mind as he lay before the Lord all day. He was filled
with perplexity. He could not understand why the Lord had led
Israel into battle—only to face defeat.

Having regrets for following God to the next level

People who are paralyzed by a presumptuous wrong turn often
wonder why they took that last risk to move forward. Joshua
expressed some regrets to the Lord:

> And Joshua said, "Ah, Sovereign LORD, why did you ever bring
> this people across the Jordan to deliver us into the hands of

the Amorites to destroy us? If only we had been content to
stay on the other side of the Jordan!"

—JOSHUA 7:7

Not only did Joshua long for "the other side of the Jordan"—the
entire nation of Israel was thinking the same thing. Some pastors
have sought renewal for their congregations without results and
are in this stage of perplexity. They may be saying, "If only we had
forgotten about this hunger for God, this fire of holiness, this pressing and struggling for new things from God. Why couldn't we just
keep having church as usual?"

There is a big temptation confronting the church today—to sell
out the vision for revival, to sell out the fervent prayers and
become content with the status quo. Those who yield to this temptation are happy to make a deal with the devil. In essence they say,
"If you don't bother me, I won't bother you. Let's make a peace
treaty. You are too strong an enemy. I will mind my own business,
and you mind yours." Yielding to temptation in that way is often
based upon perplexity regarding the actions of God.

When people go through a crisis of faith they wonder what God
is doing. No doubt they believed it was God who was leading them
to move in a certain direction or to do a specific thing. Yet after
they take that route, things do not seem to work out. This is what
we call *religious traumas*—situations that happen at church and
are unresolved in our minds and hearts.

Christians who are suffering the effects of religious trauma still
attend church, still partake of the Lord's supper and do a lot of
"religious" things. But when the time comes to step out in faith
and do something big for their God, they stop. A voice within says,
"Wait a minute; remember the defeat of Ai. Remember you didn't
have a clue why you lost—but you lost. You are going to lose
again." This voice of regret then paralyzes the people from attempting a new conquest.

PUSHING AWAY PRESUMPTION

Did you recognize any of the symptoms of presumption as being things present in your own life? Do you feel that you no longer understand God's purposes for the things He is doing in your life? Have you lost your purpose—or do you lack direction to move ahead with God?

There are some steps that we can take that lead us away from presumption—not further into it. Use these steps to regain the purpose in your life. As you take these steps, God will give you a fresh revelation of His purposes and destiny for you.

Resolve your previous defeats.

Before we can end our perplexity, we need to resolve our previous defeats. Follow Joshua's example. Get before the Lord for as long as it takes to hear from Him. Ask Him what went wrong. Ask Him to help you and to teach you. Tell Him you want to learn. You may not be able to change the situation from the past, but you can certainly change your mind-set—and the way you will work in the future.

Joshua was in a post-revival syndrome. Just before the Israelites' defeat at Ai, there had been a supernatural victory that led to the fall of Jericho. The nation of Israel had defeated the fortified city that could have hindered the Israelites from possessing the Promised Land. Israel's enemies were stricken with fear. Because of God's sovereign plan and guidance, the walls came tumbling down miraculously. They had conquered the unconquerable! Joshua should have been experiencing great confidence and hope for his future.

It does not matter how many victories you have had in your past or how many people you have led to the Lord. It will not even matter how many glorious miracles you have seen the Lord perform through you. If you have an Ai experience—an unexplained defeat—it will haunt you. It will immobilize you. If your pastor says, "OK, church, it is time to move on to the next stage," you will be unable to step forward. There will be a sick feeling in your heart. You may say, "I have tried that before." So be aware that your reluctance can turn into a transgression.

Guard God's honor.

When faced with situations that we do not understand, it is not only our name that is at stake—it is the honor of God Almighty. If we fail before the sight of our neighbors, in their eyes God fails. The only picture of Jesus that many believers can see is what they see when they look at you and your family. What do they see when they look at you? Joshua was concerned beyond his own image as a leader:

> O Lord, what can I say, now that Israel has been routed by its enemies? The Canaanites and the other people of the country will hear about this and they will surround us and wipe out our name from the earth. What then will you do for your own great name?
>
> —JOSHUA 7:8–9

Joshua wasn't concerned just about the future of Israel—he was concerned about God's reputation. Although Joshua had been seized by presumption, he actually did the right thing by expressing his concern about the honor of God. He asked the right question: "What then will you do for your own great name?"

How do you respond in the moments when you do not understand God's ways? If you lose faith and strength, Christianity may look like a failure to those around you. Our responses in situations we do not understand are important. Guard not only your own reputation; guard God's honor above all.

Be loyal.

The step of loyalty is vitally important to avoid presumption. Think of the issue of loyalty in a church staff. Too many times we have seen church staff members concerned with their own honor and reputation rather than that of their pastor. For example, there will be times when someone sitting in a pew will decide that he has been called to the ministry of correcting the pastor. So he erroneously accuses the pastor of wrongdoing or perverted doctrine.

It is very rare that such an individual would go directly to the pastor with his accusations. More often he spreads his concern through gossip. Gossip discredits people without giving them a chance to defend themselves.

When gossip begins to spread through a congregation, the pastoral staff has two immediate options. A staff member can feel defensive and become worried about how the gossip will make him or her look personally rather then rising to the defense of the pastor. If a staff member chooses personal offense over loyalty to the pastor, he or she has chosen to become a part of the problem. If that staff member chooses to continue spreading the accusation through gossip, he or she has widened the circle of conflict. Often such a staff member even gets to the point of deciding to oppose the pastor.

The other option for a staff member is to understand that his or her role involves *covering* the pastor's back—rather than stabbing him in the back. The pastor could actually be wrong, but the way to solve the situation is not through gossip and talking behind his back. Resolution will only happen through face-to-face dialogue. There is a loyalty issue at stake. The first reaction of a church staff member should be to express concern for the honor of the pastor—and the honor of God—rather than concern for his or her own honor.

My brothers and sisters, we need to protect the honor of God in this nation, as well as before our neighbors. At times it may seem that everything we touch becomes a disaster and a failure. But our attitude of concern should extend beyond ourselves. God's honor is at stake. Our response to crisis should not be one that betrays God.

Persuade God to guard His honor.

Moses prayed many times, "What will the Egyptians say if You wipe out Israel? What will people think if You allow us to fail and these people die in the wilderness?" Moses gives us some insight into knowing how to persuade God to guard His own honor. Moses said, "Even if You raise a new generation through me, what will those pagan Egyptians say about all these people who left Egypt and then died? Lord, don't wipe them out."

Moses stood in the gap between God and the people of Israel. He gives us a beautiful picture of the intercessory ministry. God was prepared to wipe out Israel because of the people's continual disobedience. But because Moses interceded for the people before God, they were spared from destruction.

In Genesis 18 we see the example of another intercessor, Abraham. When God told Abraham of His intent to destroy the cities of Sodom and Gomorrah for their great sin, immediately Abraham pleaded for God's mercy. "Will you sweep away the righteous with the wicked? What if there are fifty righteous people in the city? Will you really sweep it away and not spare the place for the sake of the fifty righteous people in it?" (Gen. 18:23–24).

So God relented and agreed to spare the cities if He found fifty righteous people living there. But that wasn't good enough for Abraham the intercessor! He came back to the Lord in intercession for the people: "What if the number of the righteous is five less than fifty?...What if only forty are found there?...What if only thirty can be found there?...What if only twenty can be found there?" (vv. 28–31).

Even when God agreed to spare the city for twenty righteous people, Abraham still interceded on behalf of the people. "May the Lord not be angry, but let me speak just once more. What if only ten can be found there?" (v. 32).

The intercession of Abraham persuaded God to guard His honor. In response to Abraham's pleading, He said, "For the sake of ten, I will not destroy it" (v. 32). Praying the kind of prayer we see from Moses, Abraham and Joshua shows that we care for the honor of God.

Accept the fact that genuine victory must be preceded by holiness.

There is no chance to win when there is sin in the camp, even if the battle is from God. If the body of Christ is not seeing revival in this land, I believe it is because the church still has not dealt with all its sin. It may be only a small percentage of the whole, but even the smallest percentage can bring defeat. We see that illustrated in Israel's defeat at Ai:

> The LORD said to Joshua, "Stand up! What are you doing down on your face? Israel has sinned; they have violated my

covenant, which I commanded them to keep. They have taken
some of the devoted things; they have stolen, they have lied,
they have put them with their own possessions."

—JOSHUA 7:10–11

There are some transgressions that we have accepted as normal.
But this is the hour for separating the evil from the good. We can
no longer put up with sin in the camp. The Lord may be saying to
the church, "This is not the time to be relenting, lamenting or
regretting. This is not the time for feeling like a victim or suffering
from inferiority complexes. Israel has sinned. They have violated
My covenant, which I commanded them to keep. They have taken
some of the devoted things, have stolen, lied and integrated them
into their daily lifestyles as normal. That is why My people have no
power to stand against their enemies."

As their leader, Joshua did not understand why the Lord had
allowed his enemies to defeat his army. Joshua was not covering
up his own sin. He personally was just doing what the Lord had
told him to do. Joshua was not living in adultery; he didn't steal
anybody's money. He was not partying and getting drunk. Yet he
was not experiencing victory—he was experiencing defeat!

You may be in the same position as Joshua. You may be doing
the right thing, yet still failing. God may have given you a clear
green light to move forward in what you know to be His will for
your life. Yet your church, your family, your community may be facing failure. Why? One explanation is the same as what happened
to Joshua—there may be sin in the camp. Disobedience opens the
door to destruction.

Destroy things devoted to destruction.

In other words, Israel was weak on getting rid of sin; they did
not destroy the sinful snares in their midst. Their weakness and
greed made them devoted to destruction.

God will not stay with those who will not destroy the items in
their lives that are devoted to destruction. The Lord is saying, "I will
not be with you anymore unless you destroy your remaining idols."

I have seen Christians from whom the hand of the Lord seems

to have been withdrawn. When we see this we ask, "Where is the blessing? Where is the fear of God?"

That state of being does not happen in a moment. Sometimes it takes years to quench the Spirit. It may take years to pollute the mind or fill the eyes with greed. But it begins—and ends—with gratifying the flesh above the Spirit of God. If we continue to feed the flesh, we will reach a point where the Lord says, "I will not be with you anymore unless you destroy whatever among you is devoted to destruction."

I heard of a Christian lady who at some point in her married life had been unfaithful to her husband through an extramarital affair. One of the gifts she had received during that time was a gold chain necklace from her lover. Eventually she broke off the immoral relationship, but she decided to keep the gold chain. After all, it was worth some money.

So, every week this Christian lady came to church with her husband and two children, wearing the gold chain. One Sunday during an altar call the Holy Spirit began to convict her of that souvenir of sin she was wearing around her neck. She made her way forward to the altar and left it there as a sin offering to the Lord. God had asked her to get rid of something in her life that had been designated by God to be destroyed.

This is the cry of God to His church today. Don't blame God for your failure and say, "Lord, what have You done with us? Why aren't we more successful? Why do we have so many traumas in our past?" First, remember that the Lord demands holiness from His people. Without holiness no one will see God.

Consecrate yourselves.

The solution that God offered for the Israelites' moment of defeat was for the people to consecrate themselves. There was no way they could win the battle in their lives until they identified and removed their own personal idols:

> Go, consecrate the people. Tell them, "Consecrate yourselves in preparation for tomorrow; for this is what the LORD, the God of Israel, says: That which is devoted is among you, O Israel. You

cannot stand against your enemies until you remove it."
                                                    —JOSHUA 7:13

On the same day that I was to minister at a conference in Sydney, Australia, the city held Mardi Gras celebration for homosexuals in a downtown location. It was a big rally with thousands of people.

Many people also came to our Christian rally, including some governmental officials who sat on the front row. These officials told me that the celebration for homosexuals had also occurred the previous year. During our conference, the Lord gave them a strong prophetic word. I encouraged them to write it down. The prophecy said, "What is happening on the streets of your city tonight is an abomination to Me [referring to the homosexual march]. But a greater abomination unto Me is the sin of My people, which has allowed a tree of unrighteousness to spring up in your city."

The Lord was telling His people that He was more concerned with the transgressions in the church than with the transgressions of the homosexuals. The prophecy continued: "This tree of unrighteousness is growing. It has grown so big that it can no longer be cut down with an ax; it has grown so large that it cannot be cut through with a saw. The only way that the tree of unrighteousness in your city will be brought down is to starve it of the nutrients upon which it feeds—the sin of My people."

This word could be applied to the church in many cities around the world. The unrighteousness in our cities is so strong that it seems as though nothing could move it—nothing will change. That is because there is unrighteousness and sin in the church.

I am not bringing an accusation of sin against any one particular church. I am saying that the body of Christ is not yet as pure as Jesus wants it to be. I look forward to the time when we no longer have to preach holiness in the churches. A time when they will say, "We do not need preachers of holiness inside the church." I look forward to the day when our cries for holiness need be directed only at those in the streets and in the stadiums—to those who have never heard the gospel.

I long for that time when we have to preach to the unbelievers because the church has already heard and obeyed. The Bible says that the Lord is preparing His bride, the church. The bride will be dressed in a garment without spot or wrinkle. The Holy Spirit is removing the last few sin spots from the church. Prepare yourself by removing the sin spot from your life.

Be united against the enemy.

In my hometown of La Plata, Argentina, we saw an awesome, history-making revival. Evangelist Carlos Annacondia came to our city in 1984 to hold an open-air crusade, and he ended up staying there for six months. More than fifty thousand people came to Christ during that time. From there, the revival spread to many cities in Argentina. It is said that more than two million people have come to Jesus during the last fifteen years as a result of that revival. Genuine miracle after miracle took place. We saw thousands saved and hundreds healed and set free from demonic oppression. Many churches grew from a small congregation of a few dozen people to several hundred members.

But as that awesome revival progressed, something else began to happen. When God moves in our midst, either we change or we will go back to where we were before we experienced revival. Some of the pastors in Argentina decided to go back to their old ways. They were content to work for their own churches, forgetting the needs of their cities. They forgot the unity, forgot the vision and concentrated on growing their own ministries and churches in isolation. In one city things got to the point that a few pastors began to criticize fellow ministers over the radio airwaves, using their microphones to slander them.

Why did this happen? They allowed sin in the church and did not take care of business. It has been said that in order for evil to abound, all the righteous have to do is *nothing*. We have seen the spiritual effect in the cities of Argentina. There are now more people addicted to drugs than ever before. Crime is up. There are people who will kill someone else for three dollars. They steal the money and then shoot their victims in the head. Insecurity and instability abound everywhere. At the time of writing this book, our cities are like a war zone because of economic collapse.

I believe it is because a visitation of the Lord came, but then we did not pursue carefully the holiness of God in our lives and relationships. We allowed a tree of unrighteousness to grow in our cities. Many pastors, myself among them, have reached the point where we cried out, "Lord, why did You ever bring these people across the Jordan to deliver us into the hands of the Amorites to destroy us?"

The revivals, blessing and instruction of the past can become our destruction if we do not pursue current holiness and purity. The counterattacks of the enemy can be stronger and more vicious than ever.

However, I am filled with hope. We have returned to the city of La Plata, where we called the city together through "Transformation Encounters." In September of 2000, we saw a sports arena fill up with more than six thousand people. When we returned again the following year, for the first time in the history of the city of La Plata we were able to hold a united meeting in the large soccer stadium. Not all churches of the city were present, but this story is still being written.

REVELATION, NOT REGRET

When things get really difficult in your family or tough in your marriage, you need to ask God why things are failing. Ask Him to reveal where things went wrong. Ask Him to tell you what to do next. Regret will not make things better. Feeling sorry about the past will not save your marriage if it is going downhill. You need revelation. You need God to speak to your heart.

If you are in a situation where you are ready to give up your church, career, ministry, prayer life or any other wholesome area of your life, you need revelation. You need the Holy Spirit to speak to your heart and give you a word of hope.

Achan's sin was the cause of trouble for the whole nation. His violation of the covenant of the Lord disgraced all of Israel.

> In the morning, present yourselves tribe by tribe. The tribe
> that the LORD takes shall come forward clan by clan; the clan
> that the LORD takes shall come forward family by family; and
> the family that the LORD takes shall come forward man by
> man. He who is caught with the devoted things shall be
> destroyed by fire, along with all that belongs to him. He has
> violated the covenant of the LORD and has done a disgraceful
> thing in Israel!
>
> —JOSHUA 7:14–15

Achan gave an explanation for why he had sinned. He described
the greed he had:

> Achan replied, "It is true! I have sinned against the LORD, the
> God of Israel. This is what I have done: When I saw in the
> plunder a beautiful robe from Babylonia, two hundred shekels
> of silver and a wedge of gold weighing fifty shekels, I coveted
> them and took them. They are hidden in the ground inside my
> tent, with the silver underneath."
>
> —JOSHUA 7:20–21

That was the explanation of their defeat. Keep this one principle in mind: When something goes wrong, God is not wrong.

We believe in the character of God. He is perfect in all His ways.
If something has gone wrong in my life, I dare say it has been something that I did wrong, either because of my evil tendencies, my
flesh or because of my own foolish ignorance.

Joshua committed the sin of presumption because he wrongly
assumed that he was going to win the battle, just as the Israelites
had won in the city of Jericho—but without taking spiritual inven-
tory. Only one problem had changed the equation—this time there
was sin in the camp.

Joshua assumed too many things. Be warned about the kind of
faith or belief that says, "If I say it many times, if I repeat something
one hundred times, God is going to have to do it, and it is going to
happen my way." We cannot manipulate God into doing things "our
way." Our prayers must be in line with God's will or they will not
be heard. I believe this truth: If we confess and declare the Word

of the Lord and the will of the Lord, it will come to pass. But if we persist in being stubborn, trying to manipulate heaven for our own selfish agenda, then we are in for disappointment.

REPENT AND FULFILL YOUR MISSION

Notice what happened later on in this story. The Israelites repented, dealt with their sin and then went back and completely took the city of Ai in a great victory. After they dealt with their presumption, they were able to possess the land.

The Lord is waiting for you to invade your city with the gospel. The Lord is waiting for you to declare victory in your home. But if there is sin in your heart, take responsibility for it and purify your heart. Then get back on the battlefield. We have no right to disqualify ourselves because of past failures.

Don't become disillusioned by mistakes you have made. Some people can no longer trust the Lord as they once were able to trust. Some people were once on fire for God, but only burn cautiously now. Maybe they made a foolish mistake in the past, but now they say, "I am not going to trust in the Holy Spirit anymore." A spirit of fear has gripped them. Be set free from that. Trust God again. Be like the child who trusts his father completely.

We need to return to the simplicity of our faith and say, "God, if You did it in the past, You can do it again. If you helped us to take Jericho, You can help us take Ai. It's not impossible." God wants to raise up Elijahs who will say to those around them, "Come here to me; the God who answers by fire will be the true God." We need challengers, people who will dare to believe.

While in high school I became friends with a young man named Marcelo. He looked so pagan, so wild, so unholy. I remember saying to another friend as Marcelo walked ahead of us, "That guy will never become a Christian."

When I led the March for Jesus in La Plata years after Carlos Annacondia's first visit, I stood looking over the crowd of more than six thousand people who had crowded into the plaza. I noticed someone on the platform videotaping the gathering. He looked like Marcelo, the fellow I had said would never be converted. After the gathering, he came over to greet me. To my great surprise, it was Marcelo!

Marcelo had been miraculously saved. We renewed our friendship, and he started attending my church. Before long he became one of the leaders in the congregation. He still attends that congregation we used to pastor, even though we have moved on. I had given up on Marcelo while in high school, but God surprised me by saving him and establishing him as a dedicated Christian worker.

Maybe you are like Joshua after his first great victory; you cannot see the future and are asking God why He brought you to this point. You may be asking if your life was destined for failure. God has a wonderful plan for your life. With God's help, you will be able to reach cities, souls, your family and your marriage for God.

Blaming God and wanting to retreat from His will when we experience failure is not just an innocent little error. It is a transgression. If Joshua would not have repented and cleansed the camp, Israel would have been wiped out. We need correction and forgiveness so that we can stand against our enemies.

If you are frustrated, God wants to give you joy. I believe the Lord will impart revelation to your heart, and you will have answers from heaven with a fresh sense of direction. You will understand more of your past and will have more faith for the future. You will move beyond your humiliating experience in Ai to take ground for the kingdom of God.

A PRAYER OF REPENTANCE

Father, forgive us for blaming You when we do not understand the reason for our failure. Purify Your church from spiritual vices and moral failures. Set us free, O God. We pray for transformation. We are like Joshua, just trying to do Your will, but good intentions are not enough. We plead with You, Lord, to expose the hidden idols in our lives. Help us to cleanse our camps and remove those things devoted to destruction. Make us effective for Your kingdom.

Lord, I pledge my loyalty to You. When I do not understand Your ways or my circumstances, I promise, O God, to defend Your honor, knowing that You are true and every man is a liar. Even though You do not heal me every time I ask, I will say as Job said, "Even though You slay me, yet I will praise You." I submit to Your sovereignty in my life. In Jesus' name, amen.

Chapter 7

The Transgression of King Saul: Allowing Foolishness to Become Sin

T*he* thought-provoking headline on a dental care newsletter I received recently from a dentist friend of mine read: "Tooth Care or Consequences." I thought about how many people challenge this law of good dental hygiene by thinking, *Maybe time will totally heal my aching tooth.* So, rather than scheduling an appointment with their dentist, they wait…and wait…until late one night the pain is so intense they can postpone the call no longer.

That headline made me think of one of my own: "Soul care or consequences." If we are not willing to expose transgressions that are present in the church today, those often unseen and unrecognized, we will eventually suffer the painful consequences. That is why there are so many moral casualties. We have not been willing to confront sin. That is why there are so many well-meaning Christians who end up in spiritual disaster.

The word *foolishness* is described in one dictionary as "lacking or exhibiting a lack of good sense or judgment; silly." A professor at my Bible school used to say, "The essence of sin is stupidity." Let's examine how foolishness led one of the Bible's central characters into spiritual ruin.

Holiness and Foolishness Can Never Mix

We could call King Saul's transgression the *sin of stupidity*. No doubt both you and I have seen a few people collapsing spiritually because of a lack of passion. But we have seen many more collapse spiritually because of the lack of wisdom. There is no holiness where there is foolishness—the two will never mix. If you want to be holy, but you enjoy your foolishness, there will be a time when you are going to have to choose one or the other.

Before we look at the example of foolishness from the life of Saul, I want to show you from my own life how the principle of foolishness operates. I remember so well how I felt when I turned nineteen years of age. I was already preaching, teaching and leading in the church. I was the president of the Royal Rangers organization (a Christian group similar to Boy Scouts) in Argentina, and I felt so mature.

I was sure that it was very important that I get married soon. After all, I did not want to turn twenty or twenty-one and not be married. So, because I was a man of prayer, I began to pray for that special young lady who was to be my wife to make her appearance in my life. Since I felt some pressure to rush this step, I decided the very nice young lady whom I had met at the Bible school might be the one. After prayer I felt OK about her and thought, *Well, God, You sure answered this one quickly!*

We became friends and started dating almost immediately. Why wait? I had the revelation. But a few months later, I realized that I did not want this young lady to become my wife! So I began to complain to the Lord. "Lord, You brought this young lady to my life," I told Him. "But I don't like her! Still, if You want me to marry her, I will marry her anyway." I felt like a martyr. I was perplexed. Because I had been bound by my own faulty concept about the will of God for my life, I had foolishly rushed ahead. I learned that when you rush, you do not hear God well. One day I decided to break off that relationship that very day. But because I had no clear understanding of God's will in the situation, for a long time afterward I was filled with doubt and confusion; I thought, *Maybe I missed the will of God. Maybe He will never use me again.*

Another instance: When I was young I found it very difficult to wait for my father to take those eternal two minutes to give me clear instructions. I would listen but keep walking. Finally my dad had to say, "Wait, son; let me speak to you, and then you can go."

Some people are rushed and tense about the will of God. Some people live with some degree of continual spiritual confusion. Others become so confused that they get mad at God. In Proverbs 19:3 we read, "A man's own folly ruins his life, yet his heart rages against the LORD." Much of our frustration with God is caused by our own haste, anxiety, misinterpretations of the will of God and our own foolishness.

While I was completing my studies at Bible school, I was also working for a man who had given me permission to hire someone to help me in my job. I hired a young man from Southern California who seemed to be a perfect candidate. But just a few days later, my boss told me, "You need to fire this fellow."

As a Christian, I didn't think I should do that. I asked my boss to give me some more time first. I assured him that his young man was a good guy and that he would someday do excellent work. But my boss (who was also a Christian) responded, "But don't you see? He is not willing to work. He does not want to learn." I tried to train the young man for several weeks, but he refused to cooperate. He operated according to "the law of the minimum effort!" Finally, weeks later, I had to let him go.

I wasted a lot of time, but I learned a precious lesson. I had idealized that person in my heart—I had not been willing to see the reality. You may be thinking, *What does this story have to do with soul care or consequences? What does it have to do with revival?*

It has a lot to do with it! Many of our revivals are discredited because of foolishness in the hearts of people. Much of the work of the Lord is minimized because the people of God do not know how to shepherd that revival. A succession of unwise decisions will discredit the revival and eventually cause it to die.

In 1 Samuel 13, we see an example of what *not* to do from the life of Saul. Although this is a long passage of Scripture, it is worth re-reading in its entirety.

> Saul was thirty years old when he became king, and he reigned over Israel forty-two years. Saul chose three thousand men from Israel; two thousand were with him at Micmash and in the hill country of Bethel, and a thousand were with Jonathan at Gibeah in Benjamin. The rest of the men he sent back to their homes. Jonathan attacked the Philistine outpost at Geba, and the Philistines heard about it. Then Saul had the trumpet blown throughout the land and said, "Let the Hebrews hear!" So all Israel heard the news: "Saul has attacked the Philistine outpost, and now Israel has become a stench to the Philistines." And the people were summoned to join Saul at Gilgal.
>
> The Philistines assembled to fight Israel, with three thousand chariots, six thousand charioteers, and soldiers as numerous as the sand on the seashore. They went up and camped at Micmash, east of Beth Aven. When the men of Israel saw that their situation was critical and that their army was hard pressed, they hid in caves and thickets, among the rocks, and in pits and cisterns. Some Hebrews even crossed the Jordan to the land of Gad and Gilead.
>
> Saul remained at Gilgal, and all the troops with him were quaking with fear. He waited seven days, the time set by Samuel; but Samuel did not come to Gilgal, and Saul's men began to scatter. So he said, "Bring me the burnt offering and the fellowship offerings. And Saul offered up the burnt offering. Just as he finished making the offering, Samuel arrived, and Saul went out to greet him.
>
> "What have you done?" asked Samuel.
>
> Saul replied, "When I saw that the men were scattering, and that you did not come at the set time, and that the Philistines were assembling at Micmash, I thought, 'Now the Philistines will come down against me at Gilgal, and I have not sought the LORD's favor.' So I felt compelled to offer the burnt offering."
>
> *"You acted foolishly,"* Samuel said. "You have not kept the command the Lord your God gave you; if you had, he would

have established your kingdom over Israel for all time. But now your kingdom will not endure; the Lord has sought out a man after his own heart and appointed him leader of his people, because you have not kept the Lord's command."

—1 SAMUEL 13:1–14, EMPHASIS ADDED

CHARACTERISTICS OF A PERSON WHO WALKS IN FOOLISHNESS

Samuel rebuked Saul for his careless decision to offer the sacrifice. From this example we can learn to identify the characteristics of people who walk in foolishness. May God vaccinate us today against whatever remains of foolishness in our lives. May we live wisely and righteously the rest of our lives.

A foolish person acts out of context.

Some time ago, a friend of mine who is a graduate of Fuller Theological Seminary in California flew to our city and came to my home to visit with me. He had many questions about the baptism of holiness that I received in 1997. "Sergio," he began cautiously, "I know you have received something like a baptism of holiness, but I want to ask you a few theological questions. What is the context of this baptism?"

I realized that he was sincere, so I began to explain my experience to him. Because he had majored in church history, he asked questions relating to history. "Have you ever seen anything like this?"

"Oh, yes!" I told him enthusiastically.

"What about in the Bible?" he asked. "Is it in there?"

"Oh yes," I answered once again, "it is there." I referred him to several scriptures on the subject. What had looked like a casual five-minute conversation when we began turned into a couple of hours. By the time I took my friend to the airport, he was asking, "Would you pray for me? I want to receive the same fire of holiness you received."

This man had first wanted to make sure the experience was not something out of context with what God was working through the entire body of Christ. Then he was ready to receive it. His caution was a sign of wisdom, not of unbelief. Like my friend, the Bereans who heard the apostle Paul preach in their city went home and searched the Scriptures to find the "context" for what the Paul was preaching (Acts 17:11).

Only a foolish person acts out of context. Saul did his own thing. He did not order his steps according to God's ways and purposes. He followed a self-centered agenda. We could say that Saul echoed Frank Sinatra's words and did it his way. He just did his own thing. There are many people today in churches who live lives of isolation. They refuse to take correction, and they will not seek advice. They operate as Lone Rangers with a maverick attitude.

Saul was unwilling to wait to do things as God had ordained. He forced the situation so his men would come to the battle. In my foolishness, I have done the same. Years ago at one of our board meetings we were discussing an area where we needed to make a decision. Dr. C. Peter Wagner was a member of our board of directors, and I did not agree with a point he was making in the discussion. Of course it is OK not to agree, but in retrospect I realize how foolish I was at that time.

Here was a man with many years of experience in the ministry who was discussing the area of his expertise in ministry. I was fresh out of seminary, yet I was trying to tell him how to do things. Thank God, since then I have done much growing and maturing. I have now learned to listen more carefully to this man's wisdom, and we have maintained a very cordial relationship all these years. We must be very careful that we do not lose our integrity by living in isolation and self-reliance. We live in a generation that tends to isolate good counsel, placing it on the shelf for easy access, but failing to take it down and use it when we need it the most.

One Christian leader in America has suggested that we should create a national council of moral accountability. He suggested that a group of one hundred leaders meet to strategize ways that Christians can become accountable to one another. I believe we need this in every nation. There are so many moral failures and casualties—and this is not the will of the Lord. The Bible does not say, "Tomorrow you shall sin for sure." The Bible says, "Sin shall not be your master" (Rom. 6:14). We can help each other walk straight by having accountability networks.

According to many of the latest national statistics, there are as many divorces occurring in America among church members as there are among the unchurched.[1] Something is not right. We need help. We need a new wave of sanctification to hit the church. It is our own foolishness that is ruining us. We need accountability; we cannot work in isolation.

A foolish person has the wrong sense of timing.

When we were just newly married, my wife, Kathy, and I wanted to serve the Lord. I had the passion and vision to go to Argentina to plant a school and orphanage and to establish a leadership training program. If possible, I wanted to do it all in one year. When I broke that news to my godly wife, she looked at me and said, "You are crazy!"

I was so hurt that I wasn't even sure my marriage would survive that blow, so I went to prayer. "Lord," I cried out to Him, "I am an evangelical Christian, so I cannot divorce my wife. But she does not want to come with me to fulfill the vision You gave me." I cried, and I prayed; I fasted, and I waited. Soon I realized that although the vision might be right, the timing was wrong. To fulfill the will of God, we need not only a green light to move ahead in His will—we also need a green light about *when* to move ahead. We need to understand His strategic timing in order to obey Him fully.

Later my wife began to ask me questions. "So what kind of school do you want to establish?" she asked. "How would you start the orphanage?" As I shared my dream with her, it wasn't long before she said, "Maybe we can do this!" And when we moved ahead to fulfill the will of God in Argentina, she became instrumental in helping to establish the orphanage, school and leadership training program in Argentina. To this day those ministries are successfully continuing.

I thank God that I did not rush. I was able to "recruit" my wife into the dream the Lord had given me. The sense of wise timing is part of our holiness (and our success!).

I remember a man who said to my father, "I am ready to be a senior pastor now, so give me my independence." But the man was not ready. Within one year he had destroyed the work that had begun in a promising location where my father had planted a new church.

It is so important to develop a divine sense of timing. We desperately need to learn to follow the Lord's calendar. People sometimes get impatient with their church leaders, believing the leader is moving too slowly or too quickly. We must learn to synchronize within the church, waiting for each other, working as one body. God may have given you powerful spiritual gifts. You may believe that everyone but you is moving too slowly. But you run the risk of destroying your own ministry by getting ahead of the church—and ahead of God.

If you are running alone, chances are you are running out of the will of God. Come back! God is bringing a revival that is accompanied by humility, unity, meekness and respect for one another's ministries. We may be able to run faster than others during the first year or so, but if we criticize everyone else and abandon the church, sooner or later we will find ourselves in trouble.

In 1 Samuel 13, Saul precipitated events. Like a child who pulls his favorite T-shirt from the bottom of the pile because he can't take the time to take things off one by one, Saul caused the whole pile to fall on top of him. Prematurely he declared a war on the Philistines. Then he became frightened by the consequences of his hasty action.

Saul ignored both the *chronos* timing and the *kairos* timing for that battle. That was foolishness in action. The *chronos* timing is that which we can observe on our watches. The *kairos* timing is the appointed time of God for His specific intervention. Sometimes we can also miss both. We may miss walking together in unity in the church or in our marriage or family, and eventually, when the visitation of the Lord comes, we miss it because we are so disorganized.

Some are always too early or too late, but never in God's time.

One afternoon when I was nine, I decided that I was such a good swimmer I could make it to the other side of a very deep pool. "I have never done this," I told my friends, "but I am going to do it for the very first time." Of course I got their attention, and I enjoyed that, even at the cost of taking a risk. There was a little pride involved. So I began to do what I had seen the older kids doing. A few yards away from the edge, I could go no further, and I'm sure I would have drowned if the lifeguards had not reached me. They pulled me out, pressed water out of my stomach, and I was saved.

Many church leaders today operate in this type of foolish rush. This is a warning to the body of Christ. Unless we walk in wisdom and unity, not even revival will help us. Our relationships, our unity and our accountability must already be established when the mighty power of God appears. The net should already be mended. Our hearts should be ready.

Part of the commitment to holiness is a commitment to the body of Christ. When the baptism of fire came into my life, one of the first changes it brought to me was an exuberant love for the body of Christ, a love that encircled all denominations. That love keeps me from rushing ahead of the body of Christ—and ahead of God—and compels me to take the time and effort, imperfect as it may be, to synchronize with others.

A foolish person does not know how to set clear boundaries.

Saul became impatient as he waited. When Samuel asked him, "What have you done?," Saul responded, "I felt compelled to offer the burnt offering" (1 Sam. 13:12). In essence, he said, "Sorry, Pastor; I could not wait for you."

Samuel had been appointed prophet and priest by God. Saul was the appointed king. Saul crossed the boundaries God had given him as king. He had a spirit of rugged individualism, which is not necessarily wrong, but it kept him from waiting for the right time. It also caused him to cross the line and step out of his own calling. In essence he decided that he could do the prophet's job along with his own.

Another king who went beyond his boundaries was King Asa. Anxious to make a treaty of peace with Ben-Hadad, the heathen king of Aram, Asa took the silver and gold treasure from the Lord's temple as a peace offering to the king. Several victories followed for him, but eventually the consequences of his foolish action caught up with him. Through a confrontation with Hanani the seer, God gave him this rebuke:

> Because you relied on the king of Aram and not on the LORD your God, the army of the king of Aram has escaped from your hand…For the eyes of the LORD range throughout the earth to strengthen those whose hearts are fully committed to him. *You have done a foolish thing,* and from now on you will be at war.
> —2 CHRONICLES 16:7, 9, EMPHASIS ADDED

One secret to keeping the fire of God burning in our lives is not to exceed the boundaries of our own calling. Develop the humility to work within the parameters of what the Lord has given you to do. Some people never learn to carry the ark of the covenant without touching it. There are grave and terrible consequences for those who touch that ark.

Foolish people often ignore reality.

Saul believed he was acting in the name of the Lord by initiating a battle with his enemies. But he did not take time to count how great the army of the enemy was or how many chariots they had. The Bible tells us they had three thousand chariots and six thousand charioteers. When Saul saw that invasion coming against him, he was terrified. Having the faith to confront your enemy is one thing—but presuming you are strong enough to defeat them is quite another thing. Sometimes it is just our own carnal courage that leads to disaster. Saul did not have the facts; he was not in touch with reality.

It is amazing how sin can blind people and make them arrive at ridiculous conclusions. I knew a man who decided to separate from his wife. He even claimed that God had told him to do this— and not to give her any money while they were separated.

Of course, it would not require a mature Christian to discern that this man had not heard from God. The Lord would never tell a person to divorce his wife and withhold support from her! But this man's sin caused him to live in a sad state of denial.

A judge in court even told this man, "You must pay, or you will be in trouble." But he continued to believe he had heard from God. He even decided that his was a "special case" even though it violated Scripture. In a few days, however, we learned that this man was in jail. Reality hit him hard, and hopefully the sentencing caused him to recognize his foolishness.

There is a price to pay for the foolishness of ignoring reality. Saul not only ignored the size of his enemy's army—he ignored his own army's lack of strength. We learn in 1 Samuel 13:22 that Saul led his army into battle against a powerful, large army without the proper weapons. Scripture tells us, "Not a soldier with Saul and Jonathan had a sword or spear in his hand." Likewise, many pastors say they want revival in their churches, but very few have counted the cost or taken the time to equip either themselves or their members (especially their key leaders) with the weapons that are necessary. They are like Saul, and their churches are like Saul's army—unequipped and unprepared.

A foolish person consumes his own resources.

The Bible says in Proverbs 21:20, "In the house of the wise are stores of choice food and oil, but a foolish man devours all he has." This seems especially appropriate in our culture, which is so drunk on debt. We live in days where we are so pushed into debt that it is hard to stop consuming.

I once preached at a church in Southern Argentina where people were bringing their credit cards to the altar at the end of the service. The pastor told me that the Holy Spirit initiated a new movement in their church. Many of their people were bound by credit card debt because they were compulsive shoppers. If they had the card, they had to use it. They were in such huge debt they could not support the work of the Lord, and eventually they could not support their own families. I began to hear testimony after testimony of marriages getting healed and stronger. They had resolved their financial conflicts by stopping compulsive shopping and facing debt with resolve.

Some experts on marriage have said that the main issue for strife in the home is finances. We live in days where we have an incredible freedom to choose what we can buy or not. Consumerism has become a sickness. You will notice when you fall into it because there is no money for tithe and nothing extra to support missionaries. We are like this foolish person who devours all he has.

John Wesley instructed his people to pray before they bought anything. I admire the wisdom of his philosophy of money in which he said, "Earn all you can, save all you can, and give all you can." At one point in his life, the Lord blessed him so much that he was able to live with 10 percent and give 90 percent to the work of the Lord.

I am not coming to you in an attitude of being holier than you are. I am coming in meekness to tell you that this is part of the holiness that God wants to bring to our families. Financial and fiscal integrity is part of being holy. Some people believe they are holy because they are moral. Holiness is not only good morality; but it is also good ethics. It is having a good testimony and presenting a good image before the pagans so that they will come to Christ.

If our holiness is not invading every aspect of our lives, then we are not holy! Some may think that they are "almost" holy. But 98 percent holiness is not enough. We all need to embrace the holiness of Jesus Christ, the Lamb of God without sin. We need to bring holiness to our checking account, to our finances, to our marriage, to our relationships, to the movies we watch and to every aspect of our lives.

The church that embraces this kind of holiness will be unstoppable. There is no demon in hell that can stop a church that is totally committed to the holiness of Jesus Christ. Revival is delayed because obedience has been delayed. As we are prompt to obey, the Lord Almighty will give us strength to usher a revival into this nation.

A foolish person will not have a good ending.

There is a hormone in plants that influences growth. Sometimes, if a plant has too much of that hormone, its stems and leaves will grow before the root system has been thoroughly established. As a result, the seedlings do not flower, and the plant usually dies before it reaches maturity. In a sense, this example from plant life reflects foolishness in the church.

Notice this disease in the spiritual realm. A particular church or ministry may be like a beautiful plant that should produce fruit in time, but the spiritual hormone of foolishness causes the young seedling to develop *foolish seedling disease*. As a result, the plant sprouts too soon. Because it does not yet have a mature root system, the ministry or church dies before maturity.

When it first grows, many people will praise the minister. "Wow! He must really be anointed. Look at how fast his church is growing!" But let's not be deceived by rapid growth. We should be more concerned about whether the church has a strong enough foundation to support the growth.

Samson, Solomon and Saul all died before they reached spiritual maturity. Many ministries have blossomed quickly but then died before maturity. There are seedling Christians out there who are saying, "God disappointed me. Through a prophecy or through the advice of friends, I believed that I was going to succeed in my ministry, but it did not come to pass."

Don't allow foolish seedling disease to affect you or your ministry. Don't let it rush you to grow fruit before you grow roots. Align yourself with God's will—and timing—for your calling. Humble yourself before the Lord and wait for His wisdom to teach you what you need to know.

I remember a dear friend I had when I was in Bible school in Argentina. We were all young during that first year of ministry training. We thought that a little foolishness was acceptable. But during that first year we progressed through a maturing experience.

My friend, however, did not change. He displayed the same kind of superficiality during his second year of school. The third year was the same; my friend still did not mature. Because he was so gifted by God and so anointed for ministry, I still thought that he would succeed in ministry. But today he is not even in the ministry. His life is a disaster.

This man was not a mean person. He was not an immoral person; *he was just a foolish fellow,* refusing to learn and to grow up. For a season, God covered him and blessed him. But after a while, it was over.

SIGNS OF FOOLISHNESS

If you want to walk in true biblical holiness, you must choose to walk in wisdom. Based on the same actions we see in the story of King Saul, here are some modern-day examples of foolishness:

- *Staying in the ministry at the cost of your soul.* Some ministers experience moral failure and yet refuse to submit to discipline and a restoration process. They continue doing ministry as normal. Wisdom calls them to confess their sins and seek restoration, but their pride will not allow them to do this.

- *Growing your local church and losing your city.* There is an unwise obsession with local church growth at the expense of a greater vision that you share with other local churches for the benefit of the entire city. Wisdom calls us to lay down personal and denominational agendas in order to walk in biblical unity, seeking both local and city ministry.

- *Fighting against others in the same kingdom.* In wartime this is known as "friendly fire." Some people in ministry attack other denominations or movements without finding out the facts first. Often this stems from pride, envy and jealousy. Someone once wisely said, "Do not criticize what God has blessed." Remember that the Word tells us we will give an account for every foolish word we say. How foolish and childish we are when we bicker and fight among ourselves over minor doctrinal matters that were never meant to divide us.

- *Refusing to release a local worker for ministry because that person is needed to further your ministry.* This is usually a sign of selfish ambition. The leader who operates in this selfish spirit of control will never experience the full blessing of God.

- *Returning to old religious habits.* There are many denominations that have explored unity and a relationship with the Holy Spirit, but then, due to fear or mistakes by leaders in the new movement, they regressed to their old practices. This discredits the cause of revival and slows down the advance of the kingdom of God. Wisdom calls us to forsake unfruitful strategies that are no longer relevant to our generation. I recently revisited a city in Asia and asked about the condition of several leaders I knew from before. They had been advancing with the move of God, but now, I was told, "due to denominational pressures," they had returned to their old formality. They were even more closed now than before the move of God.

- *Having illusions about becoming someone we have not been called to be.* Not everyone is called to be a Bill Bright or a Martin Luther King Jr. Ask God to keep you centered in the reality of the specific calling He has given to you. Don't try to be someone you are not. Ask God to deflate your ego if you are operating in this kind of spiritual pride.

- *Being a leader who does not lead because of neglect and irresponsibility.* The overused axiom, "You can lead a horse to water, but you can't make him drink," carries some spiritual significance. God may have called you to lead your church into a greater success within the kingdom. But if you neglect your calling, choosing to follow your own desires and ignoring the responsibilities of leadership to which God has called you, you fail to lead. Don't give up just because the task is hard. Don't put off what God has called you to do today.

- *Living in ministerial isolation.* We all need fathers, mentors and friends. It is a dangerous and vulnerable spot to be in if you have no one to stand with you. God has placed us in a body, and He has called us to be accountable to one another. Don't isolate yourself from those who can "father" or "mentor" you into maturity. If you are alone, then you are being foolish.

- *Putting the gifts of the Spirit first and neglecting the fruit of the Spirit.* Some Christians believe the overtly powerful gifts of the Spirit are more important than the internally powerful fruit of the Spirit. Don't be a "resounding gong or a clanging cymbal" (1 Cor. 13:1). Develop the characteristics of leadership available through the fruit of the Spirit. To value charisma over character is to set yourself up for failure and disappointment.

THE HIGHWAY OF HOLINESS

The Bible says there is a highway of holiness on which the righteous will walk, but "wicked fools will not go about on it" (Isa. 35:8). The Holy Spirit is calling those who have committed acts of foolishness to repent and make peace with God. And He wants the church as a whole to embrace godly wisdom. In my own life I have learned that God will not bless my nonsense.

During the altar call at a large meeting, I saw a vision of a young woman trying to kill herself. I began to describe to the audience the weapon I had seen her using. As I did, a young woman came forward and said, "That's me. I had specific plans to commit suicide this week." She was going to do something foolish, but God Almighty had different plans for her.

Perhaps you are quietly thinking about divorce. You might be saying, "My wife is good, but I have fallen in love with someone else." This is foolishness—and it can ruin your life. If you are about to do something foolish, do not run from God. Pray a prayer of repentance and surrender to God.

Maybe your foolish action involves criticizing what God has blessed. Do you have a critical spirit? Are you always finding fault with other people, other churches and other movements? If so, come before the Lord in repentance today. The church is suffering because of the divisiveness among God's people. Criticism will not build us up. Criticism is foolishness. There is a place to confront and to exhort, but it has to be done according to Matthew 18, face to face with a brother and speaking the truth in love.

If you have felt compelled to abort the baby you are carrying, come to the Lord. He will give you good advice.

Do you feel so much anger against your rebellious teenager that you are tempted to respond with the same intense level of screaming, insulting and bickering your child is using? Take your anger to the Lord, and ask Him to fill you with the fruit of love so you can respond in love.

If you are not a man or woman of your word, if you promise a lot of things that you never fulfill, come before the Lord today. I have been there. Sometimes our promises are very superficial. I have learned that when our word cannot be trusted it is not just a weakness—it is a sin. I have repented many times and asked God to forgive me. I want my *yes* to be yes and my *no* to be no. I want to be a man of my word.

Heed the warning given to us in Ephesians 5:17, which says, "Therefore do not be foolish, but understand what the Lord's will is." If you have fallen into foolishness, and it has led you into sin, follow these three steps to avoid it in the future:

1. *Understand that the root of foolishness is the fear of man.* If you care more about what people think of you than what God thinks, you will make foolish choices. Learn to embrace the fear of the Lord.

2. *Acknowledge foolishness as a sin, and repent.* Ask the Lord to fill you with the knowledge of His will. Soak your mind daily in the wisdom of His Word. Embracing foolishness is not a weakness but a transgression.

3. *Prioritize wisdom.* The Book of Proverbs describes godly wisdom as "more precious than rubies." Learn to treasure it. Seek it out and value it like never before.

A PRAYER OF REPENTANCE

Father, I confess my foolish actions and thoughts. I truly repent. I pray that my foolishness will not turn into disaster. Forgive me and purify me. But if I must face the consequences of my foolish acts, I pray for the courage to face them in humility and strength. I am willing to learn. Holy Spirit, burn in me a passion for wisdom and a repulsion against foolishness. Lord, You are my wisdom. Help me to be wise in my daily walk. Sanctify me through and through. In Jesus' name, amen.

Chapter 8

The Transgression of David: Failing to Set Boundaries

Just *a slice of pizza and I'll go back to the gate to catch my plane,* I said to myself. I quickly finished my pizza, but by the time I returned to the gate, the airline attendants informed me that the plane had already left. "It is not even the departure time yet!" I protested.

"The plane was able to leave a few minutes earlier than scheduled," I was told in reply. "We announced through the speakers that passengers should remain close to the gate to hear updates on the flight."

I had heard the announcement, but honestly, I had not taken it seriously. I was "hoping for the best" as I wandered away from the gate area to get that slice of pizza. And that afternoon I spent hours walking the Dallas airport and promising myself that I would not do this again. In the spiritual realm, many people just "hope for the best." But then they get the worst because they failed to set boundaries on their lives. We must learn to live within godly limits if we are to succeed spiritually and morally.

This chapter is a warning call to Christians who have not learned to live their Christian lives on alert. The fact that you do not see temptation headed your way will not excuse you before

God. He requires us to be vigilant.

When a person understands this transgression of failing to set boundaries—and avoids it—that person has taken charge of his life and will no longer be driven or out of control by the surge of sin around him or her.

Many people believe that the greatest error into which David fell was the sin of *adultery,* but I believe his greatest error was *greed.* David had so much, yet apparently what he already had was not enough for him. Unlimited desire brings an otherwise healthy soul to moral tragedy. The moral problem is the visible consequence, but greed is the invisible cause. David was rebuked mostly for his greed, not for his moral failure. The Word of God always points us to the root sin. It goes beyond the wrong action, exposing the evil intentions behind the behavior.

> For the word of God is living and active. Sharper than any double-edged sword, it penetrates even to dividing soul and spirit, joints and marrow; it judges the thoughts and attitudes of the heart.
>
> —HEBREWS 4:12

Greed has been described as "intense desire for what we should not have." Greed happens when we trespass beyond the line of contentment. Often we fail to recognize that greed is not a minor sin. It is one of the transgressions that cause social disintegration. "Thou shalt not covet" is one of the boundaries given by the Lord to preserve social order and civilization. Much of the crime committed in the streets of our nations is born out of greed and covetousness. The financial slavery of millions is caused by greed. The Bible tells us that the love (another form of greed) of money is the root of all evil (1 Tim. 6:10).

THE FERTILE SOIL OF A GREEDY HEART

Jesus described greed-filled desires as inner filth. When addressing the religious leaders of His day, who avoided the so-called *spectacular sins,* He condemned them for what was hiding in their hearts:

> Woe to you, teachers of the law and Pharisees, you hypocrites! You clean the outside of the cup and dish, but inside they are full of greed and self-indulgence. Blind Pharisee! First clean the inside of the cup and dish, and then the outside also will be clean.
>
> —MATTHEW 23:25–26

Sins of the spirit, sins of the soul and sins of the body all have consequences. But the propeller of them all is the sins of the spirit, such as greed and pride. Often unseen, these sins lurk within and infect every part of a person with their filthy disease. The first step in purification is a change of heart—"first clean the inside of the cup." Once the inside is cleaned, then, almost naturally, the outside will become clean also.

Today many stores stay open twenty-four hours a day, seven days a week. Modern life, especially in the city, creates a need for stores that are always available. Some businesses find that this round-the-clock schedule allows for a smoother operation, allowing time for better maintenance, cleaning and organizing than would be available if the business closed for a period of time every day.

In the city where we live, my wife and I are familiar with twenty-four-hour stores. Sooner or later, we know we will need their services. At times, Kathy finds it even enjoyable to do shopping during the late evening hours when the children are in bed and there is no great pressure to return home quickly. She has plenty of time to shop for great deals on things the family can use during those leisurely shopping hours.

The Holy Spirit is looking for people who are available 24/7, who have the doors of their hearts open constantly to His sanctifying work. These are people who, whether they rest or work, run or stop, are constantly in His presence. The light in their hearts never goes out, day or night. They are always pure or purifying themselves. It is this kind of people who will conquer the world for Christ!

Do you want to be a 24/7 Spirit-filled Christian? To be one you must learn to avoid five errors we can see in the life of David, who obviously had decided that he did not have to walk in holiness at all hours of the day and night.

DAVID'S STEPS TO DISASTER

The greed of David's heart, perhaps then unnoticed to him, triggered a number of wrong steps.

1. Staying at home in time of war

> In the spring, at the time when kings go off to war, David sent Joab out with the king's men and the whole Israelite army. They destroyed the Ammonites and besieged Rabbah. But David remained in Jerusalem.
>
> —2 SAMUEL 11:1

The Book of Ecclesiastes tells us that there is "a time for war and a time for peace" (Eccles. 3:8). David was living in a time for war. But he trusted his past victories and his army, and he let his men go out to fight without him. David failed to realize that leadership requires diligence. His place was with his men in battle. It is the same for us today. Our people need us near them in the time of battle. And, surprising as it may seem, we need to be near them.

I hear about so many Christian men today who become snared by the trap of Internet pornography. This is such an epidemic that entire ministries have been raised up to offer freedom from this plague of sexual addiction. I am grateful for these ministries; however, I wonder if these men would have fallen into pornography if they had been on the battlefield. If they had been engaging the devil, walking in spiritual alertness and winning people to Christ, perhaps they would not have had time or interest in looking at pornography. How desperately we need to see that we are called to the battlefield.

2. Misusing his free time

> One evening David got up from his bed and walked around on the roof of the palace.
>
> —2 SAMUEL 11:2

I have been reading articles in newspapers and magazines about the September 11 terrorist attack on New York. In all the articles I've read, there has been a consensus that since the attack the United States has had to find new ways to strengthen its defense at home. It is not enough to increase security only at major airports. Our national leaders have had to create plans to guard our water reservoirs, nuclear plants and food supplies. President Bush has asked the American people to be on the alert. One government official called our heightened awareness "The Eyes-Wide-Open Program."

David could have profited greatly by instituting the "Eyes-Wide-Open Program" in his own kingdom! Instead of joining his men on the battlefield, he had allowed himself some free time—which he was misusing a bit. He had mixed *healthy relaxation* with *toxic coveting.* He was not on the alert. He had proven the old adage, "Idle hands are the devil's workshop."

If you are serious about being "holy as He is holy," it is important to take care about how you spend your entertainment hours. Ask yourself these questions:

- Is this type of entertainment refreshing or polluting?

- Do I follow a different moral code when my entertainment hour comes?

- Do I reject indecency in real life but enjoy it as fiction?

- Have I developed a dissonance between my mental values and action values?

We must pursue "no regret" entertainment. Our families—or an individual—can have wholesome fun laughing, singing, enjoying one another and giving honor to God by the way we entertain ourselves.

There is a rise in unwholesome entertainment—even among Christians. One Christian worker told me, "I only go to the porn sites when I am very tired." Obscenity is not a healthy way to relax! If wholesome entertainment does not satisfy, maybe there is a point of greed in your soul that is pulling you in the wrong direction.

There is an important principle here: How we use our free time will affect our work performance. This can be seen in the example of Nicolino Locche, a famous Argentine boxer. He was such a talented boxer that he could spend the nights before a fight drinking and partying in the nightclubs, and still win the next day.

He was very fast with his fists, so fast that he disconcerted his opponents. He faced his opponent with hands down; when his opponent sent a bullet punch toward his face, in a split second he moved his face and dodged the punch, leaving the opponent perplexed, punching air time after time. Each time this happened, his opponents would lose points, just by missing punches.

Nicolino was an unquestioned champion, but gradually the lack of preparation and physical fitness, and his disorderly lifestyle, began to take its toll. Soon, Argentina watched as Nicolino was easily and shamefully beaten. In time, there were no fast reflexes to save him. His career ended in defeat. Nicolino was good in the ring, but he failed to manage his free time well. This caused his downfall.

Guard your free time zealously. Is relaxation time overexposing you to temptation? Don't let your guard down and allow distractions and temptations to cause you to misuse your free time. Your spiritual success as a Christian, a spouse, a businessperson or leader depends largely upon how wisely you live when you are not "on the job."

3. Letting desire dictate direction

David progressed in his journey toward transgression. He began by not being where he should have been. Then, as he indulged in free time while his friends fought on the battlefield, he stepped even closer to transgression by allowing a momentary glimpse of a beautiful woman to give rise to desire and then acting upon his desire. In two short succinct sentences, we see this progression:

> From the roof he saw a woman bathing. The woman was very beautiful.
>
> —2 Samuel 11:2

I grew up in a Christian home. My parents lived what they preached. Never has there been an obscene magazine in my house nor even a hint of an immoral joke. However, as I became a young man, I was bombarded with immoral temptations, probably much as any worldly young man is confronted with it. Although temptation is normal, the intensity of the temptation pressing upon me gave me a clue that something was wrong.

I believe there are two reasons for the temptation that confronted me and that confronts young Christian men and women everywhere.

1. *The demonic powers are not resting.* Satan and his host of demonic spirits have a priority agenda that include tempting and destroying the morality of young people. These demonic powers often target the children of ministers.

2. *Pornography is freely available and visible in the streets of our nations today.* When I was a teenager, pornography was visible everywhere in my country, especially after the military dictatorship ended. We entered a trend labeled "the uncovering." It was a period of time when an epidemic of immoral exposure arose as a reaction to the repression of free speech my country had experienced under the dictatorship that had lasted for many years in the country.

As a young child in one of the large cities in Argentina, I would see obscene pictures displayed on the newsstands positioned every two blocks or so as I walked to school. Thousands of children and young people are confronted with the same images daily on the streets of not only Argentina, but also the United States and the other nations of the world. I never quite stopped to stare at those pictures, curious as I may have been, but just walking by them and inadvertently seeing them would, in time, turn the natural temptations of a young man into an all-out spiritual battle. This is the phenomenon of oversexualization, an aberration of our modern society. What has been difficult for our grandparents will prove more difficult for our children.

My daily challenge and self-discipline is to direct my eyes according to my purpose, not to direct my purpose according to my eyes. My sense of destiny and transcendent duty govern the muscles of my eyes. My purpose provides the parameters for what I will and what I will not look at.

Each day I am on a sublime assignment, one so important that it is worth pruning anything evil or vain out of my life. Only when I long for and work toward continuous holiness am I on the right track. You see, holiness is not *positional;* it is *directional.* The place where your heart is headed is far more important than the place where your feet are positioned right now. My heart is headed toward continual holiness, and my feet are somewhere on the path to that destination. My daily assignment is to get further down the road toward the cross.

Having found myself far away from my destination so often, deeply entrenched in partial holiness instead of continual holiness, I can tell you there is a striking contrast between the two locations on the path. Advancing toward the destination leads to life and makes you stronger as you go, but taking your eyes off the destination and compromising somewhere along the journey debilitates you and eventually defeats you.

Seeking continual holiness will constantly steer your heart along the path God traces for you. The stronger the wind is that arises to try to cause you to deviate from the path, the harder you will be required to hold tightly to the steering wheel to keep moving down the path. Ask God to make you "holy to the minute." Well, to be more precise, ask God to make you holy to the second!

One day while walking down the streets of a coastal city in Argentina with my three young boys, we suddenly faced a huge billboard with a scantily clad woman on it. I saw their eyes widen as they stared at the sign in front of us. I took that opportunity to teach them the *principle of the second second.*

"You see, boys," I told them, "as we turned the corner and happened upon that billboard, we could not avoid seeing it. That was our first second. However, each of us could choose whether or not to continue to stare at that lady's nakedness. That choice was the *second* second. We need to learn to choose wisely that which our eyes will look at during the second second."

4. Misusing authority

David's progression toward transgression caused him to misuse his kingly authority. When his desire pushed him in the direction of committing an act of immorality, he used his authority to direct that the beautiful woman he had seen from his balcony be brought to him at the palace.

> And David sent someone to find out about her. The man said, "Isn't this Bathsheba, the daughter of Eliam and the wife of Uriah the Hittite?" Then David sent messengers to get her. She came to him, and he slept with her. (She had purified herself from her uncleanness.) Then she went back home. The woman conceived and sent word to David, saying, "I am pregnant."
>
> —2 SAMUEL 11:3–5

You and I may not be kings invested with the authority to command that our every desire be carried out. But you have a level of authority in your life that allows you to direct the steps you will take each day. Don't misuse your authority or privileges. Don't manipulate the events and circumstances of your life to take down the boundaries of morality and holiness. David failed to set an important boundary in place in his life. Don't follow his lead.

At times when I am strongly tempted and traveling far from home, I reflect, *This nice hotel room was paid for by the church for me to prepare for the meetings. It is a privilege. It is kingdom finances that have been used. How can I dare to use any minute here for unwholesome entertainment or wicked thoughts?* Then I resist the temptation on two grounds: love and loyalty. Love for God, and loyalty to the people of God who trusted me and treated me as their guest.

We live in a day when our nation has recognized the importance of setting in place necessary boundaries to keep evil and terror from encroaching upon our lives. Every time you walk through an airport or visit a governmental site you are confronted with these barriers. It is even more important that you erect spiritual barriers in your life to prevent evil "terrorists" from reaching your soul. Use your God-given authority to command that these influences stay far from you. Don't misuse your authority.

5. Covering sin instead of confessing it

One day soon after I learned to drive, I was driving with a friend to an annex of my dad's church in La Plata, Argentina. I was about to learn a new lesson for the road. Along the route from La Plata to City Bell there were four city blocks of unpaved roadway. On rainy days, the whole street became like a road of melted chocolate.

On this particular occasion, we got stuck in that mud. Being an inexperienced driver, I tried to get out by doing what I had learned to do—push the gas pedal to go. That day I learned that once stuck in mud, the more you turn the wheels, the deeper you get into the mud.

Finally, when the door of the car was touching the mud, we decided it was time to ask for help. We had gotten ourselves into a difficult situation. The car was so deep into the mud that I wondered if we would make it out. Some neighborhood men brought some large boards, bricks and a shovel. After great effort, during which time several people were muddied by the wheels as they pushed the car, we made it out.

In the same way, many inexperienced believers do the same thing when they get stuck in the spiritual mud of sin. They just keep pushing on the gas pedal, attempting to keep on going as usual. We don't realize that it is time to call for help!

In several nations, I have observed a similar pattern. If a known preacher falls into immorality, the leaders will ask him to take a "leave of absence" for a year or so for accountability and restoration. In many cases, his answer is the same: "I cannot afford to leave the ministry for that period of time. I will not submit to the restoration process." The result is that because the person does not leave the ministry temporarily, he or she ends up ruining the ministry altogether.

David chose to commit a third sin. First lust, then adultery and then murder. With each sin, David was getting deeper and deeper in the mud.

> In the morning David wrote a letter to Joab and sent it with Uriah. In it he wrote, "Put Uriah in the front line where the fighting is fiercest. Then withdraw from him so he will be struck down and die."
>
> —2 SAMUEL 11:14–15

Unconfessed sin triggers a terrible progression of sinful actions. Multiple sins will carry multiple consequences. It takes more sin to cover up existing sin, thus setting in motion a chain reaction. This domino effect of covered-up sin in turn conceives a "sin unto death." The person goes from a fall into sin to open rebellion and a callused heart. If the person continues in this condition over a period of time, eventually the person's conscience becomes seared. Once that happens, that person no longer feels any guilt about his sin issue. He can minister, pray and exhort others into purity, all the while continuing to commit the sins he condemns. The soul of the person is dead and on its way to eternal condemnation. What a tragic state to be in!

Be aware that falling into sin is serious, but covering up sin is devastating. If you are stuck in the mud of sin, do not get deeper into it. Call for help! Go to reliable and seasoned Christian leaders who can help you by telling you the truth in love until you are restored completely. Be willing to submit to their counsel, and don't hide any aspect of what you have done. True healing is found in straightforward confession.

THE CONSEQUENCES OF SIN

In spite of David's progression into sin with Bathsheba, David still was a success in Israel. He still had great power to lead his kingdom. And he was still greatly loved by God. In the New Testament, we see that God identified David as "a man after my own heart" (Acts 13:22). But David's sin brought consequences that he would be required to face as the result of his failure. In 2 Samuel 11:27 we read, "But the thing David had done displeased the LORD."

We must always remember that consequences will come if we displease the Lord. When I recognize that my priorities have become disarrayed, it is very helpful for me to remember an old prayer that says:

> Lord, let me please You, just that.
> If I can see Your smile over my life,
> Everything is fine for me.
> Let me please You.

Untold times I have said that prayer—at my home, while driving and in hotel rooms. It seems to give me perspective in life again and again.

David, the man who had been chosen to replace Saul as king because his heart sought after God, had now displeased God. His example stands as a constant reminder of the fact that our former righteousness or right standing with God is never enough! We need to keep our righteousness current. This principle is seen so clearly in the following verses:

> Therefore, son of man, say to your countrymen, "The right-eousness of the righteous man will not save him when he dis-obeys, and the wickedness of the wicked man will not cause him to fall when he turns from it. The righteous man, if he sins, will not be allowed to live because of his former right-eousness." If I tell the righteous man that he will surely live, but then he trusts in his righteousness and does evil, none of the righteous things he has done will be remembered; he will die for the evil he has done...If a righteous man turns from his righteousness and does evil, he will die for it.
>
> —Ezekiel 33:12–13, 18

When David recognized his sin before God, he fasted and pleaded for God to spare the life of his coming baby. He desper-ately wanted that baby to live. But God had already made up His mind. As the consequence of his failure, David experienced tragedy—the infant died. There are consequences, sometimes irre-versible, for our stubborn sin.

The consequences of David's sinning did not stop with just the death of his baby. Another consequence he faced was gross immorality in his own household. Through the prophet Nathan, God had said to David:

> You struck down Uriah the Hittite with the sword and took his wife to be your own...Now, therefore, the sword will never depart from your house...This is what the LORD says: "Out of your own household I am going to bring calamity upon you. Before your very eyes I will take your wives and give them to one who is close to you, and he will lie with your wives in broad daylight. You did it in secret, but I will do this thing in broad daylight before all Israel."
>
> —2 SAMUEL 12:9–12

Some time later, David became an outcast in his own kingdom; he experienced great shame. When we try to cover up our sin to avoid shame, in the long run we create greater shame than if we confessed and repented immediately.

There are some important lessons we can learn from the example of David's sinning. You will be able to avoid the transgression of failing to set boundaries to protect yourself from the encroachment of sin that brings lasting consequences if you follow these principles:

- *Don't go to the roof by yourself.* Most of the time when I travel, my wife or a team member travels with me. This important step in accountability protects me from unfounded accusations and helps me to stay focused. It is much easier to resist temptation when you are surrounded by godly friends.

- *Don't allow public showers around your palace.* Get rid of all sensual literature. Do your best to avoid exposure to pornographic images. Strive for both integrity and ethics. If you know of places where pornography is displayed, avoid them. Don't go to places where you know you are tempted sexually.

- *Don't forsake your people on the front lines.* Remember the dedication, sacrifice and offerings of those who are a part of your ministry. Develop a sense of loyalty to your own family members and to your friends and helpers in the ministry or at work. Don't make David's mistake of betraying a noble man, Uriah.

- *Don't let legality rule morality.* In 1 Corinthians 6:12, Paul says, "'Everything is permissible for me'—but not everything is beneficial.'Everything is permissible for me'—but I will not be mastered by anything." Just because something may be legal doesn't mean it's the right thing for you to do. God's standards for us are always higher than the world's standards.

- *Don't love the world.* We read in James 4:4, "Don't you know that friendship with the world is hatred toward God? Anyone who chooses to be a friend of the world becomes an enemy of God." This verse is not admonishing us to avoid becoming a friend to someone who does not yet know God. It indicates our need to avoid accepting worldly standards and codes of behavior. It means rejecting ungodly activities. This includes sensual gazing and even jokes with a double, obscene meaning.

- *Don't love the things that are in the world.* Not only should be avoid the behaviors and customs of the world, we should also avoid many of the things the world offers that do not honor God. God's Word admonishes us, "Do not love the world *or anything in the world.* If anyone loves the world, the love of the Father is not in him" (1 John 2:15, emphasis added).

These principles will help us to avoid transgression. We must draw the line and set up clear boundaries. When the children of Israel marched into the Promised Land to possess it for their own as promised by God, they failed to establish boundaries to keep the enemy out of the camp. Even after they defeated the enemies who attacked them from outside the camp, they were left to do battle with the enemies with whom they had established a compromising relationship. These were the enemies who threatened them with destruction.

RULES FOR GUARDING YOUR EYES

One of David's pitfalls came because he did not guard his eyes. He sat on his rooftop and let his eyes wander, and when he saw Bathsheba, he became enticed by gazing at her. You must learn to set your boundaries carefully and guard them diligently. Don't allow the enemy to sneak quietly into your heart and steal away the blessing and inheritance of God. Begin by guarding your eye-gate—one of the boundaries most threatened by your enemies. Use these rules to set a guard around your eyes.

You don't have to stare at it just because it is there.

Eye muscles are controlled by the brain—the brain is not controlled by the eyes. So when your eyes are confronted by an image that causes an ungodly response from you, use those muscles to close your eyes or to turn your gaze elsewhere. Temptation does not become sin until you act upon it—and gazing even ten seconds longer than you should at something that raises desire or lust within your spirit is the act that causes you to sin.

Think about the example we have in Genesis of Joseph. When Potiphar's wife approached Joseph one day, took hold of his coat sleeve and invited him to sleep with her, he didn't even take the time to say, "Please take your arm off my sleeve." The Bible tells us this: "But he left his cloak in her hand and ran out of the house" (Gen. 39:12). What do you think would have happened if he had taken the time to look closely at her attractiveness before he responded? He acted decisively and immediately—and so must we.

You don't have to crave it just because it is attractive.

You need to determine your endurance level. Each year I travel to more than fifty different preaching locations. I have discovered that I have an optimum endurance for being away from home nine or ten days at a time. So, with the exception of a few strategic longer trips, I schedule according to this rule. Any trip that extends beyond that length becomes more difficult for me physically and emotionally. I have recognized my limits and have learned to better administrate the strength that the Lord has given me for ministry.

If I am gone away from home too long, sexual temptation or irritability can become intense. So I know that I must manage my emotions carefully and also carefully schedule my travel so that I do not allow myself to get into a difficult situation.

You don't have to own it just because you can.

I have a friend who was traveling in North Carolina on business. After dinner he returned to his hotel to retire for the night. As he was about to park, he noticed a small paperback book in the parking lot that he had run over. After parking, this young man had a strange feeling that the book was pornographic. He did not know this because he had seen anything in it; it was really a warning from the Holy Spirit.

The young man was full of curiosity. He walked over and picked up the book—and sure enough, it was a sexually explicit novel. The young man was torn inside. *I could take this inside and read it, and no one would ever know,* he thought to himself. *My wife is not here, and no one I know is here.*

He initially took the book inside, but immediately he was gripped by conviction. He knew that even though this book literally landed in his path, he did not have to accept it. So he walked back into the parking lot and threw the book into the hotel's trash bin.

You don't have to accept it just because it's permitted.

Not all things that are legal edify. Abortion in the United States has been legal for years, but it is not right in the sight of God. In many places around the world, we have made altar calls for Christians to rid their lives of "souvenirs" of past relationships that were out of the will of God. People have brought jewelry, love letters and photos of past promiscuous relationships in their lives.

In Jude 22-23 we read, "Be merciful to those who doubt; snatch others from the fire and save them; to others show mercy, mixed with fear—hating even the clothing stained by corrupted flesh."

Some time ago, I received a nice handwritten note from a Christian lady. It was so flattering that I was tempted to save it; it was not of spiritual interest, but some kind of emotional attraction for me. I tore it up and threw it away. Even though what she said to me was not immoral or explicit, I knew that it was not appropriate for me to keep it.

Have you set a guard around your eyes? Do you know your limits? Have you accepted them? Don't foolishly say, "By faith, I disregard any limits." That is unlimited foolishness. God will never honor foolish decisions.

BE PREPARED TO PUT OUT THE FIRE OF LUST

On the doors in many hotels are posted maps indicating all the exits from each room and from the hotel in case of an emergency such as a fire. Over the past few years, there has been an epidemic of moral "fires" occurring in the church, often leaving casualties behind. These "fires" bring discredit to the gospel. Many of these fires begin with the smoldering match of lust. You can use the following practical steps to avoid being burned by the fire of lust in your life:

Memorize the route to the emergency exit.

In a moment of emergency, there might not be light or sound to guide you. However, if you know your way out, you can run toward the exit. Speed is important. It is even OK to leave valuables behind. The important thing is that you flee when temptation strikes. It's OK for you to get ruthless as you respond to the emergency.

If you feel tempted, cancel that tempting appointment, erase that e-mail address from your database, be absent in the next inappropriate Internet chat or cancel the cable service that brings moral filth into your home.

I once had an office that had glass panes on the door. But the glass panes had been painted over for privacy. I asked one of my helpers to scrape the paint off the glass. Occasionally I have to meet with female staff members. If any accusation were ever to be brought against me, my staff would be able to defend me because they could easily observe everything that happened in my office. Those glass panes were the route to my "emergency exit."

If the door is hot, don't open it.

Learn to discern when a relationship is out of God's will or is one that could "explode." While in Bible college in Canada, I experienced my first fire drill. The instructor told us, "Touch the door. If it is hot, don't open it. The room may explode!" We need to be on our guard continually. Doors that may have been normal doors just yesterday could become dangerous once a fire of lust is ignited behind it. Just opening such a door can mean serious trouble.

Keep a fire ladder handy.

My family lives in a two-story home. When we moved into that home, I bought a fire ladder so we could get out of the second story should a fire occur. We practiced fire drills with our boys, which they thought were great fun. My wife and I felt awkward crawling out of our upstairs windows to the ground, but we gained a valuable sense of security through those fire drills. The time was well worth it.

In the same way, if we tighten the security in our hearts, it may save a life—eternally! I avoid being alone with a non-relative of the opposite sex. This is, of course, not a biblical mandate, but an ethical regulation that I embrace by choice and follow in a noncompulsive way. It is a safeguard. It has become my fire ladder. It isn't necessary that I evaluate each situation as it arises to think through whether or not it would be appropriate. I just apply this personal principle. My spiritual fire ladder has safeguarded my life from confusing situations, to say the least.

Get a fire alarm that works.

Do you know if the smoke alarm in your home has working batteries? Just as we check the smoke alarms in our homes, we should check our spiritual "smoke alarms" periodically. Do your board members, your spouse or your close Christian friends sound the alarm when they see indications of moral "smoke" in your life? To whom have you given permission to confront you when they see (or smell) smoke in your character, actions or relationships? Let's humble ourselves. Let the alarm sound whenever it is necessary.

Do not wait until the next temptation strikes. When a fire starts, it is too late to order a fire ladder. You must have it ready, installed and be practiced at getting out during nonemergency times. Once the fire has started, it is too late to buy new batteries for the alarm that didn't go off.

My wife can ask me any question about my actions. She has a

right to know where and with whom I am at any time. I recently told her of a dear brother who had committed adultery. She asked me, "Would you let me know if you have a moral failure?"

"Yes," I told her, "I promise you I would." I knew that step of accountability with my wife was God's way of reinforcing my life in the right direction—unless, of course, I chose to lie to her. I have made a commitment with my wife to tell her if I watch any obscene movies at the hotels or have any inappropriate conversations or actions with a woman. By establishing these important boundaries around my life, with God's help I will continue to be able to avoid transgression. Just thinking about the necessity of needing to "report" or of falling back on my word strengthens my will to maintain high moral and ethical standards.

Fight fire with fire.

When a forest fire is raging out of control, firemen will often burn a strip of land before the destructive fire arrives so that the oncoming fire will have nothing to fuel it and will therefore be less likely to advance. In that way the firemen are able to keep a fire under control.

The fire of God is like that control fire used by firemen. It will burn fleshly passions out of our lives and stop them in their tracks. The fire of temptation is circumscribed by the burned, fleshly strips you made when you surrendered all your passions and ambitions to Christ.

Lust is a parasitic sin. It rides on a transgression—greed. Lust is an obsession with having what we ought not to have. The prophet Nathan confronted David on the basis of greed, not of lust:

> Then Nathan said to David, "You are the man! This is what the LORD, the God of Israel, says: *'I anointed you king over Israel,* and I delivered you from the hand of Saul. *I gave your master's house to you, and your master's wives into your arms. I gave you the house of Israel and Judah. And if all this had been too little, I would have given you even more.* Why did you despise the word of the LORD by doing what is evil in his eyes? You struck down Uriah the Hittite with the sword and took his wife

to be your own. You killed him with the sword of the
Ammonites. Now, therefore, the sword will never depart from
your house, because you despised me and took the wife of
Uriah the Hittite to be your own.'"

—2 SAMUEL 12:7–10, EMPHASIS ADDED

David's major wickedness was to steal the only sheep the poor
man had—to be greedy for another man's wife. It was greed that
conceived adultery and murder. Greed is the opposite of contentment. The greedy heart cannot say, "I have enough. Thank You,
Lord." Greedy souls are in permanent unrest. Greed or selfish ambition engenders all kinds of diabolic outcomes.

> For where you have envy and selfish ambition, there you find
> disorder and every evil practice.

—JAMES 3:16

If you follow the principles contained in this chapter, you will
not have to worry about falling into the transgression of not erect-
ing boundaries. If those boundaries are in place, you will experience these results:

- *A greater freedom.* Any road trip you take in your car is so much
  easier if you stay on the road and obey traffic rules. Driving
  through ditches, across open fields or through someone's back-
  yard creates difficulties, and it will get you arrested! If you stay
  of the road of accountability and avoid the ditches of transgression, you will get where you are going more quickly—and you
  will be safe while you are traveling.

- *A greater joy.* Your spirit is able to soar on the wings of joy when
  you aren't burdened with trying to find fulfillment through the
  thrills of momentary temporal success. Boundaries enable you to
  run a steady race and feel the honor and joy of doing it.

- *A greater strength.* Boundaries keep things where they belong.
  The neighbor's goats aren't going to eat your flowers if you have
  a fence around your yard. And you aren't going to wander into a
  ditch late at night if the wall keeps you away from it. With spiritual boundaries you will finally become a consistent Christian—

rock solid! Nothing will defeat you. Boundaries will keep you living in the promise of 1 John 2:17:"The world and its desires pass away, but the man who does the will of God lives forever."

A Prayer of Repentance

Dear Lord, I repent from any and all of my lustful, immoral and impure thoughts, sights and words. I renounce the root problem of greed! I unmask greed in my heart and confess any specific greed-motivated actions, words or thoughts. I proclaim my covenant to You to be satisfied with what You give me. I choose to live a self-controlled life under the leading of the Holy Spirit. I promise I will keep godly people around me with corrective access to my life.

Please help me to set both moral and ethical boundaries so that "[my] good will not be spoken evil of." I trust in Your grace. I walk in my integrity. Thank You for Jesus who has become my righteousness. Amen.

Chapter 9

The Transgression of Solomon: Fatal Distractions

Early one morning an accident happened not too far from our house. A young construction worker was on his way to work when he leaned over to pick up his hat from the floor of his truck. Unknowingly, he turned the steering wheel and swerved into the other lane, causing a head-on collision with another truck coming from the opposite direction. He was killed instantly.

When I was reading that, I thought to myself, *Life is so unfair. That man was not drinking, not trying to do any wrong purposely; he was not in rebellion or trying to bring disaster to anyone. Just because of one momentary distraction he was killed.*

However, even more dangerous than distractions while driving are the distractions that occur in the body of Christ. Sometimes we fall into a habit of spiritual absentmindedness. Chances are that fatal morning wasn't the first time the young man in the truck had been distracted from his driving. Distractions may have presented themselves to him nearly every time he drove his truck. Other times those distractions had no doubt gone unnoticed, but this one time it was fatal.

Breaking Concentration

The problem of distracted drivers is so serious in the United States that the Shell Oil Company has published a full-color brochure titled "Deadly Distractions." I read that brochure, but I must confess—I read it as I was driving. The brochure says:

> Distractions are everywhere…What is a distraction? It's anything that takes your hands, eyes or attention away from driving. It could be a billboard, passengers in your car, something going on outside your car or even something as simple as trying to set the speed of your windshield wipers.[1]

Reading the brochure made me aware of the serious danger of distractions. Even changing the radio station or dialing a cell phone can distract you as a driver. These same warnings about distractions apply to our spiritual walk.

Spiritual distractions can be just as destructive—or even more destructive—to our spiritual lives. King Solomon's life is a prime example of the danger of distractions:

> As Solomon grew old, his wives turned his heart after other gods, and his heart was not fully devoted to the LORD his God, as the heart of David his father had been.
>
> —1 KINGS 11:4

Solomon experienced deadly spiritual distractions. The distractions began when he was young and physically strong and when his ministry and kingdom were still powerful. God's anointing was strong in his life as a young king. The wisdom of God was so evident that people would come from other nations to learn from him. Not only was he a king, but he was also an educator and a teacher. He had so much potential from God because he had been gifted with incredible heavenly wisdom.

Solomon had two divine visitations from the Lord. God gave him divine revelation, wisdom and wealth. He had amazing success, but because he got distracted, eventually he ended up in spiritual disaster.

Satan can ruin the lives of Christians not only through sin, but also through distractions. When we become distracted we can no longer concentrate on what God is calling us to do. As distractions continue to come our way, the process begins to wear people out. Distractions undermine the strength of many ministries and of the servants of God. In the beginning they are nearly unnoticeable, but they can eventually destroy us.

Heed this warning about the danger of distractions. If we pay attention to this warning, God's protection and strength will be available in our lives.

STEPS TO DISTRACTION

There are some warning lights that we need to pay attention to in order to avoid the danger of distractions. We see from Solomon's life that distraction was a process:

Solomon bound his soul to women who were idolatrous.

This distraction appealed to Solomon's lusts and emotions. It attacked the normal, natural feelings that God places in the hearts of all human beings. The feelings of love and attraction to the opposite sex and the desire for marriage are things God has placed in our hearts, but Solomon got very distracted because of them.

Solomon was bound to his feelings, as we can see in the following Scripture passage:

> King Solomon, however, loved many foreign women besides Pharaoh's daughter—Moabites, Ammonites, Edomites, Sidonians and Hittites. They were from nations about which the LORD had told the Israelites, "You must not intermarry with them, because they will surely turn your hearts after their gods." Nevertheless, Solomon held fast to them in love. He had seven hundred wives of royal birth and three hundred concubines, and his wives led him astray.
>
> —1 KINGS 11:1–3

A lot of people think that Solomon's problem was adultery. But it wasn't. The deeper issue is that he committed the ultimate infidelity—idolatry. He followed after foreign gods as a result of trying to please his foreign wives. I believe this is the issue most people miss when reading this passage. They dismiss it, thinking, *I cannot relate to King Solomon; I'll never have a harem or become polygamous.* But we all, or at least most of us, can relate to the dangers of greed, lust and internal passions, all started by an initial neglect of God's specific instructions to us.

Recently a fellow believer in Europe told me he had become distracted from doing the things of God because of the Internet. Eventually he made contact online with a woman who had been his girlfriend in earlier years. Apparently there was nothing wrong with that. They just started chatting with each other occasionally. But after a few weeks, his heart became entangled with that woman. "It got to the point," he said to me, "that I am now more in love with that woman than with my wife." The man was devastated.

As we prayed together about this matter, I mentioned to him that I had noticed this attachment was not just an emotional entanglement. I sensed that demonic influence to destroy his ministry was also present in the situation. "Are you aware that this is not only emotional?" I asked him. "Witches are working against you to destroy your marriage." I continued by advising him, "Do not just feel guilty about it. That is not going to help you. Surrender this relationship to the Lord. Be aware that you are engaged in spiritual warfare right now." He did just that as we prayed together.

Many Christians struggle with emotional entanglements, which are so easy to get into. Many people who are not evil or rebellious get entangled easily in a relationship that is out of the will of God. In the fear of the Lord I tell you that if you are entangled in a friendship or relationship that you know is out of the will of God, you need to surrender that relationship to God today.

You might feel so emotionally bound to that relationship that you feel you will have an emotional collapse or even die if you break it off. But I assure you that the Lord will give you power and authority to get rid of things that are distracting you. If your dating relationship is pulling you away from the things of God, you need to change it. If you notice that day after day and week after week you are less interested in the things of God, and you have more interest in disorderly passions, you need to surrender that dating relationship to God—today! When we renounce the emotions that are keeping us from getting closer to Him, He miraculously gives us the release we need from those bondages.

If you have been distracted or have let your soul become entangled by a romance or attraction that is out of the will of God, today is the day to surrender your confusion to the Lord. If you take the first step by faith, God will help you do the rest. Take that first step by praying these words:

> *Lord, I present this relationship to You. I want my heart to be free. In my own strength I cannot completely cut off this relationship, but with Your strength and Your power in my life, I will do it.*

All the Lord wants from us is a total surrender. Then He will give us the strength we need to complete the release. You are destined to be free emotionally.

Solomon became overcome by idolatry.

There are many warnings about the "sins of our youth." But I want to take a moment to warn those who are middle-aged about the sins of old age. I have observed some ministers and believers who became aggressive, bitter, resentful or immoral in their latter years. These people eventually lose the passion for God that they had in their youth.

I remember a servant of the Lord from Argentina who, a few years before his death, became obsessed with persecuting other believers. He wrote letters about a fellow servant of the Lord and sent the letters to other ministries in the country rather than confront the fellow servant one-on-one.

I observed this process. It drew my attention. Perhaps, as with the example of King Hezekiah, it would have been better for him to die younger—before he permanently damaged his testimony in old age. (See 2 Kings 18–19.) One prayer I always present to the

Lord is this:"Lord, either let me honor You or please take me home. Do not let me become a stumbling block to others or discredit Your name." Should the Lord tarry, I plan to grow old. But I want to get there with a heart that is still sensitive to the Holy Spirit, a heart full of passion for God and love for my neighbors.

I believe the reason some people become aggressive when they get older is because roots of legalism and criticism have been allowed to grow in their hearts. These roots were never uprooted. Eventually, as these people get older, they get so worn out and distracted that they become a negative influence to others. Some things, if they are not corrected in time, just get worse—including dangerous roots that should have been uprooted years earlier.

One night not long ago, some family friends went to bed in their home just as they did every night. While they were asleep this night, however, carbon monoxide was leaking into their home, but they did not perceive it. One of the family members was awakened during the night by a noise and, with his last ounce of strength, was able to waken the others and drag them out of the house just in time to save their lives. How sad that some Christians do not even realize they are in such spiritual danger because of their sin. There is a dangerous gradualness in sin. I have addressed this more fully in my book *The Fire of His Holiness.*[2] (See the chapter titled "The Dynamics of Temptation.")

Solomon allowed the roots of idolatry to grow in his life for many years before they overcame him. The roots of sensuality, legalism or criticism can grow unnoticed for many years also. These transgressions, like a dangerous invisible gas, can be present without our even perceiving them. We need to check our hearts continually, asking the Holy Spirit for discernment to help us detect any hidden sins. We need the purification that goes beyond our lists of known things that may be wrong in our lives. We need the purification that comes by the holiness of Jesus in our lives.

Solomon became an expert on partial obedience.

Solomon did not follow the Lord completely. He *did* follow the Lord partially.

> He followed Ashtoreth the goddess of the Sidonians, and
> Molech the detestable god of the Ammonites. So Solomon did
> evil in the eyes of the LORD; he did not follow the LORD com-
> pletely, as David his father had done.
>
> —1 KINGS 11:5–6

I have been there. Until the Lord baptized me with His holiness
in 1997, I followed the way of the Lord the best I knew how to
do—but my best was only partial obedience. I lived the way I had
been trained to live, and I thought that was my measuring stick. I
thought my best was all that I could do. But when a revelation of
the holiness of Jesus came to my heart, I knew the Lord was calling my heart to be totally pure and totally committed. God would
not allow even 2 percent of unholy thinking. God's call is the same
for every believer. He wants our hearts to be totally pure and
totally committed to His will.

Solomon used his gifts for God—and also for the devil.

God had given Solomon the gifts of wisdom, administration and
construction. He could lead people. He could motivate people. He
could pull together resources to accomplish great things. But the
same gifts he used to build the temple were the gifts he also used
to build a house for foreign gods.

> On a hill east of Jerusalem, Solomon built a high place for
> Chemosh the detestable god of Moab, and for Molech the
> detestable god of the Ammonites. He did the same for all his
> foreign wives, who burned incense and offered sacrifices to
> their gods.
>
> —1 KINGS 11:7–8

Our gifts are taken captive by the enemy when we are distracted. When we are bound in emotional entanglements, sooner or
later, whether we like it or not, we are going to be building things
for Satan instead of for God. The Lord is present to help us, and He
will purify our thoughts and the motivations of our hearts, but we
must be warned that it is dangerous to be distracted. How tragic
that the man God used to build the temple in Jerusalem later built

an infrastructure for demonic powers to establish their control in Israel!

Solomon continued with partial success, even though he lost the anointing.

Why was Solomon still successful? This is so puzzling. There are people today who do things that cause them to lose character or even to be immoral, and yet they can still be "serving God" and doing something significant with a measure of success. How can this be?

The Bible helps us to understand how Solomon could still be successful. We read:

> Ahijah took hold of the new cloak he was wearing and tore it into twelve pieces. Then he said to Jeroboam, "Take ten pieces for yourself, for this is what the LORD, the God of Israel, says: 'See, I am going to tear the kingdom out of Solomon's hand and give you ten tribes. But for the sake of my servant David and the city of Jerusalem, which I have chosen out of all the tribes of Israel, he will have one tribe.'"
>
> —1 KINGS 11:30–32

Solomon was no longer blessed, but he was still under the blessing of his father, David. He was enjoying the short-term benefits of a borrowed anointing.

It wasn't until his reign as king ended that we see the disaster his distractions brought. Sometimes we do not see immediate disaster in our own lives as the result of our carnal natures, our flirting and our wrong passions. But we may be initiating a very negative influence upon the next generation. We might reap a harvest of tears unless we repent. There will be a consequence for our sin. Scripture clearly states, "You may be sure that your sin will find you out" (Num. 32:23).

I always remind myself that whatever I do with my eyes will affect the eyes of my children someday. This principle keeps me away from lust and helps me to keep my eyes pure. It is very easy to fall into lust today; pornography invades our living rooms— without our buying anything. That's why it's so important to remind myself continually about the effect I may have on my children's lives. If I become distracted in my thinking, and my thoughts are not pure before the Lord, I may see the effect in my marriage and on my children. Tension may arise in my family—even a diabolical oppression that invades my home. I do not want to open a window to any such oppression. I am sure you do not want to see it happen in your home either. It is for that reason we much keep our minds pure.

Be aware of the principle of emotional adultery. That is what happens when a man or woman says, "I wish I could be married to someone else." It occurs when a person longs for someone else's spouse. Even if there has never been a relationship or a dialogue about it, if that thought has been entertained, then that heart has already become unfaithful and disloyal to his or her spouse.

We are confronted with hundreds of temptations every week. Temptation will continue to come, but if we have a strong passion for God, we do not need to allow one single thought to go in the wrong direction.

I have received a baptism of fire, and I would not give it up for anything. Yet I tell you, there is no baptism, no visitation or no experience with the Lord that exempts a person from temptation. As long as we live here on Planet Earth, we will be tempted.

But I also tell you that you can develop a divine, anointed discipline to keep you focused on Jesus Christ and a willingness to repent immediately. If you have this discipline, you will not fall. There have been times—in airports, airplanes, anywhere—when I realized I had dwelt too long on an ungodly thought. One second would have been OK; I would just call that *temptation*. But when I allowed my thoughts to move to two...three...or fifteen seconds, it was too long! So right there, wherever I stood at the time, I knelt down and repented. "God," I cried out, "for fifteen seconds, I betrayed You. Forgive me and purify me."

Perhaps you think that is a yoke of discipline you cannot bear. No, friends, what we cannot bear is a lethal mixture of holiness with sin—that is a deadly cocktail!

Solomon was prepared for success, but he ended up in disaster. He began his reign with a godly anointing upon his life. He had even been blessed with two visitations from the Lord (1 Kings 11:9). He also had promises given to him from the Lord, but those promises were canceled because of his distraction.

> So the LORD said to Solomon, "Since this is your attitude and you have not kept my covenant and my decrees, which I commanded you, I will most certainly tear the kingdom away from you and give it to one of your subordinates."
>
> —1 KINGS 11:11

Even though there was peace in Israel during his reign, it was while he was king that God began to raise up the coming enemies of Israel. The victories of the previous generation became persecution in the next generation.

When we get distracted, Satan regroups. Old temptations return with greater force. When we do not fill our hearts with the will of the Lord and with the power of the Holy Spirit, allowing them to become empty, demons move back in with greater numbers than before. The temptation becomes stronger than the original one that oppressed us. It comes to deter us and to destroy us.

DISTRACTIONS TO AVOID

Let's take a closer look at some of the distractions we must learn to avoid if we want to be all that God wants us to be. Don't let any of these things pull your concentration away from your devotion to Christ.

The distraction of consumerism

As I mentioned earlier, while in the southern part of Argentina, I spoke in a church that was doing a strange kind of fast—they were fasting credit cards! Several people testified about how they were set free from debt as they fasted. This spontaneous work of the Holy Spirit broke the distraction of consumerism, which breeds compulsive shopping.

The "noise" of the media

Turn off the noise so that you can hear the "still, small voice of God." Any continual sound entering through your ears can distract you from the voice of God arising from deep within your spirit— even if it is "Christian" noise. Don't let media "noise" become a substitute for communion with God.

Half-hearted work for God

God's Word advises us, "Whatever you do, work at it with all your heart, as working for the Lord, not for men" (Col. 3:23). Don't be distracted by your own impatience or lack of enthusiasm for the things of God. Work for Him with your whole heart.

Constant disagreement with the vision of the church

If you are constantly criticizing the direction of your church or trying to make it perfect, you are distracted. Billy Graham once said, "If you ever find the perfect church, don't join it; you will wreck it!" It is counterproductive to work *against* the body of Christ; make a decision to work with it.

Not having any goals in life

Determine now to set some godly goals for your life and for your family. If your goals line up with the will of God for your life and for your family, He will honor many of your goals and help you to reach them. Without goals, you will be easily distracted.

The presence of immoral passions in your life

The Bible condemns any kind of mental impurity—not only overt acts of adultery and fornication. Any kind of lascivious fantasy is out of the will of God. Jesus is very clear about this subject. If any man lusts after a woman, *in his heart* he has already committed adultery.

Waiting for recognition

Don't be distracted from working for the Lord by waiting until you receive recognition and honor. That time may never come. Even if others fail to recognize your efforts, will you work for the Lord and serve Him anyway?

CHARACTERISTICS OF THE UNDISTRACTED

The servant of God who avoids the transgression of distraction has a clear sense of direction. Below are some of the characteristics of people who avoid distractions:

- They have a constant desire to be like Jesus.

- They have a passion for lost souls.

- They are reliable because of their ability to keep a straight course.

- They love the entire body of Christ.

- They are effective in their work for God.

- They have a sense of dignity—even when completing small tasks for God.

Do you have the characteristics of the undistracted? Do you have a holy love for God's people—and for the lost? Do your prayers unite people instead of separating people? Do you feel good about serving God, whether your ministry is a great, important ministry in the eyes of men or just a small ministry?

Jesus is our example. He was a man of commitment. He was a man of direction. In Luke 9:51 we read, "As the time approached for him to be taken up to heaven, Jesus resolutely set out for Jerusalem." He would not let even His disciples distract Him. Because of "the joy set before him [he] endured the cross" (Heb. 12:2). Jesus had high goals, a high objective for the human race. Because of His objective for mankind, He was willing to suffer a humiliating death.

We live in a day in which the Lord is asking us to grow roots and to become spiritually established. We cannot afford to continue our Christian walk with distractions. We know from Solomon's example that even great men and women of God—who have accomplished mighty feats for Him in the past—can get off track quickly because of distractions. We must keep our eyes on the prize and refuse to be lured away from reaching our destination.

A Prayer of Repentance

Father, thank You for warning me with Your Word. Give me a heavenly freedom right now to break away from any relationship in my life that is not within Your will. Help me to break away from any passions that are not Yours.

God of great mercy, come now and make Your presence tangible. Send Your angels to help me. Break the yoke of sin. May every addiction be broken by Your power. May every evil habit be broken to pieces. Come, Lord, and set me free from deadly distractions. May I do Your will every day of my life. In Jesus' name, amen.

Begin to release your distractions to the Lord. Let go of envy and jealousy. Let the Lord touch your eyes. If family is on the brink of a breakdown, be sure to come before Jesus today. The distraction of a lack of commitment will destroy you. Indecisiveness will distract you from His will.

Jesus is an *embracer,* not a *rejecter.* Renounce every emotional bondage that is drawing you away from Jesus. Stay focused on Him and His will for your life.

Chapter 10

The Transgression of Jonah: Serving God With Reluctance

A missionary on furlough stood before a church audience to share about his call to the mission field. Before he preached, his wife shared also. She went to the platform, stood behind the pulpit and told how difficult it was for her to leave her hometown and live in a distant country. She spoke of the nights she had spent crying about the decision. She told about her close relationship with her mother. She shared how much her children had enjoyed living near their grandmother and how they missed it. She then began to cry. Through her tears, she said, "I am going to be obedient, though. I *will* go where Jesus wants me to go." By the time this woman finished her sad story, half the congregation felt like saying to her, "Maybe you should just go home!"

I knew of a pastor who, throughout his thirty years of serving his congregation, hardly ever let a week go by without reminding the congregation of the good job and position he had left to become a pastor. "You just don't realize the sacrifice I made to come here," he would say. "I never wanted to come here, but I chose to obey God." I am not sure that he regretted being a pastor, but at least he wanted to be sure that everyone knew of the great sacrifice he had made to serve them.

DISAGREEING WITH THE VISION OF GOD

In front of King Agrippa, the apostle Paul once said, "I was not disobedient to the vision from heaven" (Acts 26:19). Perhaps not every Christian can say the same thing. There are people who are quietly rebellious, disobedient or who disagree "quietly" with God Almighty. How arrogant that we think we can pick and choose what aspects of His will we will obey!

The word of the Lord to Jonah will be especially meaningful for you if God has been repeating something in your heart for the second, third or more times—and you have not yet responded to His promptings. Is God telling you, "Go," but you have resisted His commission? Through this story about Jonah, God is about to repeat something in your heart that was given to you a long time ago.

Jonah had heard the voice of the Lord. He had received revelation. He knew what to do, but he had a problem: He was in sharp disagreement with God.

> The word of the LORD came to Jonah son of Amittai: "Go to the great city of Nineveh and preach against it, because its wickedness has come up before me." But Jonah ran away from the LORD and headed for Tarshish. He went down to Joppa, where he found a ship bound for that port. After paying the fare, he went aboard and sailed for Tarshish to flee from the LORD.
>
> —JONAH 1:1–3

Jonah heard this first word from the Lord—but he ran in the opposite direction. We do not know all the reasons why he ran. Perhaps he was afraid of facing the people. Perhaps he was prejudiced toward them because they were Gentiles. We do know that he wanted vindication against the cruel Ninevites instead of compassion. Whatever the case, he said *no* to God. But God graciously gave him a second chance, even though he blew the first one.

> Then the word of the LORD came to Jonah a second time: "Go to the great city of Nineveh and proclaim to it the message I give you."
>
> —JONAH 3:1–2

You may be tempted to say, "Why did God give the guy another chance? He didn't deserve it!" But as for me, I cannot be too critical about Jonah's delay in responding to something God had told him to do—because I have had that same attitude.

CALLED TO GATHER THE CITY

Soon after I had a special visitation from God in 1997 with a baptism of fire in my life, the Lord called me to gather the congregations together in my city of La Plata, Argentina. He actually gave me a vision of revival there. When I closed my eyes, I could see a sports arena packed with people seeking the holiness of God.

After seeing that vision, I followed the conventional route and began to talk to some of my pastor friends who were leaders in the city. They discouraged me totally from trying to do such a thing. Pastors will not pray or work together, they assured me. They told me that the city was divided, so much so that the pastor's association in the city had split into two groups.

Even so, I printed some posters to announce the event. But when I found out that the city was holding a secular festival during that same time, I let the matter drop. *Oh well,* I thought. *I guess that idea was not from God.*

Three years later, the voice of the Lord began to grow silent in my life. I went for weeks without hearing anything from Him. I traveled to England to minister in a conference there, but He did not speak to me. I would go to meetings and see His presence manifested, but He remained silent toward me. The glory would come, miracles of transformation would happen, but when I returned to my hotel room, God was so strangely quiet. I could not sense the presence of the Lord. Concerned, I began to ask Him about it.

One afternoon I went jogging and took my tape recorder with me. I was listening to the sermon of the speaker who had preached prior to me in that conference. I wanted to get an overall view of what God was doing in that conference before I spoke.

As I jogged, I heard the speaker say, "God doesn't like to repeat Himself. He will speak to us once and then silently wait for our obedience." By the time he finished saying those words, I was no longer running. At first I continued to walk slowly, and finally I ended up kneeling down and saying, "Lord, that's me. Three years ago you asked me to call the churches together in my city, and I didn't obey. Forgive me. If You will give me a second chance, I promise that You won't have to say it again. This time I will obey." In that moment I began to relate to the reluctant prophet Jonah!

I sensed a green light. God gave me that second chance. However, by now we were not even living or pastoring in the city of La Plata. The first time God had asked me to gather the church, I was one of the pastors in the city. Since then, we had resigned our local congregation to embrace a worldwide vision the Lord had given to us.

So I started recording radio programs for the Christian radio station in La Plata. I planned a citywide meeting for all the churches. On the radio programs, I talked about the meeting and invited the churches to participate. I talked with one of the pastors in La Plata and asked for his support and cooperation. He replied, "This is the worst time to organize a rally! Pastors are divided. We just had a new split in the city, and the spiritual atmosphere is not good. If it was bad before, it is worse now. Do not try to rent the sports arena; you are going to lose a lot of money." But this time I did not allow the voices of doubt to deter me.

I knew I had received clear direction from the Lord, and I had given Him my word. So I decided to go ahead with my plans if they would just grant me permission—with or without their support. Eventually I received an e-mail basically giving me "permission to fail," but that was enough. I must admit that I too thought we might fail, but I was convinced that I would rather fail in doing God's will than to succeed in doing my own.

"Lord," I said, "I know that people will not come. Some pastors have already let me know they are not supporting us and that churches are not coming. Some of them are forbidding their congregations to come to these meetings. There is no way we can pull this together. But Lord, in obedience to You, I am going to rent that sports arena. Even if only fifty people show up, I will do it, and I will fulfill my duties in that city and maybe never do anything there again!"

A few weeks before the meetings started, the pastors began sensing that the meetings were God's will. Young people gathered from different congregations for a youth rally. They printed flyers and distributed them to the city. Something new had started to happen.

By the time my wife and I walked into that sports arena, the place was packed. On the second day, I still had my doubts—and as though to support my doubt, we had a downpour all day. But that night the arena was packed again. On the third day, the place was overflowing. The local newspaper reported that more than six thousand people packed that sports arena, which supposedly seated only three thousand.

The results of those meetings continue to be seen today in La Plata. The pastors began to call the churches together and hold united meetings on a monthly basis. Subsequent large gatherings have taken place. Momentum for a citywide revival continues to build.

GOD GLORIFIES HIMSELF IN THE IMPOSSIBLE

Even if something looks impossible, God can glorify His name through it. The Book of Jonah is really a book of victory, even though Jonah did not enjoy his own participation that much.

In the first two chapters of the book, we see that Jonah did the wrong thing by running from God. In chapters 3 and 4, Jonah did the right thing but with the wrong attitude—he was still a loser. Even his success made him frustrated and angry. The word of the Lord came to Jonah the second time and said, "Go to the great city of Nineveh and proclaim to it the message I give you."

God has a sense of humor. He chose a conservative Jew to go to a city that was hated by the Jews. It was a city of the oppressors, a city of cruelty. There was something in the heart of Jonah, and it was not revival—it was revenge. His prayer was, "Lord, bring Your justice—hold Your grace. Help us to get even with these people." He had a religious, judgmental attitude toward these unclean

Gentiles. He didn't realize that God was trying to show him that His plan was to take His word to all nations.

So many times our conclusions, even as Christians, are blatantly opposed to the conclusions of God. The New Testament uses a word to describe these wrong conclusions: They are called *strongholds*. A stronghold is a lie, a wrong conclusion that we have accepted as truth. It is usually so set in our minds that the light of the Holy Spirit cannot penetrate it.

How do you demolish a stronghold? You demolish it with the power of God. It takes the power of the Lord to pulverize those invisible walls in our hearts that resist the will of the Lord and the truth of God.

Evidently Jonah had a stronghold in his heart against the Ninevites. He did not want to go to Nineveh, and neither did he want God to be there. However, the second time God called, he obeyed:

> Jonah obeyed the word of the LORD and went to Nineveh. Now Nineveh was a very important city—a visit required three days. On the first day, Jonah started into the city. He proclaimed: "Forty more days and Nineveh will be overturned."
>
> —JONAH 3:3–4

In those two short verses is contained the entire message Jonah preached to the city. He forgot to include the second part, "If you repent, God will forgive you." In essence, he forgot the last point of the sermon! The Bible tells us that the Ninevites believed God. The king instructed all citizens—rich and poor—to fast. They put on sackcloth, which was a symbol of repentance and humility before God.

> When the news reached the king of Nineveh, he rose from his throne, took off his royal robes, covered himself with sackcloth and sat down in the dust. Then he issued a proclamation in Nineveh:
>
> "By the decree of the king and his nobles: Do not let any man or beast, herd or flock, taste anything; do not let them eat or drink. But let man and beast be covered with sackcloth. Let everyone call urgently on God. Let them give up their evil

ways and their violence. Who knows? God may yet relent and with compassion turn from his fierce anger so that we will not perish."

—Jonah 3:6–9

Wouldn't you be thrilled to see your entire city turn to God? Imagine what could happen if our civic and religious leaders issued a proclamation like this! Your city is not beyond the grace of God. God has so much power He could transform your city in one day.

As Jonah began to make this proclamation over the city of Nineveh, suddenly a sense of urgency came to the people, and they recognized their need to repent. They were so serious about repenting that they even put their animals on a fast. When God saw what they did and how they turned from their evil ways, He had compassion and did not bring upon them the destruction He had threatened. His mercy triumphed over judgment.

Now if this were the only chapter of Jonah, we would assume that the preacher was fulfilled and gladdened by the people's response. But in the next chapter we learn that this preacher had drawn his own personal conclusions about what the outcome should be. He was actually upset that Nineveh had been spared!

Nowadays, some people have ideas about revival. They might think, *If a revival comes, it will have to be in this style of worship, with this kind of people.* When we have our own preconceived notions about how God should work already set in our hearts, those thoughts may rise up against the knowledge of Christ. Then, even if we obey, we may not enjoy the fruit. As a result, we might live in frustration for the rest of our lives unless something changes.

Jonah obeyed, but he ministered without passion. He had no compassion for the city of Nineveh. He actually wanted judgment to fall on the city. He may have learned that the results of disobedience were so terrible that it was better to obey—but he hadn't learned to embrace God's will joyfully.

Enjoy the Plan of God

God is calling the church today to a higher level. He is telling us that transformation is possible. Zechariah 3:9 proclaims, "I will remove the sin of this land in a single day." God can revive a city in one day—just as he did in Elijah's and Jonah's day. In one afternoon the entire atmosphere can change. The time we spend in prayer, fasting and proclaiming will not be in vain—God will send the harvest.

The problem occurs when our stubborn will refuses to *enjoy* the plan of God. When we decide that we want God to do things our way and only our way, we set ourselves up to miss the real blessing that He is sending our way.

Jonah became experienced in disobedience. He began by running away from the Lord (Jon. 1:3). When the sailors started asking questions about where he was from and where he was going, he admitted to the men that he was running away from God. Then, terrified, "They asked, 'What have you done?'" (v. 10).

In essence, Jonah replied to the men by saying, "I'm going anywhere away from the will of the Lord." He had negative purpose. He knew only where he did not want to go and from whom he was running. His disobedience caused several problems. One of them was delay. If you disobey, you delay the will of God for your life and your city.

There is a law with which all human beings must comply, no matter how spiritual we are. It is the law of time. Time is not forever on this earth. If we resist, question and disagree with the will of God, our resistance begins to cause delay. We never have the right to postpone obedience.

At the church I used to pastor, one of the leaders called me one day to make an appointment with me. He said he had something very important thing to tell me. When he arrived at my office, he said, "Pastor Sergio, I want to tell you this. I have been working in this church for more than twenty-five years. This week I made a decision—I am going to give 100 percent of my life to God."

I was happy but perplexed. I realized there are Christians who have been in ministry as much as a quarter of a century who have never said, "Lord, I give You everything. Tell me what to do and I will do it." How could this man be in the ministry that long and yet not be surrendered to God's will?

Not every Christian is at the 100 percent point of obedience. There are Christians who slow down the will of God by bargaining, negotiating and giving excuses and conditions to God. In essence, we are dragging our feet as we serve Him. That is why the church is advancing so slowly. If we would let Him take us with Him, the Holy Spirit could move much faster.

The real problem with delayed obedience is that it becomes disobedience. We can believe ourselves to be very spiritual, but we may even have forgotten what the voice of the Lord has whispered to us in the past. But God does not forget, and He does not change His mind.

As my wife and I entered that sports arena in La Plata for the united meeting we had finally planned in obedience to God's voice to me earlier, a wonderful thing happened. People in the crowd began to stop me. One man shook my hand and said, "Pastor, do you remember me? I was the taxi driver you witnessed to." Another lady came down from the bleachers and said, "Pastor Sergio, do you remember me? I was your neighbor, Coca. You stopped at my house and told me about Jesus. Now I am a committed Christian." My heart rejoiced!

I remember the day I went to Coca's house in obedience to the Holy Spirit. She gathered her teenage girls around her and made them turn off the television to listen to me. When I finished talking, I led her to the Lord. How happy I am that I did not postpone talking to her!

One year after that first city gathering, we went back to La Plata to hold another united meeting. My wife, Kathy, went back to our old neighborhood to knock on each door and personally invite our previous neighbors to the meetings we were holding. As she arrived at Coca's house, she rang the doorbell. A man came out to the gate. Kathy asked, "Is the lady of the house here? Her name is Coca, right?"

"Coca is dead," the man replied. "She died in December of last year." That had been just three months after we saw her in the united meeting. I was so thankful that we had not delayed in obeying God about speaking to her about Jesus. She would not have heard if we had even waited to make a second visit to her house until we came to La Plata for that first meeting.

DISOBEDIENCE: A NEGATIVE INFLUENCE

Another problem caused by our disobedience is the negative influence it has upon those around us. If we are not totally committed to the Lord and filled with joy about what God wants us to do, our family will be impacted by our negativity. Our marriage will be impacted. Our churches will pick up on our attitude, too. It is unavoidable. If you are not in the will of God and are refusing to do what the Lord tells you, it is inevitable that there will be an influence on others that is not good.

In the case of Jonah, the negative influence was very evident. The boat he was in was about to sink! A big storm came, and the people began to ask, "Who is guilty? Why does this punishment come upon us?" They cast lots, and the results pointed out to Jonah.

When we are not in God's will, we become the main problem, not the unbelievers around us. It was not those idol worshipers in the boat who were the problem at that moment. It was the servant of the Lord who was hiding from the will of the Lord. We become the problem and create new and unnecessary crises with our disobedience.

The men on the boat asked, "What should we do to you to make the sea calm down for us?" (Jon. 1:11). What a question! Instead of saying, "Let's hold hands and repent before God and pray," Jonah simply said, "Pick me up and throw me into the sea."

Jonah was ready to die rather than comply with the will of the Lord. His reluctance made him negative and despondent. He was also so angry that he said he would rather die. So they threw him into the ocean, and a big fish came and swallowed him without killing him. The things God has to do with rebellious people is amazing! All the creativity of heaven needs to surround us so that somehow we get back on the right track.

Once Jonah was entombed alive in the belly of that big fish, he began to pray and repent. Then he said:

> What I have vowed I will make good.
>
> —JONAH 2:9

Finally, after being inside the fish, Johan was willing to go where God had directed.

EXTERNAL OBEDIENCE

In other words, Jonah finally agreed to give God what he had promised. Here we note a change in *behavior*, but not in *attitude*. A lot of people comply externally to the vision of their church or to what God is doing in the city, but inwardly their hearts are not there. When our hearts are not in sync with our actions, there is no enjoyment.

Jonah finally made it to Nineveh to preach. After his proclamation, the people repented. What was Jonah's reaction?

> Jonah was greatly displeased and became angry.
>
> —JONAH 4:1

When our hearts are not in tune with the will of God, even if revival comes, we will be angry. I have met people—I know them by their first and last names—who became very angry after the revival came to the city of La Plata. You may wonder what could make a genuine Christian upset when a revival comes.

Some were upset because they had lost their "personal pastor." Before the revival, some pastors would have the time to stand at the doors of their churches to greet each person personally as the congregations left the services. When thousands of new people began cramming into the churches, the pastors could not always shake hands with each person. In fact, some people could not even find a seat, so a few of them began to complain.

Some people called their pastors to express their displeasure. Their hearts were not impassioned for the city. They just wanted a church that served *them*. They were not mean or bad people—some of them had been faithful Christians for many years. But sometimes even the most faithful Christians fail to stay updated with the new things God is doing. The very essence of faithfulness requires that it be current.

In my heart, I know that when I begin to complain and become discontent, it is a sign that something is wrong. When that happens I go to prayer and say, "Lord, set me free from resentment, from a victim complex and from thinking I am the only one who is sacrificing by doing so much traveling." Many times when I feel like complaining, I think about the precious pastors who live in persecuted nations and risk their lives daily for the sake of the gospel. I am not worthy to share a platform with them.

When my wife and I went to the Czech Republic to minister, the meetings were powerful—they were packed with people and overflowing with the presence of the Lord. While there, we learned that the pastor who had invited us to come was the leader of a denomination with many people who had spent long months in Communist jails. I trembled when I heard that, because I realized that some of the people sitting in those meetings knew suffering and persecution from firsthand experiences that we had never known and, hopefully, will never experience. Knowing of their sacrifice humbled me and caused me to stop focusing on my own problems—which were minimal compared to theirs.

HAVING PASSION TO OBEY

The fire of God gives us passion to do the will of God. The fire of God is not a feeling—*it is a direction.* It is a passion for God and for souls. Jonah had the ministry, the calling and the title, but Jonah did not have the passion. Even though God used him, he did not enjoy the work of the Lord.

Even after the city repented, Jonah continued to be stubborn.

> He prayed to the LORD, "O LORD, is this not what I said when I was still at home? That is why I was so quick to flee to Tarshish."
>
> —JONAH 4:2

When we argue with God for too long, it gets ridiculous. It doesn't make sense, but we keep arguing *with God,* saying, "Lord, I told You so. You should have listened to me. I was right."

Even though Jonah argued with God, God was merciful to Jonah. The Lord answered him:

Have you any right to be angry?

—Jonah 4:4

If you have become angry with God while doing His will, the Holy Spirit is bringing this question to your heart. Have you any right to complain? Have you any right to be angry? Have you any right to continue to disagree with the calling of God for yourself… your home…your church…or your city?

There are many people who are rebellious, but they would never take a boat somewhere to run from God. Their rebellion and disobedience are subtler. But they still refuse to believe the destiny of God for their cities. They are in quiet resistance.

We long to see the day when congregations will join the pastors who have a vision for their cities, becoming an encouragement to those pastors. We pray that those who have been on the sidelines will jump into God's dream for their region and make a tangible commitment of time and finances to win their cities.

God is waking up the vision to see revival in our cities, and He is awaking us to the reality that He has called every one of us to be a part of the harvest. In the time of Jonah, God called to Jonah through a direct call. Today God has appointed leaders and pastors in the church—people to lead us in the right direction.

It is time to give up any anger or discontent. It is time to crucify our flesh and obey His will. Notice that Jonah was doing the right thing outwardly. He did go to Nineveh and preach. But his attitude was still not right.

Jonah waited to see what would happen to the city.

—Jonah 4:5

Jonah was still hopeful that these rebellious, evil and wicked people would be destroyed by God. So he sat there watching them. Perhaps you are just sitting and waiting, spiritually speaking, to see if God will change and do things your way.

Maybe you were offended years ago and said, "Until this is made right, I will not cooperate with the church again." You are waiting to see what will happen. Jesus is standing in front of you and saying, "Forgive. Let go. Pray for your enemies. Move on with the vision that I have for you." Don't let offense cause you to fall into Jonah's trap!

Some people think they are always hearing the same thing from God. It may be because they are not yet doing what God said to them in the first place. Some people prefer to quench their days in sadness rather than to let go of the hurt and disappointment and move on with the will of God.

The Lord is asking, "Should I not be concerned about Chicago... Buenos Aires... Bombay... or about the city you come from?" Why do we insist on a more comfortable Christianity? Why are we so tempted to give up our efforts? Why do we say it has been too long? Why not be refreshed with the vision of God for your city and the hope that if He could change Nineveh, He can change your city?

God is going to use consecrated people to complete His will in our cities. I pray that you not only consecrate your outward actions but also your inner attitudes. I pray that you will be able to say, "Yes, Lord," to His calling for you.

In a meeting recently, one young man came and said to me, "I was called by God to the ministry when I was a child. Then I went into a time of confusion, and to this day I have been confused. But today I come to the altar to tell the Lord that I am going to fulfill my vows and obey the calling of the Lord on my life."

In Southern Texas, just as I finished my sermon, my young translator turned to me and said, "I WILL study Japanese!" He then explained that years earlier he had been instructed by God to learn the language and to be ready to be a missionary to Japan. He had delayed in his obedience, but now he was ready to obey. Have you put some of God's directives on the shelf?

Jesus said, "What shall I give this generation? I will give them the sign of Jonah. Like Jonah I am going to be three days underground.

But then I am going to resurrect." There were many human reasons why Jesus could have chosen to avoid the will of God. In His humanity He prayed, "Father, if you are willing, take this cup from me" (Luke 22:42). But He also prayed, "Not my will, but yours be done."

There are ministries that are going to be rekindled with the fire of God. I believe that part of God's agenda on earth today is to revitalize ministries that are totally asleep. These ministries will be like vitamins to the body of Christ that were missing.

Jonah never became an official backslider. He never quit believing in God, never stopped being a member of the people of God. *But his heart was far from the will of God.* Perhaps you are an active church member and do not consider yourself a backslider. Yet you have constantly resisted the voice of God. You may even be confused about what the will of the Lord is. Disobedience will always bring confusion, but obedience will bring clarity. The way to pierce through the fog created by disobedience is to begin to take steps of obedience one at a time.

Rise up, O man and woman of God. Align your heart once again with the complete will of God for your life. Reach out to your city for God. Stop dragging your heart. Proclaim the day of salvation to those who need to hear it. Don't let negativity, offenses or excuses prevent you from embracing His will. Be a part of what God is doing in this day in your city.

If you are struggling with being willing to give everything to the Lord, it is because you do not trust the Father who loves you. Remember that God's will is perfect, it is good, and it is pleasant. (See Romans 12:2.)

Grasp this wonderful reminder of the goodness God has for your life:

> LORD, you have assigned me my portion and my cup; you have made my lot secure. The boundary lines have fallen for me in pleasant places; surely I have a delightful inheritance.
>
> —PSALM 16:5–6

A PRAYER OF REPENTANCE

Lord, I thank You for Your Word. I pray that You set my heart free from this transgression of disagreement with Your will. Set me free from discontentment that is worldly. Set me free from the spirit of complaining. Holy Spirit, come and embrace me now. I ask You to transform my life and ministry.

Lord, I want to change. I want not only my feet to follow Your will, but my heart also. I renounce discontentment, regrets and my unhappy heart, and I am going to follow Your will with joy. Whatever You ask me to do, I will do it, Lord. As You teach me how to do it, as You equip me to do it, I will obey Your will.

Father, I pray that before You build anything in my life, demolish the old wineskins. Disarm the old arguments. Pulverize my excuses. Lord, set me free from my own inner conflict. Yes, Lord, I plead with You, do this before You plant and build—uproot and destroy. Come and perform Your divine demolition in my heart. Destroy every work of the flesh, every diabolical thought, every thought of confusion, rebellion and disobedience.

Lord, I renounce my ways and choose to follow Your ways. I renounce that judgmental and critical attitude that always questions the vision of the leaders or the programs of the church, but never does anything to help.

Forgive me, forgive my foolishness, forgive my pride and my arrogance. Lord, I am not going to feel like a failure anymore. It doesn't matter how weak I might be; I am Your servant. You can use me.

Lord, my finances are for Your kingdom. As You give me Your grace, I will administer them wisely and give to You everything You ask me to give. Selfishness, be gone in Jesus' name. Self-centeredness, be gone from my life in Jesus' name. Come, Holy Spirit, and burn the character of Jesus into my heart. I empty myself of anything that belongs to the old way of doing things. I am in Christ. Old things have passed away, and all things have become new.

Lord, come now and breathe life into my thinking, into my ministry and into my work. Father, I pray that You touch the eyes of my understanding and that suddenly I will see the vision so clearly. Father, I pray that I will never be a backslider in heart, but that I will serve You wholeheartedly.

In Jesus' name, amen.

Chapter 11

The Transgression of Peter: Fearing Man More Than God

I participated in some wonderful revival meetings in New York City several years ago. The pastor had invited other area congregations to participate in those services. The glory of the Lord descended, and it seemed as if we were in the kinds of glorious outpourings of the Holy Spirit that you only read about in history. Many people repented, and there were tears and brokenness. The place was totally packed; even the aisles were full.

On the day I was leaving, the clerk at the hotel desk told me that everything was OK and that the church had taken care of my bill. The pastor had also already told me everything was taken care of and not to worry about a thing. Just as I was just about to leave with my luggage, the thought came to me, *I ought to look at the bill.* It seemed almost "nosey" that I would ask to look at the bill and see how much the pastor had paid for my stay there. But I knew the Holy Spirit was nudging me to ask to see the bill for some reason.

So at the front desk, just before leaving, I asked for a copy of the room charges. I had never done this in all the times that I had been traveling. The clerk gave me the bill without hesitancy, and when I looked at it, I realized that there was a charge on the bill for a pay-per-view movie. Generally, such movies are pornographic. I smiled and spoke to the person at the front desk and said, "When I entered my hotel room, I unplugged the television set! I have not even turned it on, yet on my bill is a charge for a pay-per-view movie." They quickly removed the charge from my bill—almost too quickly. I wondered how many people had paid for these movies without ever knowing that such a charge had been added.

By the time the pastor came to pay the bill, I explained to him what happened. I now believe the Holy Spirit's prompting to me to look at the bill was God's protection upon me and my ministry's reputation. I left New York saying, "Thank You, Holy Spirit, for preserving my integrity before these people." Even though I was innocent, this could have ruined my testimony unless they asked me personally about it.

LEARN TO CULTIVATE YOUR INTEGRITY

Since that time, every time I check out of a hotel, I always ask for a copy of the bill. I now realize that it is my responsibility to guard my integrity in the eyes of people the best way I can. We need to protect the Christian image we project.

Holiness is a gift of God. Integrity is something that we have to cultivate. You and I have to "grow" integrity in our daily lives. In fact, the Bible tells us that it is our responsibility to guard our reputation:

> Do not allow what you consider good to be spoken of as evil.
> —ROMANS 14:16

We learn from reading the New Testament that one of Jesus' closest followers fell into the trap of compromising his integrity. Peter had spent three years in the Bible School of Jesus. He had walked next to the Master and witnessed His miracles. This was the man to whom God had given the grace to carry the gospel to the Gentiles. He received the keys to the kingdom.

Yet Peter stepped into a situation in which he lacked integrity. Even if you are a teacher, preacher or worker in the church for many years, it is easy to break the principle of integrity. But *it is not necessary* to fall into this transgression of hypocrisy, even though many have been entangled by it. This happened to Peter not long after the apostles had taken the gospel outside of Judea.

> When Peter came to Antioch, I opposed him to his face, because he was clearly in the wrong. Before certain men came from James, he used to eat with the Gentiles. But when they arrived, he began to draw back and separate himself from the Gentiles because he was afraid of those who belonged to the circumcision group. The other Jews joined him in his hypocrisy, so that by their hypocrisy even Barnabas was led astray. When I saw that they were not acting in line with the truth of the gospel, I said to Peter in front of them all, "You are a Jew, yet you live like a Gentile and not like a Jew. How is it, then, that you force Gentiles to follow Jewish customs?"
>
> —GALATIANS 2:11–14

Peter had begun to act hypocritically. He was more concerned with "looking right" to the other Jewish believers from Jerusalem than he was with maintaining his Christian witness to the Gentiles to whom he was ministering. He played it safe. He followed the traditions and rules of man—and in so doing showed himself to be a hypocrite by his actions. And it was his fear of religious people that caused him to fall into this trap.

A LACK OF INTEGRITY IS HYPOCRISY

John Wesley, the great preacher of the seventeenth century, designed a list of twenty-two questions that he asked in every one of his "holy clubs." He had more than two hundred thousand people participating in his cell groups in England during his ministry years. He traveled by horseback thousands of miles each year, visiting churches and igniting fires of holiness. Some of the questions he asked them were about their integrity. They discussed these questions in their small groups.

One question asked, "Are you consciously or unconsciously creating the impression that you are a better person than you really are? In other words, are you a hypocrite?" Another question asked, "Have you tried to appear better than you really are?" These questions got my attention. There are very few people today who are asking questions like these.

Appearing to be something better than we are has become commonplace among Christians. It has become normal for some people to put on a mask and make others think we are doing better than we really are. But it is a lack of integrity to make something appear different than what it really is, to play a game of faking spirituality. We don't realize that we are risking our integrity when we pretend.

In times of old in Rome, the artists of that day were dedicated to creating beautiful sculptures, many examples of which we still find today in museums and private collections. History tells us that when an expensive sculpture created of marble would break, the broken part was replaced with wax, which was then painted over to look exactly like the marble it replaced. Many sculptures that had been repaired with wax were sold, often without indicating that the replacement had been made.

In the Latin language, the words they used were *sine,* which meant "without," and *cera,* which meant "wax." It is from those Latin words that our English word *sincere* is derived. There was a time in history when this practice was so prevalent that when buyers wanted to purchase expensive statues, they would first ask for one that was *sine cera* (without wax).

People who are sincere are people without falsehood. They are people who are morally cohesive and who do not have some parts of their lives that are "made out of wax." They do not have falsehood in their character.

The world is asking to see sincere Christians—believers who do not deceive, lie and who are truthful in their work practices. If the world sees Christian role models like this, it will believe in the gospel these Christians preach. One of the greatest hindrances impeding the world from believing the gospel is the evidence of falsehood in the lives of many Christians. These believers look like the real thing and have made themselves out to be sincere, but because they lack integrity they have become stumbling blocks to the spread of the gospel. They are full of wax!

Some people quickly announce that they are Christians, but others do not want to take them on as employees because of their lack of honesty. They add hours onto their work week that they did not work. They dishonestly take things home with them from the workplace. Even if we can raise the dead and heal the sick (and we need more of that in the church), such acts of dishonesty will break trust and cancel the effectiveness of our ministries.

I remember hearing of a secretary who was newly hired to work in a church. After being there a few days, she began receiving phone calls from collection agencies asking for the pastor. She explained that the pastor was not in and offered to take a message. One man replied, "I need to talk to him now. He has not paid his credit card bills for over seven months!"

When the secretary mentioned the calls to the pastor and asked a few straightforward questions, she was soon released from her position. The pastor explained, "You have done nothing wrong; the Holy Spirit told me to release you from your duties." The pastor took special care to keep those who would ask questions at a distance. He was a dishonest man without integrity. What does the world think of the church when even our leaders behave like this?

LITTLE WHITE LIES?

Some of us, because of our social and cultural backgrounds, were taught to lie. My social and cultural background taught me to say things that were not so. These were not said out of evil intentions; rather they were errors out of ignorance. For example, we were taught, "Don't tell that person you do not want to buy that item. Tell them that it is nice, but just don't buy it."

Going to the marketplace with my grandmother when I was a little boy was a favorite experience. I remember how people would use cunning and deception in order to buy things cheaply. They would look at the tomatoes and say to the vendor, "How expensive the tomatoes are today!" But after they had purchased the tomatoes, they would say to the person with them, "Did you see how cheaply I bought those tomatoes?" It was like a game.

Their intentions were not bad or evil; it was just a trick to buy things at a bargain price.

My grandmother was a precious saint of God, but she often used this method. She would ask the butcher, "How much does that meat cost?" When he told her the price, often she replied, "That is so expensive."

Then she would say to me, "Be real still; this meat is very cheap, but I think I can get it at a better price!" In those days none of us realized that this was a point of deceit in our society.

Another kind of lie that is common, especially in Latin American countries, often occurs when your child has a fever and you say to him, "No, son; you don't have a fever. Don't worry." The point is to keep your child from becoming fearful, but what we are really teaching him is that sometimes it is all right to tell a little lie. We are teaching him that at times, when something is not in your favor, you can use a lie. Some people call these "white lies." They may be small lies, but there is really nothing harmless about them.

Habits like these stay with an individual when he or she has grown to adulthood. The child buying tomatoes in the marketplace may one day become a pastor. Maybe you now say things like this to the church treasurer: "Just round it off a little bit, otherwise we will have to pay more taxes."

The Bible tells us that those who are dishonest in small things will not be trusted to administer great things. Telling lies, even small ones, is dishonest. People who lie lack the integrity they need to be the people God wants them to be.

There is no minimum for dishonesty. It can be one million dollars or one dollar. One of the places where I have personally learned not to be dishonest is at the customs checkpoints in international airports. The customs booth at the airport in Buenos Aires, I have to confess, is one place that makes me a bit nervous.

It used to be that a few hours before I was scheduled to arrive there, a struggle would begin inside of me. "Lord," I would pray, "should I declare this? Should I show them that?" There had been a history in Buenos Aires of corrupt practices such as bribery, inventing laws or overcharging people for the things they wanted to bring into the country.

This is not considered a matter of right and wrong because customs agents have been known as blatantly dishonest people. Travelers coming through the customs checkpoints have been basically subject to the whims of the person inspecting his or her baggage.

As time passed, I realized that the customs laws were beginning to change and become more defined. As I would think about all the things I was bringing into the country in my bags, I realized that often I was more ready to lie about what I had than to tell the truth. At times like that, the cultural training from my past would try to dominate me. The commandments of the Lord would fade out.

When I realized that I needed to make some changes in this regard, I began to pray silently, "Lord, give me the strength to be truthful at whatever cost, even if they take my shoes at the airport." Once I made the decision to be totally honest, I have to admit that it made me feel stupid. I thought of others from my culture who would tell me how stupid I was for paying to bring things into the country. Some would tell me I should not have paid because, after all, the equipment was going to be used for the service of the Lord.

For years now, my thinking has been changed. The Holy Spirit has renewed my mind. I now look at these customs inspections as an opportunity to show the airport officials that there are some Christians who are honest. I often let them know I am a Christian. When they inform me, in a low voice, that I will pay less if I do not ask for a receipt, I tell them that I am a preacher. I let them know that I want to do what is right.

God has blessed me at customs because I have adopted this attitude. For example, recently I had to pay $100 to bring in a box of ministry materials. The officials were ready to take a smaller amount as a bribe. However, I chose to pay the $100 required by the law. When I arrived at La Plata, a fellow believer who did not know anything about what had happened at the customs booth handed me an envelope. It contained a donation of $100! I know from this and many other examples that God rewards integrity and truthfulness.

A GRADUAL AND PROGRESSIVE EXPERIENCE

Holiness can fall upon you in a moment of faith, but then you need to learn to walk in it. Once holiness has come upon you, then, by the grace of God, you must learn to walk in integrity for the rest of your life. Holiness came upon my life, and it purified me. But it will take the rest of my life, in a gradual and progressive experience, to learn to walk as Jesus walked.

I do not bring condemnation to you about this subject. I know that laws vary from country to country, but there comes a time when a red light goes off in our conscience. When that light begins to flash, we had better pay attention. It could be a warning light from the Holy Spirit to inform us of impending danger. It says to us, "Danger ahead! You are about to compromise your integrity." Do not ignore that signal!

I remember a person who was driving from Buenos Aires to Mar del Plata, a four-hour trip. While he was driving, a red warning light came on the dash. Because he did not want to be distracted, he put a cloth over the red light. About halfway to his destination, smoke began billowing out from under the hood of the car. He had burned up the motor of the car because he didn't take time to heed the warning and check what was wrong with the car. Do not burn up the motor of your life. When the Holy Spirit sends you a warning light, take heed.

The person without integrity will lose the trust of those around him, no matter what other thing he does well in life. The father who lies will never have the respect of his children, unless, of course, there is repentance, confession and change. The children will remember that their father had lied and will think, *Maybe he is lying to me again; maybe this is not truth either.* Sometimes we disqualify ourselves over things that are insignificant. Solomon said, "Catch for us the foxes, the little foxes that ruin the vineyards, our vineyards that are in bloom" (Song of Sol. 2:15).

The little foxes got into the vineyards when things were in full bloom. They would dig in the ground and ruin the roots without any outward signs. They could destroy a whole vineyard this way. In the same way, the small lies and deceitful things that we do can begin to destroy the roots of Christianity in our lives. On the outside, our lives may appear to have a lot of "greenery," yet the vines may be drying up. It is often the little foxes in our lives that end up bringing the most destruction.

CHARACTERISTICS OF A PERSON WHO LACKS INTEGRITY

There are some common characteristics that can be found in the lives of people who lack integrity. It is important to recognize these characteristics and to check our own lives continually to be sure none of these characteristics have become identifiable in ourselves. Let's take a closer look at these qualities.

The person who lacks integrity has a mantle of condemnation.

A person who wears the mantle of condemnation no longer falls under the blessing of God. He is actually under the disapproval of God. In Galatians 2:11, Paul confronted a fellow believer named Cephas (Peter), a man who wore the mantle of condemnation. We read: "But when Cephas came to Antioch, I opposed him to his face, because he stood condemned" (NAS). The church today needs face-to-face confronters like Paul, not anonymous criticizers.

You might say, "But I believe in the grace of God, and He has pardoned all of my sin." That is true, but the person who is not living in integrity is condemned and no longer wears the mantle of God's blessing and approval. Instead that person has God's disapproval.

If you live a life filled with lies—big or little, you can count on God's disapproval. If you are a businessperson who changes the scales in your favor, you are robbing God—even if the extra income you earn by adjusting the scales is part of your offering to the church! The offering will not sanctify or purify you. Stealing is stealing. Unless you have confessed your sin and sought to make restitution, you will not sense God's forgiveness.

Some people wrongly believe that integrity is a leadership gifting that doesn't apply to the average person. Integrity is not a "gift" for leaders—it is a requirement for all Christians. Every believer is mandated by God to walk in Christlike character. Whatever your position in life, whatever your career, whether you are the president of a bank or a garbage collector, you must consistently live your life with integrity. No one is above the requirement of accountability.

The person who lacks integrity operates out of fear.

Some people are so anxious to please the people around them that they are willing to make decisions to "look good" by doing things that show a lack of integrity. To these individuals, *looking good* becomes more important than *acting good*. This is the mistake Peter made when he fell into the transgression of fearing man more than God. He seemed to change his behavior depending on the crowd he was with.

> Before certain men came from James, he used to eat with the Gentiles. But when they arrived, he [Peter] began to draw back and separate himself from the Gentiles because he was afraid of those who belonged to the circumcision group.
>
> —GALATIANS 2:12

Peter went from saving faith to "saving face." For fear of what the Jews would say, Peter began to behave strangely. Once he became afraid of the Jewish believers and what they would think of him, he decided that he could not eat or be with the Gentiles any more. He separated himself from the Christian Gentiles to be accepted by the Jews.

Remember, this was the man who had said that he was willing to die for Jesus. According to tradition, Peter died crucified upside down on a cross. He paid a high price for his willingness to serve Christ. But in this moment of weakness, he had a fear of what others would say. This is a transgression we commit to make us look good. It is a dangerous transgression to fall into. There are people who, in their desire to look good, can even lose their salvation.

My grandparents were converted to the gospel because my mentally ill aunt was healed of epilepsy. My grandparents took her to a service at Christian church, and she was miraculously healed. Because of their background and culture, at that time their house was filled with religious idols. Superstition had been their way of life. But they now gave their hearts completely to the only true God.

Some of their friends began to come to them and say, "Why are you getting involved with those poor evangelical Christians? You are of another religion." After a time the pressure of being concerned about what others thought about them caused them to return to their idolatry. As strange as it may seem, my aunt became sick again. This got the attention of my grandparents, and when my aunt became sick once again, they returned to the Lord. My aunt, however, was never healed again and died at the age of forty. Because of the fear of man, my grandparents chose to cling to pagan idols.

In the late fifties, evangelist Tommy Hicks ministered in Argentina. He filled stadiums to overflowing; he saw thousands of healings under his ministry. One day he went to visit my grandparents' house. When he prayed for my aunt, she did not get healed. Evangelist Hicks told my grandmother, "Her soul is in peace."

Although this woman was granted entrance to heaven, she never was healed. Why? I believe it is because my grandparents had abandoned the way of the Lord. The Lord did not want them to depart any more. My grandparents are now with the Lord. They became people of great integrity—a man and a woman who did not care what other people said about them. They gave it all up for the Lord. Until the last day of their lives, they were people of prayer and integrity.

The person who is a hypocrite drags other with him.

In his desire to please man rather than God, Peter transgressed. But he didn't remove just himself from the point of God's blessing—he caused others to transgress also. His sin created a stumbling block for many.

> The other Jews joined him in his hypocrisy, so that by their hypocrisy even Barnabas was led astray.
>
> —Galatians 2:13

The person who is a hypocrite will indirectly encourage others to do the same. If he can bring others along in his transgression with him, he does not feel so condemned or different than others. Such a person has a negative influence in the church. That person begins taking others with them in lies and deceit.

The person who lacks integrity is on a path of error.

Without walking in integrity, it is not possible to stay on the path of God's blessing and approval. A person who lacks integrity is on a crooked path leading away from the Lord. In our example of Peter, Paul confronted Peter publicly with his hypocritical behavior and pointed out to him the foolishness of his actions.

> When I saw that they were not acting in line with the truth of the gospel, I said to Peter in front of them all, "You are a Jew, yet you live like a Gentile and not like a Jew. How is it, then, that you force Gentiles to follow Jewish customs?
>
> —GALATIANS 2:14

Paul, the newest member of the apostles, decided to stand up against Peter because of the dishonest simulation. Peter had chosen to return to the legalism of the Jews.

My father and I worked on a study together about our church in La Plata. We designed a test about issues of integrity to go along with it. We gave it to the whole congregation.

We were able to draw some enlightening conclusions about the believers in the church. During the first five years after conversion, most believers continued to grow spiritually. But there seemed to be a five-year turning point. We discovered that a majority of the people who left the church did so in their fifth year of conversion. It was as if they had finished a cycle. The first phase of Christianity had ended for them, and their earlier enthusiasm for the Lord had begun to wane. They began to lose their first love—just as we read about the church of Ephesus in Revelation 2:4.

Some of these believers became bitter, critical and divided from the rest of the body. In our study, we discovered that at the end of five years, believers had done one of two things. Either they had become very involved in ministry, evidencing spiritual maturity, or they had left the church completely and returned to the world. It was as though there was a tendency to return to the past after a certain amount of time.

It is important for every believer to be aware of this human tendency. We should not return to our past. Hypocrites tend to rebuild the shady habits that were canceled at conversion, even though they may hide their sinful behavior behind a religious façade. We read a clear warning in this context: "If I rebuild what I destroyed, I prove that I am a lawbreaker" (Gal. 2:18).

Those who lack integrity waste the grace of God.

Those who lack integrity want to please others in the flesh so much that they would even lie to look good. They waste the grace of God. Yet the apostle Paul said:

> I do not set aside the grace of God, for if righteousness could
> be gained through the law, Christ died for nothing!
> —GALATIANS 2:21

What Paul is saying is that if someone returns to legalism, he returns to be bound to certain things he must do or say to look good. In doing so he is setting aside the grace of God. The person who is a liar, hypocrite or deceitful—the person who tries to look spiritual, but is not—is setting aside the grace of God.

Those who lack integrity are obsessed with details.

In Galatians 3:1, Paul addresses the Galatians by saying:

> You foolish Galatians! Who has bewitched you?
> —GALATIANS 3:1

When the believer is not careful, magical blinders can begin to cover his spiritual eyes. He cannot see truth.

There are people who have a form of holiness but do not yet have integrity. What I am going to share now is not a biblical principle but rather an observation, one I believe will help the church. I believe that there can be people who have been sanctified, but they lack integrity.

I have known servants of the Lord who loved the work of the Lord and who would give their lives for it, but they would use deception in small situations. They would do things that were not honest. I think that for a time they are covered by their ignorance. However, after a time, that allowance of ignorance is spent, and it becomes time to know the truth of God. These individuals need to pay attention to the red warning light that is blinking on their dashboard. If they continue to resist that voice of the Holy Spirit in their hearts, it is no longer ignorance; it has now become open rebellion.

> In the past God overlooked such ignorance, but now he commands all people everywhere to repent.
>
> —Acts 17:30

It is possible for a Christian to fall into shady practices for a short time and not realize it. This is a temporary state of foolish ignorance. But if that individual fails to apply true honesty and purity in the situation, he or she will lose their state of holiness. We need informed holiness; we need to be saturated with the Word of God.

Those who lack integrity will lose everything.

How sad it is to see an individual who was once a person of integrity…one who walked in the blessings and approval of God …fall away into a sinful and unrepentant lifestyle. Integrity is the glue that keeps us on the pathway to God. Without it we risk losing everything.

> Have you suffered so much for nothing—if it really was for nothing?
>
> —Galatians 3:4

In his confrontational words to Peter and the church at Galatia, Paul asks the believers, "Are you really willing to throw it all away?" In other words he was asking them, "Brothers and sisters in Galatia, you have worked hard; you have suffered for the gospel, and now it seems that it was all in vain. Are you about it lose it all?"

Why were the Galatians in danger of losing it all? Because of their legalism and hypocrisy, their pretending and religiosity.

One of the things that my wife and I have been asking God for is more honesty, especially with our children. Of course, every parent wants to impress his or her children. But so often in our desire to impress our children, we say or do something that is not completely honest. I want to leave that kind of thing to one side as I would leave trash. I want to be completely honest with my children.

A few weeks ago I was spending some time in my home with my children when I noticed that the atmosphere seemed to be very tense. Almost immediately I realized that I was the one who was tense! Sometimes when I return from my ministry trips I am very tired and stressed—as I was that day. As a result, I was looking for something to be wrong. I criticized my kids for every little detail in the house that was not right. When I realized this, I knew I needed to make a change.

My kids know that I am a preacher of holiness. As such, I often feel as though I should be perfect for them. Unfortunately, I'm a long way from perfect—as we all are. And I know that it is not good to pretend to be something I am not—it is better to be transparent.

That day I went to the sink in our laundry room and picked up a plastic tub. I filled it with warm water and carried it into the living room along with soap, a towel, perfume and body lotion. I called my family all together there.

"Family," I said to them after they gathered there, "I have been a bit tense. Boys, I want to wash your feet, and I want to ask your forgiveness for being tense these days." One by one, I began to wash their feet. I dried them and rubbed on body lotion and perfume.

When I finished, one of my boys said, "Daddy, could you wash my feet again? I love the warm water!"

I love to preach with the Bible in my hands. Sometimes I stand in the middle of my living room and say, "Children, I have a lesson I want to teach you." But there are times when we need to preach with the wash tub. It is a way to recognize our errors. There have been times when my wife and I have knelt before our children and said, "Boys, we have had a bad character, we have been screaming, and this is not of God. Will you forgive us?" They forgive us right away. Children have a virtue that seems to disappear as we become adults—they can go from anger to forgiveness in thirty seconds. I need to walk in integrity and honesty at all times—but especially in my home with those I love the most. As a part of my marriage vows, I said this to my wife at the ceremony: "My first ministry will be to you and my children. You will be, I trust, my most eloquent sermon to the world."

Jesus preached before the masses while He walked on earth. His words transformed lives and are eternal. But He also preached the gospel with a towel—and with His servanthood. It's not always necessary to figuratively "hit our children over the head with a Bible." Instead we minister best to them with love and by acknowledging our own defects. Recognizing our error and asking forgiveness when we have made a mistake are signs of integrity that speak loudly and clearly.

CHARACTERISTICS OF A LIFE OF INTEGRITY

We have looked at the characteristics of someone who is not walking in integrity. We should avoid those characteristics. But just as important are the positive qualities that are demonstrated in the life of a person who lives a life of integrity. Let's take a close look at these characteristics:

A person of integrity speaks the truth.

Jesus said that our yes should mean yes and our no, no (Matt. 5:37). How easy it is to say, "Yes, I will be there," but inside think, *I will not go.* If Christians would become more truthful, Christianity would be demonstrated in a more powerful way.

A man of integrity is sincere. Just like the statue that was made totally out of marble and did not contain any wax, the person who has integrity is also made out of one solid piece. He has no need to pretend—and nothing to hide.

A person of integrity has pure motives.

But the wisdom that comes from heaven is first of all pure;

then peace-loving, considerate, submissive, full of mercy and
good fruit, impartial and sincere.

—James 3:17

Pure motives are so vital. They arise from a purity of heart. This
verse in James indicates that the first requirement for wisdom is
purity. A person who is pure is not mixed with corrupt or unholy
things. He does not have mixed intentions, but is motivated by only
one thing—pure love for God.

One problem that happens in many ministries is that we allow
faith to get complicated. You notice it when someone begins to say
things like, "I have already been working a year in this position;
they need to give me more honor. When the pastor mentions the
ten people who have worked hard during the past year, he forgot
to mention me! I am going to go to another church because they
did not recognize me."

This kind of thinking happens when our disorderly passions
begin to direct our thinking. Disorderly passions cause our ego-
centric desires to rise up, and the church is unable to satisfy
them. However, we read in this passage in James that the wisdom
that comes from heaven is not mixed, but rather it is pure. I
believe purity calls us to return to simplicity.

A person of integrity has perseverance and consistency.

One of my friends in the ministry is evangelist Carlos
Annacondia. I meet up with him in different cities of the world.
When we are ministering in the same city, I always try to find an
opportunity to talk. One of the important characteristics I have
noticed in this servant of the Lord, who has brought more than
two million people to the Lord in his evangelistic campaigns, is the
fact that he is a person who perseveres.

Annacondia has ministered in crusades where eighty thousand
people attended. But I have also seen him preach in small meetings where there were less than one hundred fifty people present.
I have seen him in places where his tent almost blew away
because of high winds. He has been in poor places and in places
where the ground was muddy.

Do you know what message he preaches to a crowd of a hundred or so? The same message that he preaches to a crowd of eighty thousand. He preaches with consistent passion a message of salvation. He often stays there until 1 or 2 A.M. to pray for people and to minister to those who need ministry.

His example has left a mark on my life. People of integrity are the same in big and small situations. They are there when there is sunshine and when it rains. They have perseverance and a strong sense of purpose. They do not become fickle when there are storms, persecution or obstacles of any kind.

If you want to have success in the kingdom of God, be consistent in doing what God has called you to do! Those who are hypocrites are ever changing in principle, and they back up in the face of difficulties. Today they attend one church, but they are looking at another one to see if it would give them more privileges. When another opportunity comes up, they leave that church as well, ignoring whether it is God who moves them. They are unstable in their ways, always trying out a new opportunity but with no solid sense of direction. They are like clouds that go from one place to the other. Resolve today to become solidly rooted in the Word of God! Become stable in the place where God plants you.

A person of integrity stretches himself beyond his own life.

The person of integrity guards the principle of integrity and the commandments of Jesus, no matter what. If he or she has to lose his life in the process, he loses it, but he does not break the commandments of the Lord.

A person of integrity is called to live and to die for Christ. He or she has nothing to lose. He is not like the Christian who is called to live for Jesus, but who, when things get tough, is not willing to sacrifice. Decide to be a hero for Christ, even if it requires you to be a martyr. Crucify your flesh and say, "Lord, if I live I will live for Christ. If I have to die, I will die for Christ." When you do, your fear of man will leave you forever.

The Pharisees came to Jesus and said, "Leave this place and go somewhere else. Herod wants to kill you."

Jesus' response was, "Go tell that fox, 'I will drive out demons and heal people today and tomorrow, and on the third day I will reach my goal'" (Luke 13:31-32). He was a man of great sorrow and pain, but also of great determination. He set His face like a rock; He went to Jerusalem and did what He had to do. In Hebrews we read:

> Let us fix our eyes on Jesus, the author and perfecter of our faith, who for the joy set before him endured the cross, scorning its shame.
>
> —HEBREWS 12:2

I can imagine the Lord saying, "This shame does not matter to Me. The fact that they beat Me, spat on Me or hung Me up seminaked does not matter to Me. I put this pain aside. This will pass. I am going to fulfill the will of God. I will defeat death, and I will do what God sent Me to do. I will see the awesome results, and My soul will be pleased."

If you desire to have deep roots in the gospel, you should be able to pray this prayer right there where you are: "Lord, I am willing to live for You and to die for You."

A person of integrity is careful about the image he projects.

Holiness is a gift, but ethics must be cultivated. It is now a popular concept to take care of your image, but the image that we are told to care for has a lot to do with our exterior. We hear a lot about projecting a good business and professional image. We are told we should "dress for success." There is an entire industry focused upon taking care of our image, but it is dedicated to making sure we have the right car, clothing, hair, face, nails and weight for our chosen profession. This is not the image I'm talking about.

We need to be more concerned about the image of Jesus that we project in our ministry. The person of integrity is a person who has learned to project holiness. Holiness is like a video God places within your life. He removes the worldly video and gives you a new tape. However, if there is not a screen on which to view it, it cannot be seen. Many Christians have kept their new video of holiness on the inside, but in the image that is projected at the workplace it is not seen. Either it is turned off, or it is carelessly presented. A mixed message will confuse the listeners.

A Christian who correctly projects holiness at the workplace does not sign false statements. He or she does not carefully work only the minimum time required or shirk his duties when the boss is not around. A Christian who walks in integrity has turned on the holiness video and has placed a monitor upon his or her life so that he clearly projects an image of Christ.

The screen where the image of holiness is projected is our daily behavior. That is why John the Baptist said, "Produce fruit in keeping with repentance" (Luke 3:8). Not only do we repent, but we also produce fruit that shows the world the evidence of our repentance.

Take care of your image—not your fleshly image—but the image of Jesus in your life. Follow the advice given in 1 Corinthians 10:23-24:

> "Everything is permissible"—but not everything is beneficial.
> "Everything is permissible"—but not everything is constructive. Nobody should seek his own good, but the good of others.

This verse is talking about the image we need to care for. The Bible does not tell us specifically how to dress, but there are principles of modesty. Before a person gets dressed, whether he is poor or rich, he should ask himself, "Lord, am I projecting holiness? Am I giving an image of Jesus Christ?" What we choose to put on is not dictated to us by specific rules of dress—it is godly principles that arise out of our love for Christ that mandates our appearance.

I heard the testimony of a lady who once was a secular singer of Latin music. She said that she would dress seductively and show as much of her body as possible as a secular singer because it was good for her music career. However, after she accepted Christ as her Savior, out of the deep love she had for Christ, she changed her appearance and began to dress to please Him even though no one told her what she should or should not wear. When she looked at herself in the mirror, she could sense if what she was wearing would be pleasing to Jesus.

The apostle Paul carefully explained to us in the verse above that everything is permissible, but not everything is beneficial. Everything is permissible, but not everything is constructive. He gave us examples from his own life to show us how carefully he guarded his integrity. He said, "If eating barbecued meat is offensive to a brother who does not eat meat, then out of love for him, I am not going to eat meat, even though doing so is not a sin. Because I love others, I want to project an image of godliness to them." It was an image to attract others to Jesus.

HOW TO OVERCOME HYPOCRISY

Do you want to avoid the transgression of Peter? In conclusion, let me offer these seven additional steps to complete freedom.

1. Find a confronter, and grant him generous permission into your inner circle and access to speak into your life as needed. Paul confronted Peter, and the prophet Nathan confronted King David (1 Sam. 11; Gal. 2:11). Each of us needs someone who is willing to challenge us when we are out of line.

2. Become a secure person. Not only are people-pleasers never good leaders; they are never holy (Gal. 2:12). Your insecurities will always lead you to embrace hypocritical behavior.

3. Put a wise distance between you and those who are hypocritical. Beware! Hypocrisy is contagious (Gal. 2:13). It can spread through a church just as yeast spreads in a lump of dough.

4. Consider hypocrisy to be spiritual poison. It is sin—not just a little mistake (Gal. 2:14). Never underestimate the evil power of hypocrisy. When Paul saw it, he confronted it with boldness.

5. Be consistent. Identify your areas of inconsistency, and pray to change them (Gal. 2:14).

6. Preach principles, not just rules. Avoid legalism, which focuses on self-righteousness, not on faith (Gal. 2:15).

7. Under pressure, do not regress. Do not rebuild the old worldly habits (Gal. 2:18).

Our goal should be to be able to say with the apostle Paul:

I have been crucified with Christ and I no longer live, but Christ lives in me. The life I live in the body, I live by faith in the Son of God, who loved me and gave himself for me.

—GALATIANS 2:20

A PRAYER OF REPENTANCE

Lord, may Galatians 2 be sealed by fire in my heart. I humble myself before You and ask that You take away any negative traits I have assimilated from our society, all of the bad habits I have learned from the culture and all tendencies to put on an appearance of what I am not. Remove all dishonesty, exaggerations, lies and everything else that lacks integrity from my life. Make me a person of integrity and sincerity. Amen.

Chapter 12

The Transgression of the Rich Young Ruler: Refusing to Give Up the Last Idol

Some time ago I took my notebook computer to be analyzed by some computer technicians. Two of them, one more skilled than the other, worked for more than two hours on my machine. They tried everything as I stood there watching. They finally handed the computer back to me and said, "Sir, there is nothing wrong with your computer. Everything is working fine, including the modem, but we just cannot get it to connect to the Internet."

Now I was puzzled. I wondered how everything could be right when it wasn't working for me. I do not know how many of you have computer traumas and software crises, or how you handle them, but I began to pray about this. I asked the Lord what I should do. I was deeply concerned, because I need to connect to the Internet in order to keep up with correspondence with my staff and family.

Then I remembered that the technician had told me that it looked as if I would have to reformat the entire hard disk. Reformatting means you save all the information first, then wipe out all of the memory from your computer. The saved information can then be reentered in an organized way, and supposedly it will work. It is like wiping the slate clean and starting over.

I did just that. My computer began to work and is still working. I came to this realization: There are times when it seems that everything is just fine in our Christian life. We find no terrible sin, and our lives comply with the Scriptures. It seems that we are OK, but somehow we are ineffective for the kingdom of God. We need to be reformatted!

There are people who live that way. They do the best they can, but they never get results. They feel they never count for the kingdom of God. They don't believe they will ever make a difference. They might have been in the church for years, but they cannot point out any significant thing they have contributed to that church. Ineffective, unfruitful Christianity is so tragic because the entire Bible calls us to use the power of God to reach out to people so they can be transformed.

If you get the message of this final chapter, you will understand all of the other chapters about transgressions. It is so radical, so conclusive, that if we get this lesson right we are ready and positioned for effective ministry. If you avoid this transgression, my brother and my sister, you will become a five-star Christian.

DISCOVERING THE LAST IDOL

During Jesus' ministry He had an encounter with a wealthy young Jew. This young man was most likely born into a privileged family. He obviously had been exposed to religious teaching. Scripture tells us:

> A certain ruler asked him, "Good teacher, what must I do to inherit eternal life?"
>
> "Why do you call me good?" Jesus answered. "No one is good—except God alone. You know the commandments: 'Do not commit adultery, do not murder, do not steal, do not give false testimony, honor your father and mother.'"
>
> "All these I have kept since I was a boy," he said.
>
> When Jesus heard this, he said to him, "You still lack one thing. Sell everything you have and give to the poor, and you

will have treasure in heaven. Then come, follow me." When he heard this, he became very sad, because he was a man of great wealth. Jesus looked at him and said, "How hard it is for the rich to enter the kingdom of God!"

—LUKE 18:18–24

Jesus was able to detect what was wrong with this young man's "hard drive." He saw into his soul and detected the unseen idol that was a spiritual blockage. In the same way, God wants us to find that "little thing"—we do not know what it is sometimes—and change it. If we are ineffective, if our conscience is not clean, it is because there is something that needs to change, even though it is undetectable. If you are a sincere and committed Christian, the good news is that the Lord is not calling you to change everything. He is calling you to change the last transgression, to tear down your last idol.

The rich young ruler, supposedly a ruler of a synagogue, was a successful person. Yet he had one burning question in his heart, "Jesus, what do I do to inherit eternal life?"

Jesus answered this question differently on different occasions. To a lawyer who asked the same question He told him to love God and love his neighbor (Luke 10:25). But this young man He told to sell everything he had, give to the poor and then come and follow Him. The Lord did not call every rich person to give up wealth. But this was His directive to this young man. There is a principle behind this.

The Lord pierced through the heart of this young man and found his last idol. *The last transgression is always an idol.* It is always something that we love more than God. It is always hidden in a secret corner of our hearts. We might say, "Holy Spirit, I'm sorry. This is the only area You cannot enter." Be assured that Jesus will zoom in on this area of your heart with His piercing light! He knows that a hidden idol is lurking in the darkness of your soul.

Many Christians are ineffective because, although they have given 90 percent of their lives to the Lord and are living according to the commandments of the Lord, they have carefully guarded that last 10 percent—or perhaps 2 percent or 1 percent—hanging on tightly to it for themselves.

The problem is that if anyone fulfills all the points of the law except one, he becomes guilty of breaking them all (James 2:10). We cannot live on the fence. None of God's laws are trivial. All of them are to be honored. Many times because we have a high percentage of surrender in our lives, we might think we have fulfilled all of God's will. Even some full-time ministers of the gospel believe that they are allowed to hide small idols in the "closets" of their lives. But it is these tiny idols that can keep us from being fruitful for the kingdom of God.

You may be saying, "I am not sure I have given 100 percent of my life to the Lord. Maybe there is an idol left in my heart. Perhaps there is some area that I have not surrendered to Jesus Christ." Don't be discouraged. You can take the following steps to total surrender.

STEPS TO TOTAL SURRENDER

If you have hidden idols in your life, decide today to remove them from your life. These six steps will destroy the last barrier that hinders your spiritual life and your effectiveness in ministry:

1. Call Jesus *good,* but know He is *God.*

The young man in Luke 18 was very well meaning. In the account of his story in another Gospel, it says he "ran up to him and fell on his knees before him" (Mark 10:17). He was very reverent to Jesus, and he called Jesus a *good teacher.* But that was not enough. It was as if Jesus were saying to him, "If you call me *good,* you better know that I am *God.* If not, do not call me good." This is what happens to Christians today.

Religion can become a casual thing. Those who have always been in the church can be tempted to develop a very nonchalant attitude about God, saying, "Good Lord, I admire You, You're great." But they demonstrate no reverence, respect or genuine fear of God, and they do not have the willingness to obey immediately. Perhaps it is because we become so familiar with Jesus that we treat Him like a good teacher.

Jesus is more than a good teacher. He is the Lord Almighty. Jesus Himself said that those who worshiped Him would do it "in Spirit and truth" (John 4:23). It would not be worship done in the flesh, not a casual coming to a religious site, but rather a total commitment to the will of the Lord. We must move from *admirers* to *adorers.*

So the first thing is not only calling Jesus good, but obeying Him as God. In Matthew 7:21–23, we are told that many in that day will say, "Lord, Lord, in Your name we have done these things," but the Lord will tell them, "Away from Me, you evildoers." They called Him "Lord, Lord" in a casual way. They expressed good words to Him, but they were not willing to give everything to obey Him completely—to obey Him as God.

2. Keep the commandments *and* listen to the Commander.

In Luke 18:19, Jesus asked the young ruler why he called Him good. He then assured him that no one is good except for God. He was calling for more than nice words. He was calling for obedience, for receptiveness and for full surrender. Many people try to keep the commandments, but they do not listen to the Commander. Their eyes and their ears are not tuned in to what God is saying to the church today. They may keep a list of religious rules, but they ignore the voice of the Lord.

Some time ago at a crusade where I was speaking, one man came to the second meeting with a truckload of kayaks, boats, rowing materials and sports items. At first I didn't understand because I had not said anything about sports at the meeting the night before. Upon talking to the host pastor, however, I learned that involvement in sports had become his idol. Outdoor activities, which are not evil in themselves, had become the main focus of his life.

When he became aware of that, he came to the crusade that day and gave it all up. He did not want to have any idols. This man was not only doing his best to keep the commandments, attend church regularly, pay his tithes and serve the Lord as best he knew how. He had also heard the voice of the Lord speak to him about the things he idolized. Unlike the rich young ruler, he was willing to obey.

Did you know that the human heart can make anything into an

idol? I know a woman who had to go on a "fast" from buying new clothes because fashion became an idol to her. For others, food can become an idol. Sometimes even certain relationships can become idols that prevent us from obeying His voice.

3. Thank God for past religious fidelity, but don't count on it for present spirituality.

Jesus told the rich young ruler:

> "You know the commandments: 'Do not commit adultery, do not murder, do not steal, do not give false testimony, honor your father and mother.'"
> "All these I have kept since I was a boy," he said.
>
> —Luke 18:20–21

In other words, this young man was stating, "I have the right doctrine. I have the right background. I am an obedient and disciplined person. What else can I give you?" We will always encounter a problem when we believe that our past obedience or our correct doctrine will save us.

The prophet Ezekiel dealt with this thinking, stating clearly and unequivocally how we should look at our past obedience:

> Therefore, son of man, say to your countrymen, "The righteousness of the righteous man will not save him when he disobeys, and the wickedness of the wicked man will not cause him to fall when he turns from it. The righteous man, if he sins, will not be allowed to live because of his former righteousness." If I tell the righteous man that he will surely live, but then he trusts in his righteousness and does evil, none of the righteous things he has done will be remembered; he will die for the evil he has done.
>
> —Ezekiel 33:12–13

All of your religious past, all of your good education, all of your good preparation and training in the ways of the Lord will amount to nothing if you are presently walking in disobedience. If there is still idolatry in your heart, it doesn't matter what good you did in the past, what position you served in the church or how many

Bible verses you memorized. Today you are at fault with your God. Present idols cancel previous obedience.

I have been there. One time I was in a meeting where there was a preacher calling people to the altar of repentance. As I listened, I found myself counting my righteousness. I thought to myself, *My whole life is OK. I am a servant of the Lord. I attend a lot of conferences and prayer meetings.* But there was one idol left. There was something in my heart that I had not surrendered. I went forward with many others to repent and renounce that idol.

Once we are in the presence of the Holy Spirit, He has a way of speaking to our hearts and showing us our idols. Don't resist the Lord's searchlight when He begins to probe your soul.

We also need to be on our guard for condemnation as we move toward greater holiness. There is a big difference between the ministry of the Holy Spirit and the work of Satan in our lives. If we have not been taught to distinguish between them, they might both look the same. Satan brings a sense of vague, general guilt to our hearts and minds. The Bible calls him "the accuser of the brethren" (Rev. 12:10, KJV). Even though the Book of Revelation says that Satan has been thrown down from heaven, he still lies to us with accusations. He brings guilt trips; that is Satan's work.

Some Christians confuse this work of the devil, thinking that it must be the Holy Spirit who is tormenting them. That is not how the Holy Spirit works. The Bible teaches us that the ministry of the Holy Spirit is not putting on us guilt trips, but rather He brings specific conviction. The Holy Spirit points out something specific in our hearts and says, "This is your idol." And He not only points out the sin, but He also offers a way of escape.

Jesus did not say to the rich young ruler, "You are a guilty man. Something is wrong with your life, but I am not going to tell you what it is. You cannot make it." Rather, Jesus said, "You lack one thing, only one thing. Once you obey Me in this area, you can follow Me." He pinpointed his love of money.

The Lord is very specific with us. If there is still an idol remaining in your heart, I pray your heart will listen to what the Holy

Spirit will point out to you. Conviction of sin is not a curse; it is a blessing. Conviction is a token of the love of God to our hearts saying, "There is one thing that is hindering you, My son or daughter. One thing that you are lacking." Once you remove that final idol, you are going to be free.

While preaching in a city in southern Argentina, I saw a vision of a watch. I gave the following invitation: "If anyone in this room has a stolen watch, please bring it to the altar." Two young men came. They were both Christians. One of them was carrying the watch as if it stunk. He held it out before him at arm's length by his thumb and forefinger. He dropped the watch on the platform. For these young men, this stolen watch for their last idol.

Unlike the rich young ruler, the Lord did not ask these men to get rid of their wealth. Chances are they did not have any wealth. But they still had an idol—a stolen item they had refused to give back. After the meeting was over, I advised them to take the watch back to its original owner now that they had surrendered to the Lord. That one act freed them from the power of sin and set them on a path of obedience.

4. Be willing to identify, define and destroy the last idol.

In Luke 18:22, Jesus said to the rich young ruler, "You still lack one thing." He did not ask him to change everything in his life— just one. You may lack just one thing, and once that idol is removed, your soul will be free to serve God like never before. Your ministry will become effective in areas where it has previously been unfruitful.

When I was a child, one of my relatives gave me a special ring that had a tiny compartment where you could hide things. I decided it would be really fun to hide a little piece of paper with all the answers in code to my next exam at school. I prepared the paper, put it in the ring and, during a class break, showed it to all my friends. "Look what I did!" I told them. "No one will ever notice." I thought my plans to cheat were very clever.

I put the paper back in the ring and, during the exam, copied from the list of answers. Looking back, I think it took me more time and work to prepare that miniscule set of answers than it would have taken me to study. Chances are I already knew the material by heart because I spent so much time writing the answers down.

One day a sister in the church said to me, "Do you know that what you did is sin, and that you are deceiving and lying by cheating on that test?" I repented before the Lord. I asked the Lord to forgive me for cheating. Conviction of sin came to my heart. I knew it was wrong, and I changed.

Recently I heard about a new trend among students called "Internet cheating." Children, teenagers and college students can find someone else's essay on the Internet, put their name on it and turn it in as their completed assignment.

This new form of cheating is just one example of the industry of deceit we see emerging in our culture today. Turning in an essay you did not write is a lie. When you put your name on that assignment, you are saying that you created the report—even though that is not true. It may look like just a little sin. I must admit that it did not seem like a big deal to me at first to cheat on a test, until conviction came into my heart. In some schools, cheating has become a habit. People become addicted to the thrill of cheating, lying and deceiving their teachers. That habit can be translated into adult behaviors such as writing falsified checks, assuming false identities or listing false hours at work. These behaviors are blatant acts of lying and cheating. Even though they do not seem to be as offensive as committing adultery or killing someone, if you do these things you are guilty of breaking all of the law.

One time during a church service, a young lady, who was probably fourteen or fifteen years old, brought a book filled with pictures of secular singers and actors and left it on the platform. There was nothing bad about the pictures; they were not lewd or sensual. When I asked the young lady what made her bring this book to the platform, she flipped the pages over, again showing me the pictures. Then she said, "Pastor, these people were my idols, and I want to get rid of them."

Another time Christians brought their cigarette packages to the platform. Some of them crushed them in anger, saying, "I don't want to have anything to do with this vice. It is harming my lungs." I have seen Christians bring drugs and all kinds of immoral pictures to the altar.

It is wonderful to witness believers getting rid of their last idols. It is an indication that God is cleaning the church and purifying His people.

You may be a person who has already lined your life up with the Word of God. You may have developed a lifestyle of godliness—and be living it. Perhaps your home is orderly and organized according to the patterns of the Bible. Yet if there is even one area of sin, God is calling you to give up your last idol.

Your idol may not be something tangible. It could be pride, religious superiority or lack of forgiveness for an offense that the church did against you. Maybe your idol has caused you to determine that you will never allow yourself to be vulnerable again. Because a fellow believer or Christian leader is the one who hurt you, you may have made the decision that you will never serve God wholeheartedly again as you used to do.

Those kinds of vows can hinder you for the rest of your life. I call them "religious traumas." You need to get rid of them today. I pray that this last transgression will be taken away from your heart. May you become like a little child in the kingdom of God. May your trust in the Lord be renewed, and, because of that trust, may your trust in Christ's body—your fellow believers—be renewed also.

A young fellow who was leading the worship for one of our crusades could hardly wait to tell me something on the second day of the meeting. When I finished preaching, he walked over to where I was and said, "Brother Sergio, I want to confess this to you. Yesterday I was convicted of watching immorality in movies and on TV. Even though I am a youth leader and I lead worship, I watched those programs and films anyway. I knew they were wrong, so I have made a new commitment to the Lord. I have decided to give up immorality forever."

Testimonies like I've included in this chapter keep me going because they are the testimonies of people who have been completely set free. They do not want to leave even the last transgression in their heart.

5. Embrace a radical philosophy regarding money.

People who are serious about giving everything in their lives to the Lord are radical in regard to their money. John Wesley used to say, "Earn everything you can; save everything you can; then give everything you can." I believe this is one of the best, most biblical philosophies for financial stewardship.

I am not preaching poverty; I am preaching diligence. We can make as much money as the Lord allows us to make. We should have a good savings plan. And we should be ready to give generously when the Lord needs some of our resources for His work. I believe the coming revival is going to cost us a lot financially because the revival needs to go around the world. We need to develop a financial passion—not a passion to accumulate, but a passion to save and make the savings available for the Lord. As He instructs us, we will reach many people by using the resources He has given us.

To the Jewish people, temporal prosperity was considered a sign of divine favor. Perhaps this is why the rich young ruler struggled with a love of wealth. First, he knelt down before Jesus (Mark 10:17). But when he heard what Jesus had to say to him, then he said, "Lord, I don't know that I can do that. What You are asking me creates a religious conflict within me because I have been taught all my life—I come from a school in the synagogue—that prosperity is a blessing of the Lord. I don't want to be poor!"

Jesus never denies that prosperity is a blessing of the Lord. But the problem is that prosperity can become a curse when we refuse to submit it to the will of the Lord.

Some believers need to "fast" from the use of credit cards for a month or so. If you are caught up in compulsive buying, consumerism and materialism, you may be called by God to put away your credit cards. If you are married, you should do this in agreement with your spouse. Not only could this be an indication that you have given away your last idol—you may be pleasantly surprised, after a season, to discover that you have also gotten rid of your outstanding debt. This also is biblical and wise.

6. Practice radical work ethics.

Jesus worked very hard. He told the rich young ruler, "I don't just want you to be My admirer and call Me good; I want you to give up your idol and follow Me. I have work for you to do."

This young ruler was the disciple that could have been but never was. He represents an aborted ministry. As far as we know, he never made it to becoming a follower of Jesus. The Bible says that he was very sad when Jesus asked him to give up everything. In Greek, the word *paralepos* means that he was grieving; he had an inner conflict. He could not be happy about his decision.

Those who refuse to give up the last idol, who refuse to commit wholeheartedly, will grieve. They know they missed the greatest opportunity of their lives—the chance to join Jesus' team. If you do not join His team, there will be something in your spirit that convicts you, asking why you did not give Him all. The rich young ruler really wanted to be a follower of Jesus, but he also wanted to keep all his treasure. Don't be like him!

Recently I read this statement, "Our spirituality is not seen in what we want to do, but in what we choose to do." We are spiritual people not because we have nice desires to be so, but because we choose to follow Jesus. We are spiritual when we choose to submit everything to the Lord. The secret of holiness is *followership*— being ready to follow the commands of Jesus.

One day my wife and I landed in the city of San Francisco on a flight returning from Asia, and we were excited about taking the next plane and returning to our family. My wife went to the counter to get a boarding pass while I did some paperwork at another counter. Somehow she made it to the plane before I did. When I got to the gate just a minute later, I was very surprised to discover that the plane was gone.

If you have flown before, you know, as I did, that missing a flight by one minute is no different than missing it by one hour. When it is gone, it is gone! Airplanes are probably one of the only vehicles on earth that do not have a reverse gear, at least in the air! The door of the plane had been closed, and the plane was pulling away from the gate. There was no way to stop it.

I explained to the airline officials that I had done my very best to get to the gate on time. I had hurried across the airport full speed. I told them about the crowds, the luggage that had been late clearing customs and that my wife was already on that plane. While we were talking, another fifteen people came running up to the gate—also late, like me.

Suddenly, the plane, which had only pulled away a few yards from the gate, stopped. I could see the airline officials talking intently on the radio. To my amazement, I saw that huge airplane backing up. It took more than fifteen minutes to back that plane up the few short yards to the gate. Soon the doors were opened again, and all of us late passengers were allowed to get on board!

There are some people who feel that they have missed the last spiritual "airplane." They believe they will never be happy or fulfilled again. Maybe you are one of these people. Maybe you think you missed the plane and have no way to get to your heavenly destination. But I want to tell you that there is still opportunity. We still live in the age of salvation; we are still under the grace of the Holy Spirit. Final judgment has not come yet. It is not too late.

There is still time to repent of any unforgiveness, bitterness of spirit or purposeful refusal to help the body of Christ and fulfill all the duties of your ministry. There is still time to give up your last idol.

In Luke 19, one chapter after the story of the rich young ruler, there is another story in the Scripture. This one tells the story of Zacchaeus, a rich man who renounced his love of money and made restitution for his dishonesty. He then committed his life to follow Jesus.

Zacchaeus was not very religious. In fact, he was a thief and a deceiver. But his response to Jesus shows us that he was ready to commit his life wholeheartedly to the work of the Lord:

> But Zacchaeus stood up and said to the Lord, "Look, Lord!
> Here and now I give half of my possessions to the poor, and if

I have cheated anybody out of anything, I will pay back four
times the amount."

—LUKE 19:8

Some very smart hunters in Africa decided to use an ingenious
trap for little monkeys. They would use a bottle with an opening
just large enough for a monkey to be able to squeeze its hand
inside. Inside the bottle would be peanuts or candies—something
very desirable to these animals. The monkey would reach its hand
into the bottle, but once it closed its fist around the peanuts, it
would not be able to get its hand out. In that short moment when
the monkey was deciding to refuse to give up the candy, a net
would fall upon it, and the monkey would be caught.

Satan wants to entice the people of God with little things. Some
people are trapped by insignificant things, and because they
believe these sins are not a big deal, they refuse to give up these
small enticements. Their hands are clenched tightly in a fist around
their tiny idols. They are determined never to let go. They keep
pulling and pulling to get these things, and they do not know a net
is about to fall on them.

The net does not come from God—it is the trap of the
destroyer. The Bible tells us that Satan "prowls around like a roar-
ing lion looking for someone to devour" (1 Pet. 5:8).

I plead with you to open your hand and let go of whatever it is
that keeps you from fully following Christ. It could be a relationship that has turned from being good *Christian dating into an
immoral snare.* It could be a love relationship or an affection of
the heart that is not in the will of God. Perhaps your emotions are
entangled with the wrong kind of friendship or relationship, and
you know it. You are saying, "Yes, I want to serve God." But you
have your fist wrapped tightly around that relationship. It may be
material blessings or a professional career. It may be attitudes or
emotions in your heart that have not been resolved God's way. It
could be something that only you know about—a secret idol that
is stashed away in a tiny crevice of your heart.

What is it that you need to lay on the altar of the Lord?

The rich young ruler was very sad because he was unable to renounce what represented his last transgression, his last idol. But Zacchaeus was happy when he met Jesus because he was willing to give his all.

It does not matter how much sin or how many transgressions have been part of your past. If you repent today, God will clear the page completely. He will purify you fully. He will completely erase your hard drive and reformat your spiritual life!

Nor does it matter how much righteousness or religious activity there is in your background. If you refuse to give up your last idol, then you are in a state of sin, and God's favor will be withheld from you.

My heart's desire is that you turn over your last idol to God and experience His power transforming your life into committed, wholehearted love and devotion to Him.

A Prayer of Repentance

Father, I pray for a miracle right now. I pray that any idols left in my life will be pulverized by the power of Your Spirit. I pray that barriers will be destroyed and any shackles still around my feet will be opened so that I can hear the spiritual sound of chains of bondage breaking off my life.

I pray, O God, that all bitterness, resentment and depression would be gone. Set me free, Lord. I ask that You come and speak to me once again and say, "This is the one thing you lack." Father, please speak to me once again. I plead for another opportunity. Now, by faith, I surrender every idol. Thank You for Your forgiveness. I don't deserve it, but I accept it.

Lord, wake up my ministry, which has been dormant. Set me free to live in the excitement of Your will. Make me an effective believer, Lord.

In Jesus' name, amen.

Notes

Chapter 1
When Weakness Becomes Sin

1. Source obtained from the Internet: Signs and Wonders in the Writings of the Early Church Fathers, www.geocities.com/Heartland/Fields/2418/Church_Fathers.html. Accessed June 11, 2002.
2. John Foxe, *Foxe's Book of Martyrs* (Springdale, PA: Whitaker House, 1981), 24.
3. Ibid., 22.

Chapter 2
Using Carnal Means to Obtain Divine Blessing

1. Allan Redpath, *Leadership,* Vol. 3, No. 2.

Chapter 3
Charisma Without Character

1. Joshua Harris, *I Kissed Dating Good-Bye* (Sisters, OR: Multonomah Books, 1997), 32.

Chapter 4
Using Godly Anger in an Ungodly Way

1. Fox Butterfield, "Man Convicted in Fatal Beating in Dispute at Son's Hockey Game," *New York Times* (January 12, 2002). Also, source obtained from the Internet: Court TV Online, "Mass. v. Junta," www.courttv.com/trials/junta/012502_ctv.html. Accessed June 3, 2002.
2. Source obtained from the Internet: Pursuing Victory With Honor: The Arizona Sports Summit Accord, www.charactercounts.org/sports/accord.htm. Accessed June 6, 2002.
3. Source obtained from the Internet: National Alliance for Youth Sports, www.nays.org/about/index.cfm and www.nays.org/pays/code_of_ethics.cfm. Accessed June 6, 2002.

Chapter 5
Embracing Disillusionment

1. Jane Brody, "Indoor Air Pollution More Harmful," *Saint Paul Pioneer Press* (January 23, 2001): 7F.

Chapter 7
Allowing Foolishness to Become Sin

1. Source obtained from the Internet: Barna Research Online, Family/Divorce (2001), www.barna.org. Accessed June 4, 2002.

CHAPTER 9

FATAL DISTRACTIONS

1. Source obtained from the Internet: "Deadly Distractions," #8 in a series by Shell Oil Company, www.shellus.com/products/booklets/pdf/Deadly_Distractions.pdf. Accessed June 14, 2002.
2. Sergio Scataglini, *The Fire of His Holiness* (Ventura, CA: Gospel Light, 1999).

...Igniting hearts with the message and fire of His holiness

Also by Sergio Scataglini...

The Fire of His Holiness:
Prepare Yourself to Enter
  God's Presence

In Spanish

El Fuego De Su Santidad:
Preparese Para Entrar En
La Presencia De Dios

To order this book or to find out
about our other products

Call: 1-877-551-7729
or
Visit: www.scataglini.com

Sergio's now on the radio

visit us at www.momentsofprayer.com

Scataglini Ministries

PO Box 6847
2410 N Grape Rd.
South Bend, IN 46660

Phone: 574-259-7729
Fax: 574-252-7729
Email: info@scataglini.com
Web: www.scataglini.com

Keep Pressing In!

We pray that God has used Sergio Scataglini to touch your heart and change your life! Here are some additional resources from Charisma House that will also refresh your spirit...

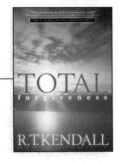

Best-Selling Author of the U.K.!

Total Forgiveness – By R. T. Kendall

"This is a book that should be read around the world." —Dr. D. James Kennedy

Dr. Kendall will help you step into freedom as you learn to let go of grudges and stop pointing fingers at others. God is adamant about this, and He wants you to understand what it means to forgive—totally.

#889-8 $13.99   Save 20% Now only $11.19

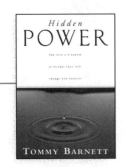

Hidden Power – By Tommy Barnett

Tap into a kingdom principle that will change you forever! Pastor Tommy Barnett, pastor of one of the largest churches in America, explains how to give yourself away and never run out of anything. Learn the secrets to a successful, happy life with an unending supply of resources and blessings. This is his life-message!

#771-9 $13.99   Save 20% Now only $11.19

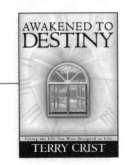

Awakened to Destiny – By Terry Crist

God wants to shape history through you! Don't miss the greatest moments in history because you are spiritually asleep! It's time to wake up and step into the incredible plans and destiny that God has just for you.

#770-0 $13.99   Save 20% Now only $11.19

Call **1-800-599-5750** to order these life-changing messages!
Visit our website at www.charismawarehouse.com and save even more!

BK12